Contents

☑ Use the tick boxes to check off the topics you've completed.

Exam Advice

Before you start your exam practice, it's a good idea to find out exactly how the exams will work.

Get Familiar with the **Exam Structure**

If you're sitting the AS-level in Biology rather than the A-level, you'll be sitting a different set of exams to the ones described here.

For **A-level Biology**, you'll be sitting **three papers**:

Paper 1 (topics 1-4, plus practical skills)			**Short** and **long** answer questions.	
2 hours	**91** marks	**35%** of your A-level	**15 marks** of **extended response questions**.	
Paper 2 (topics 5-8, plus practical skills)			**Short** and **long** answer questions.	
2 hours	**91** marks	**35%** of your A-level	A **15 mark comprehension** question.	
Paper 3 (topics 1-8, plus practical skills)			Section **A**: **practical** techniques.	
2 hours	**78** marks	**30%** of your A-level	Section **B**: a **25 mark essay** question.	

1) The **short** and **long** answer questions in Papers 1 and 2 will test you on the **facts** you need to know, on whether you can **apply your knowledge** to unfamiliar contexts, and on **practical skills**. There will also be a few **calculation** questions. Similar questions can also be found in Paper 3, but there'll be more emphasis on **practical techniques** and **15 marks** in this paper will be awarded for **critical analysis** of **experimental data**.

2) The **extended response** questions in Paper 1 require you to write a **longer answer** with a **logical structure**.

3) The **comprehension** question in Paper 2 will require you to **read a passage of information** and answer the question parts using both the information provided, and your own scientific knowledge.

You'll Have a **Choice** of **Two Essay Titles** to Write About in **Paper 3 Section B**

Your essay should include a **range of material** from **both years** of your A-level course. Here are some **top tips**:

1) **Before you start** your essay, scribble down a **rough plan** — this will help you to present your ideas clearly and stop you missing out any important points. You should aim to write about **at least five** different topic areas.

2) You'll need to show clearly how **all** the information you include is **relevant** to the **essay title** — don't just write down everything you know about a topic. The information you include must be **scientifically correct**, **detailed**, and of **A-level standard**. Make sure you use appropriate **scientific terminology** too.

3) To get the **very highest marks**, your essay should show evidence of **wider reading** — this means writing about things that aren't explicitly on the specification, but are still **relevant** and of at least A-level standard.

Manage Your Time Sensibly

If you get stuck on a short question, it's sometimes worth moving on to another one and then coming back to it if you have time.

1) For **Papers 1** and **2**, you get **just over a minute per mark**. Bear in mind that you might want to spend a **bit longer** than a minute per mark on the **extended response** and **comprehension questions**.

2) For **Paper 3**, it's a **similar story** — you'll want to **spend longer per mark** on the **essay question** than on the shorter questions, so make sure you **leave enough time** for this at the end.

Command Words Tell You **What You Need** to do in a Question

Here are some of the **most common ones**:

Command word	What to do
Give / Name / State	Give a brief **one or two word** answer, or a short sentence.
Describe	Write about what something's like. E.g. describe the structure of a cell.
Explain	**Give reasons** for something.
Suggest	Use your **scientific knowledge** to work out what the answer **might** be.
Calculate	Work out the **solution** to a mathematical problem.

Some questions will ask you to answer '**using the information/data provided**' — if so, you must **refer** to the information, data or figure you've been given or you won't get the marks.

63483X

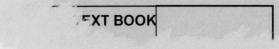

EXT BOOK

A-Level
Biology

Exam Board: AQA

Getting to grips with A-Level Biology can be strenuous, but with this CGP book your brain muscles* will be beautifully toned by the time the real exams arrive.

It's brimming with a massive range of exam-style questions covering both years of the AQA course — perfect for testing your skills and knowledge.

What's more, we've added a sprinkling of exam tips and a whole section of in-depth answers that'll tell you exactly how the marks are dished out for every question. There's no better way to shape up for the exams!

*Note from CGP: the rest of this book was written by Biology experts. This page was not.

A-Level revision? It has to be CGP!

Published by CGP

Editors:
Charlotte Burrows, Ellen Burton, Daniel Fielding, Christopher Lindle, Emily Sheraton, Hayley Thompson.

Contributors:
Mark Ellingham, Emily Lucas, David Martindill, Ciara McGlade, Bethan Parry, Megan Pollard, Duncan Wiles.

ISBN: 978 1 78294 910 7

With thanks to Alex Billings, Emily Forsberg, Sarah Pattison, Rachael Rogers,
Camilla Simson and Karen Wells for the proofreading.

With thanks to Ana Pungartnik for the copyright research.

Printed by Elanders Ltd, Newcastle upon Tyne

Based on the classic CGP style created by Richard Parsons.

Biological Molecules — 1

There's a huge variety of life on Earth, but all organisms share the same few groups of carbon-based compounds. There might only be a few of these groups, but I've still managed to put plenty of exam-style questions together for you to have a go at. Best get to it — you can thank me later.

1 **Figure 1** shows a polymer.

Figure 1

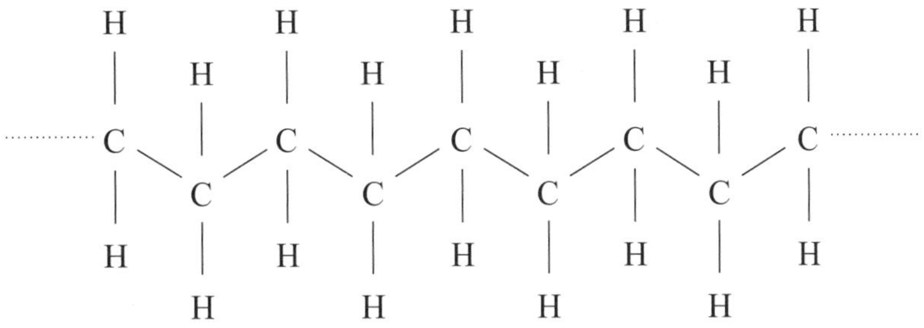

1.1 What is a polymer?

....

(1 mark)

1.2 Draw a circle around a single monomer in **Figure 1**.

(1 mark)

1.3 Give **three** types of monomer found in biological molecules.

....

....

(1 mark)

2 **Figure 2** shows a reaction between two monomers that produces a disaccharide.

Figure 2

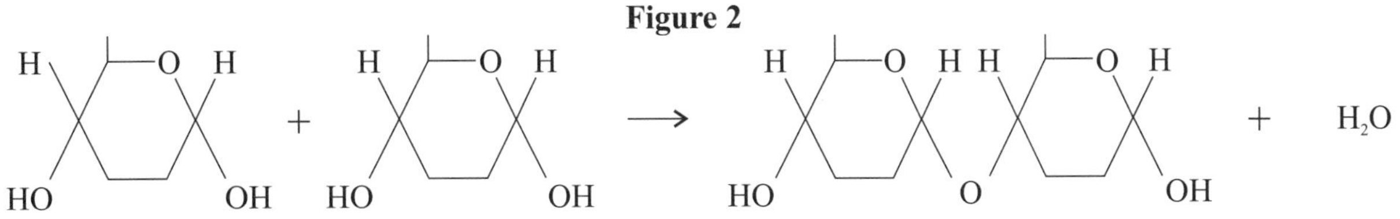

2.1 Name the monomers shown in **Figure 2**.

....

(1 mark)

2.2 Name the disaccharide produced in **Figure 2**.

....

(1 mark)

2.3 Disaccharides can be broken down.
Describe this reaction.

....

....

....

(3 marks)

3   Proteins have four levels of structure.

Figure 3 shows part of the secondary structure of a protein.

Figure 3

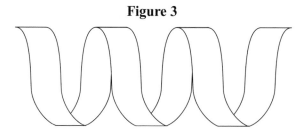

3.1   State which secondary structure is shown in **Figure 3**.

....
(1 mark)

3.2   Compare and contrast the bonding in the secondary and tertiary structures of a protein.

....

....

....
(2 marks)

3.3   Explain why the tertiary structure of proteins is important for metabolic reactions.

....

....

....

....
(3 marks)

3.4   Haemoglobin is a quaternary protein.
        What does this information tell you about haemoglobin's structure?

....

....
(2 marks)

Haemoglobin is the oxygen-carrying molecule in red blood cells.
At low pH, haemoglobin's ability to bind to oxygen is reduced.

3.5   Suggest why a low pH affects haemoglobin in this way.

....

....
(2 marks)

EXAM TIP: Take your time to really read the question — every word is carefully chosen. You need to look out for command words. The phrase "compare and contrast" means the examiner wants you to talk about the similarities <u>and</u> differences. It'd be really easy to forget to mention the differences here and just talk about the similarities, but you'd lose yourself marks that way.

Score

18

Biological Molecules — 2

1   Proteins are polymers of amino acids.

Figure 1 shows the amino acid alanine.

Figure 1

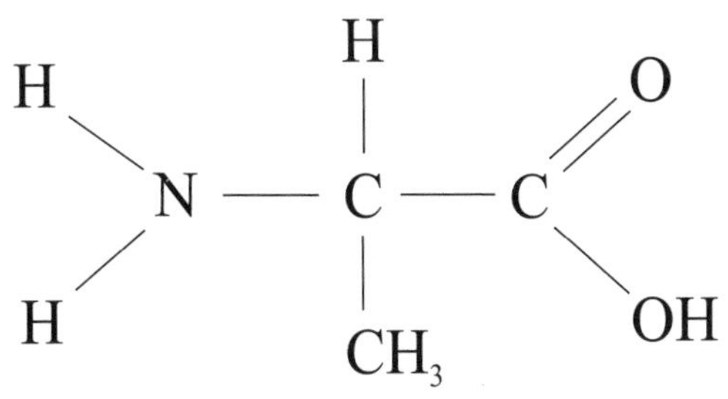

1.1   On **Figure 1**, circle and label the carboxyl group, the R group and the amino group.

(3 marks)

1.2   How is alanine different to the other 19 amino acids?

....

(1 mark)

1.3   Draw a diagram of the dipeptide formed from the reaction between two molecules of alanine.
Label the peptide bond.

(2 marks)

1.4   Name the molecule required to break the peptide bond between two amino acids.

....

(1 mark)

1.5   If this molecule alone is added to a dipeptide under neutral conditions in a laboratory,
the peptide bond does not break down.
Explain why the bond is able to break down in the human body but not in the laboratory.

....

....

(2 marks)

6

2   Three food samples (**A**, **B** and **C**), each containing carbohydrates, were tested using different techniques.

The results of these tests are shown in **Table 1**.

Table 1

Sample	Test Results		
	Test with iodine dissolved in potassium iodide solution	Test with Benedict's solution	Test with Benedict's solution (after heating with dilute hydrochloric acid)
A	Negative	Negative	Positive
B	Positive	Negative	Positive
C	Negative	Positive	Positive

2.1 Describe how to carry out a Benedict's test and what would indicate a positive result.

....

....

....

(2 marks)

The tests shown in **Table 1** allow the type of carbohydrate in each sample to be identified.

2.2 Using the information provided in **Table 1**, complete **Table 2** by placing a tick (✓) in the column that correctly identifies the type of carbohydrate present.

Table 2

Sample	Type of carbohydrate present		
	Reducing sugar	Non-reducing sugar	Starch
A			
B			
C			

(2 marks)

Two more samples were tested and found to contain reducing sugars.

2.3 Describe how the amounts of reducing sugar in the two samples could be compared.

....

....

(1 mark)

The reducing sugar present in one of the samples was identified as lactose.

2.4 Name the **two** monomers that form a lactose disaccharide.

....

(1 mark)

3 **Figure 2** shows a type of biological molecule.

Figure 2

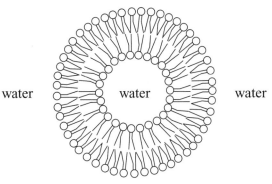

3.1 Name the type of molecule shown in **Figure 2**.

....
(1 mark)

A droplet of these molecules was placed in water.
The molecules took the arrangement shown in **Figure 3**.

Figure 3

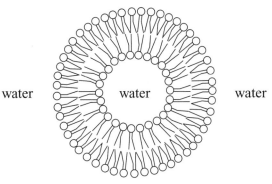

water   water   water

3.2 Explain why the molecules arranged themselves in this way.

....

....

....

....
(3 marks)

3.3 Describe **one** role that the molecules shown in **Figure 3** have in a cell.

....

....

....
(2 marks)

4   **Figure 4** shows two different fatty acids.

Figure 4

Fatty Acid 1

Fatty Acid 2

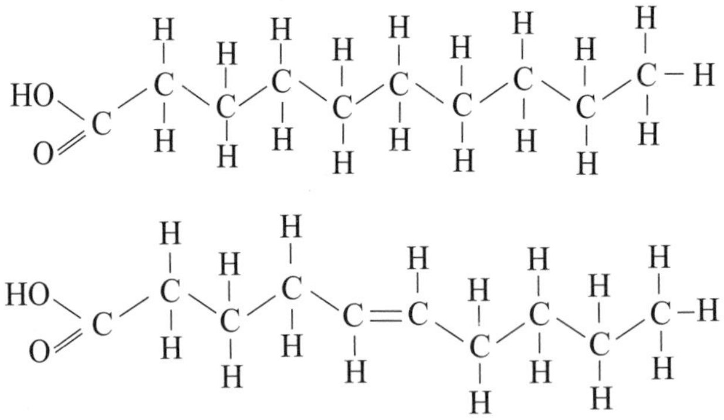

4.1   Explain the difference between these two fatty acids.

....

....

....
                                                                                                               (2 marks)

Triglycerides contain fatty acids.

4.2   Describe how triglycerides are formed.

....

....

....
                                                                                                               (3 marks)

4.3   Give **one** function of triglycerides and relate this to **one** of their properties.

....

....
                                                                                                               (2 marks)

The emulsion test can be used to test for lipids.

4.4   Describe the emulsion test, including a positive result.

....

....
                                                                                                               (2 marks)

4.5   An emulsion is droplets of one liquid suspended in another liquid.
      Using this information, explain why lipids give a positive result in the emulsion test.

....

....
                                                                                                                (1 mark)

EXAM TIP

You need to be really familiar with the structure of proteins, lipids and carbohydrates. You might get asked to identify a type of molecule or one of its groups from a diagram. Practise drawing these molecules out at home to help you visualise them — and don't be afraid to take a minute to quickly sketch out a molecule in your exam if it helps you to answer the question.

Score

31

Biological Molecules — 3

1 Glycogen, starch and cellulose are all polymers of glucose.

1.1 Explain how the structure of glycogen makes it well-suited to its function.

....

....

....

(2 marks)

Starch is made of alpha-glucose molecules and cellulose is made of beta-glucose molecules.

1.2 Draw the structure of beta-glucose below and explain how it is different from that of alpha-glucose.

....

....

(2 marks)

1.3 The beta-glucose molecules allow cellulose to form long, straight chains with multiple hydrogen bonds between the chains. Explain how this makes cellulose well-suited to its function.

....

....

(2 marks)

Starch is a mixture of two polysaccharides of alpha-glucose, amylose and amylopectin.
The structures of amylose (**A**) and amylopectin (**B**) are shown in **Figure 1**.

Figure 1

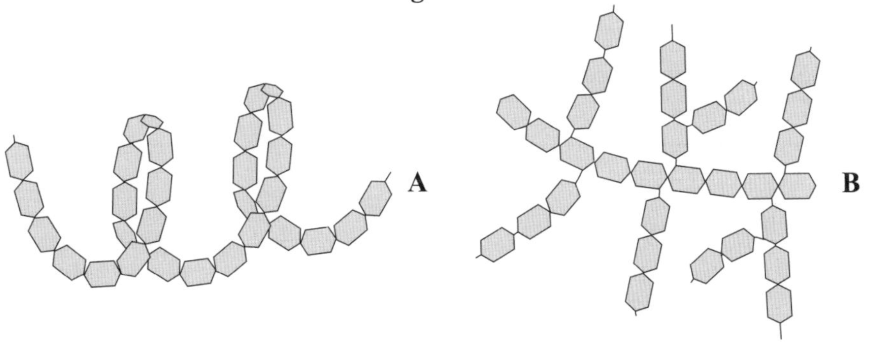

1.4 Different starches are made up of different proportions of amylose and amylopectin.
Using **Figure 1**, suggest **one** advantage and **one** disadvantage of using amylose to store excess glucose, rather than amylopectin.

Advantage: ....

Disadvantage: ....

(2 marks)

2   **Figure 2** shows the activity of two different enzymes (**A** and **B**).
The enzymes are involved in respiration. One enzyme is from an insect that
lives in the UK and one is from an insect that lives in a tropical climate.

Figure 2

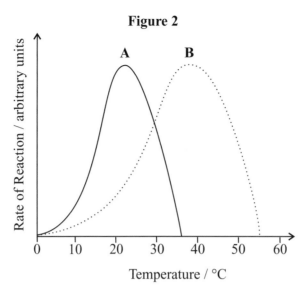

2.1   Explain the shape of the curve for enzyme **A**.

....

....

....

....

(3 marks)

2.2   Suggest which enzyme (**A** or **B**) is from the tropical insect. Explain your answer.

....

....

....

(2 marks)

Insecticides are chemicals that kill insects.
Scientists have developed an insecticide that works as a competitive inhibitor of enzyme **A**.

2.3   How would the addition of the insecticide affect the shape of the curve for enzyme **A**?

....

(1 mark)

2.4   Describe how the insecticide works.

You need to use information from the introduction to question 2, as well as your knowledge of how competitive inhibitors work, to answer this question part.

....

....

....

....

(4 marks)

3 Four molecules were tested and found to be proteins.

A biuret test was used to test these molecules.

3.1 Describe how to carry out a biuret test and what a positive result would be.

....

....

....

(3 marks)

Further analysis showed that each of the proteins had a slightly different structure.

Protein **A** was made of long polypeptide chains lying parallel to each other, with cross linkages between.
Protein **B** had tightly folded polypeptide chains and was roughly spherical in shape.
Protein **C** was made up of two light polypeptide chains and two heavy polypeptide chains.

3.2 Protein **A** is a structural protein. Explain why its structure makes it well-suited to this role.

....

....

(1 mark)

3.3 Suggest how proteins **B** and **C** are used by the body.

Protein **B**: ....

Protein **C**: ....

(2 marks)

The fourth protein was found to be a channel protein.
It had a hydrophobic region and a hydrophilic region.

3.4 Describe the function of a channel protein and explain how its structure allows it to carry out this function.

....

....

....

....

(3 marks)

4 A student investigated how an enzyme-controlled reaction is affected by changes in enzyme concentration. The student used the enzyme catalase to break hydrogen peroxide down into water and oxygen.

4.1 Identify the dependent and independent variables in this investigation.

....

....

(1 mark)

The results of the student's first experiment are shown in **Figure 3**.

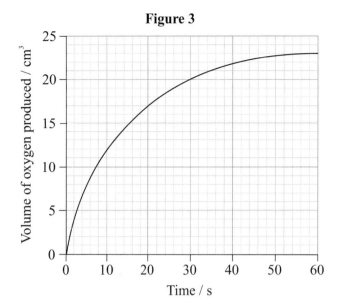

Figure 3

The student collected the oxygen in a measuring cylinder submerged in water.
The measuring cylinder measured to the nearest 1 cm³.

4.2 Give the uncertainty of measurements associated with this measuring cylinder.

uncertainty = ... cm³
(1 mark)

4.3 Suggest **one** way that the student could have obtained more accurate results.

....
(1 mark)

4.4 Calculate the average rate of the reaction shown in **Figure 3** for the first 20 seconds.

rate = ...
(2 marks)

4.5 Calculate the initial rate of the reaction shown in **Figure 3**.

To calculate the initial rate, you need to draw a tangent.

rate = ...
(1 mark)

4.6 Sketch on the same axes the curve you would expect if the experiment were carried out with a higher enzyme concentration.

(1 mark)

Pen, pencil, ruler, calculator... Oh, that's just my shopping list for my exam. Sometimes examiners will ask you to draw, measure or calculate, so you need to make sure you've got all this stationery — a ruler that can measure in millimetres, a calculator, a pencil (for drawing graphs) and a pen with black ink. In fact, make sure you've got a couple of spare pens too.

Score

34

More Biological Molecules

DNA, water and ions are essential for cell function in living organisms, and being able to answer questions about them is essential for your exams. This one might only be a short section, but make sure you give it a go.

1   Inorganic ions play many important roles in organisms.

1.1   Give **one** role that sodium ions (Na^+) play in living cells.

....
(1 mark)

1.2   Explain how the concentration of hydrogen ions (H^+) affects the internal environment of an organism.

....

....
(2 marks)

1.3   Suggest why nitrate ions (NO_3^-) are needed to make DNA.

....

....
(2 marks)

2   Animals living in hot, dry climates have developed behaviours that help them keep cool.

Kangaroos have been observed licking saliva onto their forearms in hot weather.

2.1   Using your knowledge of the properties of water, explain why this behaviour helps the kangaroos to keep cool.

....

....

....

....
(3 marks)

Koalas have been observed to hug trees in hot weather.
This is thought to be because the trunks of trees are usually cooler than the surrounding air.

2.2   Tree trunks contain a lot of water.
Explain how this could contribute to the tree trunks being cooler than the surrounding air.

....

....
(2 marks)

2.3   Explain how water is able to flow up a tree trunk, from the roots to the leaves.

....

....
(2 marks)

3   RNA carries genetic information from DNA to the ribosomes.

Figure 1 shows part of the structure of an RNA molecule.

Figure 1

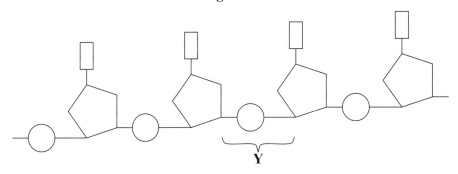

3.1   Name the bond labelled **Y** in **Figure 1**.

....

(1 mark)

3.2   What type of reaction results in the formation of the bond labelled **Y**?

....

(1 mark)

Some RNA molecules are capable of folding into structures known as stem-loops.
An example of a stem-loop structure is shown in **Figure 2**.

Figure 2

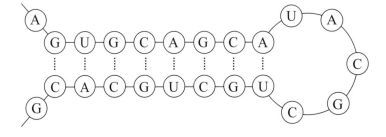

3.3   Looking at the sequence of the structure shown in **Figure 2**, explain how you can tell that this is part of an
      RNA molecule and not a DNA molecule.

....

....

(1 mark)

3.4   Using your knowledge of how DNA molecules can form a double helix, explain how the stem-loop
      structure shown in **Figure 2** is formed.

....

....

....

....

(3 marks)

4 A scientist is investigating the role of enzymes in DNA replication.

4.1 Describe the roles that the enzymes DNA helicase and DNA polymerase play in DNA replication.

....

....

....

....
(4 marks)

The scientist mixes a bacterial DNA sample with the enzymes and substrates required for DNA replication. He does this in both the presence and the absence of ATP, and using active and inactive ATP hydrolase. He then measures the amount of DNA produced to determine whether DNA replication has taken place.

Some of the results of the investigation are shown in **Table 1**.

Table 1

DNA replication enzymes	ATP hydrolase	ATP	Has DNA replication occurred?
Present	Active	Present	Yes
Present	Active	Absent	No
Present	Inactive	Present	No
Present	Inactive	Absent	No

4.2 With reference to the structure of an ATP molecule, explain why ATP is known as a nucleotide derivative.

....

....

....
(2 marks)

4.3 Outline the reaction catalysed by ATP hydrolase.

....

....
(2 marks)

4.4 Describe and suggest an explanation for the results in **Table 1**.

....

....

....

....

....
(3 marks)

Score

29

Cell Structure and Division — 1

All cells share some basic structural features, but there are plenty of differences you need to know about too.
The structural differences between cell types are important for their particular functions and replication methods.

1   A student investigated mitosis in plant tissue.

1.1   A 1 cm length was cut from the tip of an onion root.
This tip was incubated in dilute hydrochloric acid for 5 minutes at 60 °C.
It was then rinsed well with cold water and left to dry.
Describe how the student could have prepared a microscope slide to view the cells in this root tip.

....

....

....

....

(4 marks)

1.2   Give **two** safety precautions the student should have taken when preparing the slide.

1. ....

2. ....

(2 marks)

1.3   Explain why the student used the tip of the root for this investigation.

....

....

(1 mark)

The student's observations are shown in **Table 1**.

Table 1

Type of cell	Number of cells
Dividing	240
Non-dividing	80

1.4   Explain how the student was able to distinguish between dividing cells and non-dividing cells.

....

....

(1 mark)

1.5   Calculate the mitotic index of the root tip.

Mitotic index = ...

(2 marks)

2   Bacteria and viruses can cause disease when they infect humans.

Staphylococcus aureus can cause a range of illnesses in humans. The electron micrograph in **Figure 1** shows an intact *S. aureus* bacterium (right) and one undergoing lysis (left).

Figure 1

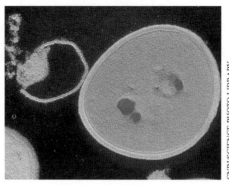

2.1   Give **one** reason why an electron microscope was used to view these cells rather than a light microscope.

....

....
(2 marks)

2.2   Name the type of electron microscope that was used to produce the micrograph seen in **Figure 1**.
        Give a reason for your answer.

....

....
(2 marks)

2.3   Give **two** ways in which you could distinguish between a prokaryotic cell and a eukaryotic cell in an electron micrograph.

        1.   ....

        2.   ....
(2 marks)

2.4   Penicillin is an antibiotic that can be used to treat infections of *Staphylococcus aureus*.
        The drugs cause cell lysis, as shown in **Figure 1**, by inhibiting cell wall synthesis.
        Explain why these drugs have no effect on human cells.

....

....
(1 mark)

2.5   The infection of human cells with West Nile Virus (WNV) can involve the cell surface receptor,
        $\alpha_v\beta_3$ integrin. Using your knowledge of the structure of viruses, suggest how a treatment that
        interferes with the function of $\alpha_v\beta_3$ integrin in human cells could prevent WNV replication.

....

....

....

....
(3 marks)

3 Sperm cells are specialised for their function of delivering genetic material to the egg.

Figure 2 shows the structure of a sperm cell.

Figure 2

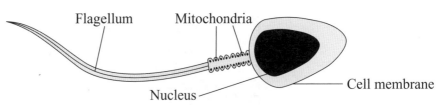

3.1 Using **Figure 2**, give **one** similarity and **one** difference between a sperm cell and a bacterium.

....

....

....

....

(2 marks)

3.2 Suggest why the mitochondria are located close to the sperm cell's flagellum.

....

....

(1 mark)

3.3 A scientist wanted to observe the mitochondria in a sample of sperm.

Which type of microscope should the scientist use to study the internal structures of the mitochondria? Explain your answer.

....

....

....

(2 marks)

3.4 DNA is related to the function of a sperm cell and a mitotic body cell.
A mitotic body cell has many ribosomes, but a sperm cell does not.

With reference to the functions of these cells, explain why there is this difference in organelles.

....

....

....

....

(3 marks)

For questions on cell structure, you can be given a micrograph. It can be tricky to interpret these and to spot the different cell structures, but they are there. Trust me. To prepare yourself for the exam, make sure you learn what all the different cell structures look like.

Score

28

Cell Structure and Division — 2

1   A team of scientists studied the organelles in **two** types of cell
(**A** and **B**) taken from the body tissues of a eukaryotic organism.

Table 1 shows the volume, as a percentage of the total cell volume, of **three** organelles.

Table 1

Organelle	Percentage of total cell volume / %	
	Cell type **A**	Cell type **B**
Lysosomes	4	1
Rough endoplasmic reticulum	8	16
Nucleus	7	7

1.1   Cell types **A** and **B** are both specialised cells. Define the term 'specialised cell'.

....
(1 mark)

1.2   The relative volume of the nucleus is the same in both types of cell. Suggest why.

....

....
(1 mark)

1.3   The role of one of the two cell types is to ingest invading pathogens, and the other is to secrete enzymes.
Use **Table 1** to determine which of these two roles is carried out by cell type **A** and which is carried out
by cell type **B**. Explain your answers.

....

....

....

....

....
(4 marks)

1.4   Two other organelles that can be found in eukaryotes are mitochondria and chloroplasts.
Contrast the structure and function of these organelles to give **two** differences.

1. ....

....

2. ....

....
(2 marks)

2 A student observed a sample of plant cells under a microscope.

2.1 Describe how to observe the cells in a prepared slide using a light microscope.

....

....

....

....

....

....

....

(5 marks)

The student used an eyepiece graticule to calculate the size of some of the plant cells.
Figure 1 shows the student's eyepiece graticule and stage micrometer.
The stage micrometer measures in millimetres.

Figure 1

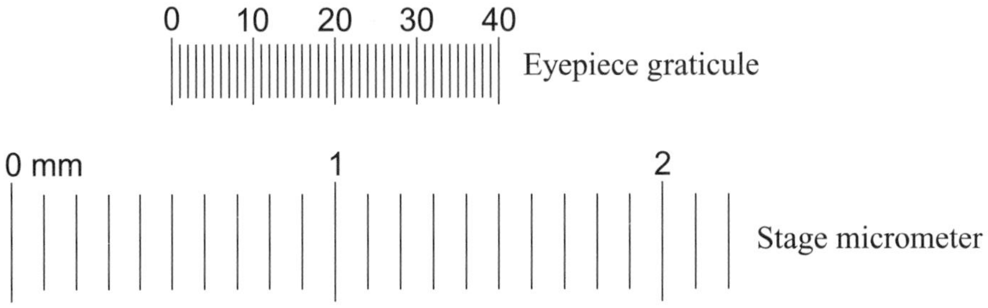

2.2 Use **Figure 1** to calculate the size of **one** division on the student's eyepiece graticule, in micrometres.

.... μm
(2 marks)

2.3 The student increased the magnification, so he needed to recalibrate the eyepiece graticule.
Explain why the student needed to recalibrate the graticule.

....

(1 mark)

Another student calculated the size of a cell from an image.
Figure 2 shows the cell at × 100 magnification.

Figure 2

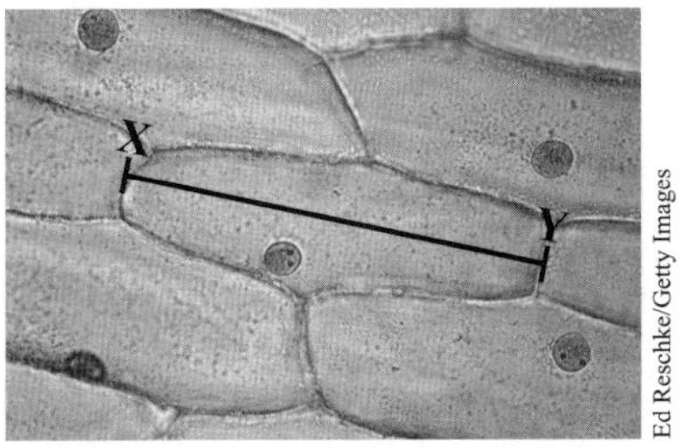

Ed Reschke/Getty Images

If you need to measure something in an exam, do it in millimetres. This'll make it easier to convert to micrometres (mm × 1000) or nanometres (μm × 1000).

2.4 Using **Figure 2**, calculate the real length of the cell (**X** to **Y**) in micrometres.

.... μm
(2 marks)

3 Abnormal mitochondria have been found in diseased heart tissue, suggesting a link between mitochondria and heart disease. Scientists investigated this by producing a strain of mice with abnormal mitochondria. The abnormal mice developed symptoms of heart disease after one year.

3.1 Describe the main function of mitochondria.

....
(1 mark)

3.2 Suggest why abnormal mitochondria might be problematic in heart tissue.

....

....
(2 marks)

Figure 3 shows mitochondria in normal mice and the abnormal mice.

Figure 3

Normal mice

Abnormal mice

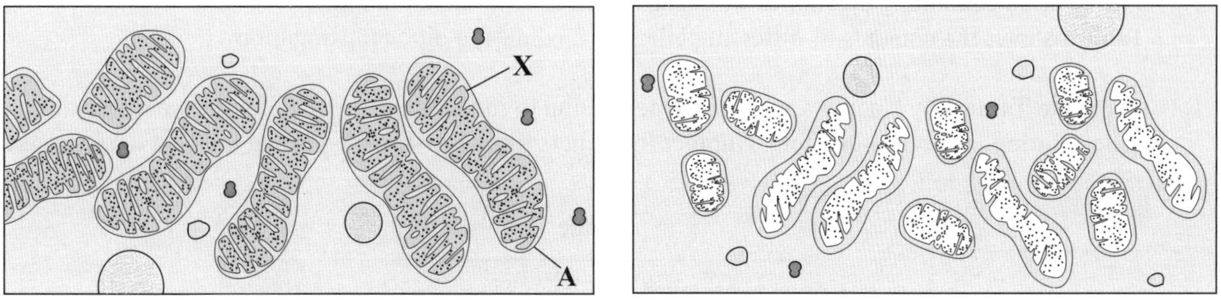

3.3 Name the part of the mitochondrion labelled **X** in **Figure 3**.

....
(1 mark)

3.4 Describe **two** differences between the mitochondria found in the abnormal and normal mice. Suggest how each difference may impair the function of mitochondria in the abnormal mice.

1. ....

....

2. ....

....
(4 marks)

3.5 The mitochondrion labelled **A** in **Figure 3** is about 1.5 μm in length. Calculate the magnification of the image.

....
(2 marks)

EXAM TIP Maths always manages to worm its way in. You really need to make sure you learn some formulas, like the one for magnification (magnification = size of image ÷ size of real object). And make sure you *really* know them — you need to be confident rearranging them.

Score

28

Cell Structure and Division — 3

1   A scientist was separating organelles from a sample of plant cells.

1.1   Describe how the scientist could separate the organelles from other plant cell components.

....

....

....

(3 marks)

1.2   After separation, the solution containing organelles was kept in an ice bath.
Explain why.

....

(1 mark)

The solution containing organelles was centrifuged to separate them out.
Table 1 shows the contents of different pellets formed during ultracentrifugation.

1.3   Complete **Table 1** by placing a number in the column to indicate the order of formation of the different pellets during ultracentrifugation. Number the pellets from **1** to **4**, with 1 being the first to separate out.

Table 1

Contents of pellet	Sequence of separation
Mitochondria and chloroplasts	
Nuclei	
Ribosomes	
Endoplasmic reticulum	

(1 mark)

1.4   A student commented on the results and suggested that the sample of plant cells were from a root.
Explain why the student is incorrect.

....

....

(1 mark)

1.5   Nuclear pore complexes (NPCs) control the passage of substances in and out of the nucleus.

In the scientist's study, cells from mutant plants with reduced NPC function were also centrifuged.
The cells from mutant plants produced a smaller pellet containing ribosomes, compared to cells from non-mutant plants. Explain why.

....

....

....

....

(3 marks)

2 *Chlamydia trachomatis* is a bacteria that replicates within a host cell.

Once inside the host cell, *Chlamydia trachomatis* replicates normally. The replication of the bacteria causes the host cell to swell and eventually burst, releasing structures that can infect other cells.

2.1 Compare and contrast the replication of *C. trachomatis* with the replication of a virus.

....

....

....

....

....

(3 marks)

C. trachomatis infections can be treated with azithromycin, a drug which inhibits ribosome function.

2.2 Explain the effect of this drug on bacterial growth.

....

....

....

(2 marks)

2.3 Explain why azithromycin can't be used to treat viral infections.

....

(1 mark)

A scientist compared the relative DNA content of a bacterial cell to its daughter cells, after the parent cell had divided to produce **two** daughter cells. The scientist's results are shown in **Table 2**.

Table 2

Cell	DNA content relative to the parent cell
Daughter cell A	1.4
Daughter cell B	0.8

2.4 Explain the results shown in **Table 2**.

....

....

....

....

(2 marks)

3   A scientist was studying the stages of the cell cycle.

The scientist used a microscope to observe some cells undergoing mitosis.
Figure 1 shows an image of **one** of these cells.

Figure 1

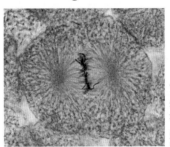

Ed Reschke/Getty Images

3.1   Name the stage of mitosis shown in **Figure 1** and explain your answer.

....

....

(2 marks)

Cyclins are proteins that play an important role in the cell cycle.
A scientist recorded the concentration of **two** cyclins (**E** and **B**) during part of the cell cycle
shown in **Figure 2**. He also recorded the mass of DNA present in the parent cell during this period
(also shown in **Figure 2**).

Figure 2

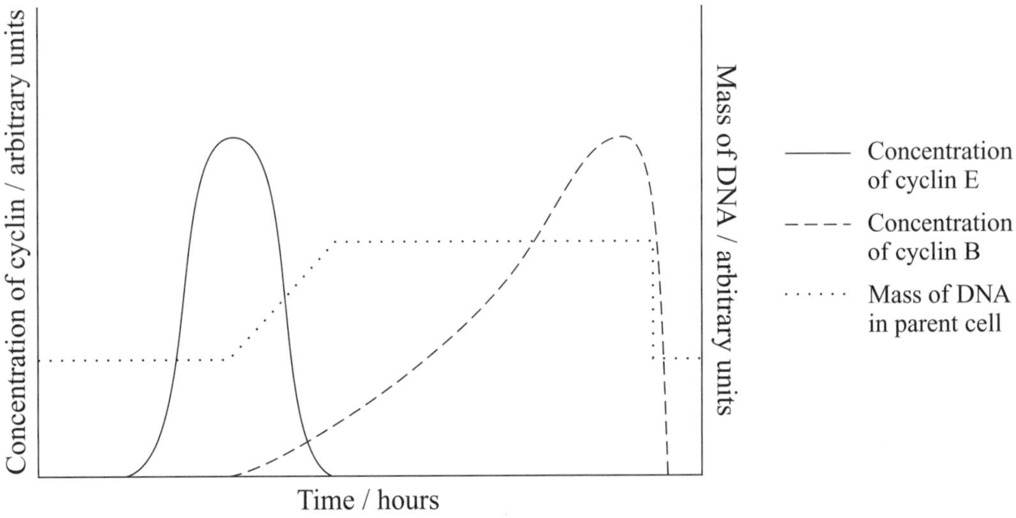

——— Concentration
of cyclin E

– – – Concentration
of cyclin B

······· Mass of DNA
in parent cell

y-axis (left): Concentration of cyclin / arbitrary units

y-axis (right): Mass of DNA / arbitrary units

x-axis: Time / hours

3.2   Using the results shown in **Figure 2**, suggest the functions of cyclins **E** and **B** in the cell cycle.

....

....

....

....

....

....

(4 marks)

4   Chemotherapy is a type of drug treatment against cancer.

4.1   Chemotherapy can prevent the production of enzymes needed for DNA synthesis.
Using your knowledge of the cell cycle, explain why this prevents cancerous cells from dividing.

....

....

(1 mark)

4.2   A hair follicle is a sac at the root of a hair. Cells in the hair follicle divide frequently, causing hair growth.
Suggest why non-cancerous cells in the hair follicle are more affected by chemotherapy than other non-cancerous body cells.

....

....

(2 marks)

4.3   A scientist took a sample of cancerous cells from a patient and calculated a mitotic index of 0.9.
The scientist observed a total number of 200 cells in the sample.
Calculate how many of the cells in this sample were undergoing mitosis at that time. Show your working.

....

(2 marks)

Aurora kinases are important molecules for the formation of spindle fibres during mitosis.
Recent evidence suggests that an inhibitor of these molecules can be used to treat cancer.
The inhibitor causes shortened spindle fibres to form during prophase, as shown in **Figure 3**.

Figure 3

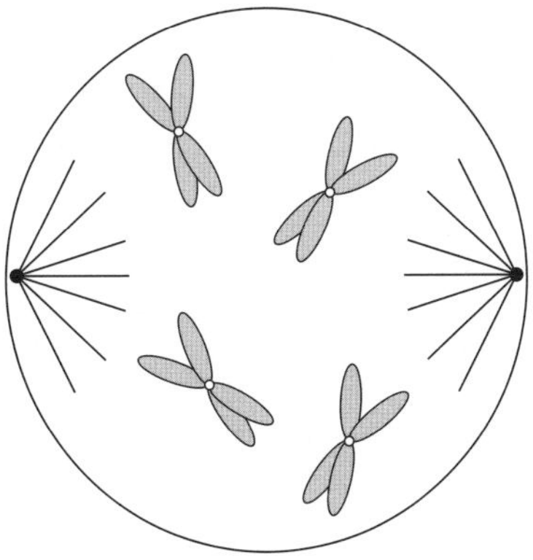

4.4   Using **Figure 3**, explain why these drugs could potentially be used as a method of treating cancer.

....

....

....

....

(3 marks)

EXAM TIP

Exam questions on the cell cycle often describe a way that the normal cycle is altered and ask you to explain what effect (if any) this has. As long as you know what usually happens during the different stages of the cell cycle, you should be able to work out what happens if something changes. It's important to be clued up about what happens during interphase and mitosis.

Score

31

Cell Membranes — 1

Cell membranes may look simple through a microscope, but nothing's as simple as it first seems. In fact, they're actually pretty complex and really important for cells. These questions will make sure your knowledge is tip top.

1   Cell membranes vary in structure due to the adaptation of specialised cells to their functions.

Figure 1 models the arrangement of molecules in a typical cell membrane, observed from above.

Figure 1

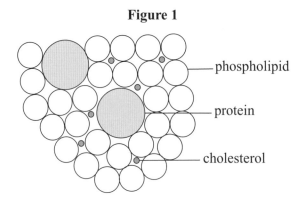

1.1 Describe the model illustrated in **Figure 1**.

....

....
(2 marks)

1.2 Explain the effect that a higher percentage of cholesterol would have on the model in **Figure 1**.

....

....
(2 marks)

Epithelial cells in the mammalian ileum absorb nutrients from a mammal's food.

1.3 Suggest and explain **two** ways in which the cell-surface membranes of these cells might be adapted to their function.

1. ....

....

2. ....

....
(4 marks)

The function of a neurone cell relies upon the rapid movement of cations across its cell membrane.

1.4 Suggest and explain an adaptation that you might expect to observe in the cell membrane of a neurone cell.

....

....
(2 marks)

2 **Figure 2** shows part of the phospholipid bilayer in a cell-surface membrane.

Figure 2

Cell exterior — water potential = –0.5 kPa

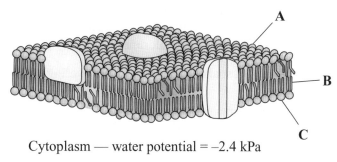

Cytoplasm — water potential = –2.4 kPa

2.1 Which letter (**A-C**) represents the hydrophobic part of the phospholipid bilayer?

....

(1 mark)

2.2 When phospholipids come together to form a cell membrane, a bilayer structure is always formed. Explain why.

....

....

....

....

(3 marks)

2.3 Using the information in **Figure 2**, describe the direction of movement of water across the cell membrane. Give a reason for your answer.

....

....

....

(2 marks)

3 Explain how co-transport is used to transport sodium ions and glucose into cells in the mammalian ileum, across their cell membranes.

....

....

....

....

....

....

....

(5 marks)

4 Beetroot cells contain a vacuole. The vacuole contains red pigments called betalains, which are contained within the vacuole by a phospholipid membrane. A scientist wanted to investigate the effect of temperature on the permeability of this membrane.

Sections of beetroot were cut from the main plant and soaked in distilled water overnight. The cut sections were then placed in fresh samples of distilled water and incubated at different temperatures for 30 minutes. The beetroot sections were then removed from the water and discarded. Each sample of water was then analysed using a colorimeter.

4.1 Why were the cut sections of beetroot soaked in distilled water overnight?

....

(1 mark)

4.2 Suggest a negative control that could have been used in this investigation.

....

(1 mark)

Table 1 illustrates the results that were obtained from the colorimetry analysis.
The percentage absorbance illustrates the proportion of transmitted light at blue/green wavelengths that was absorbed by the pigments in the water.

Table 1

Temperature / °C	Absorbance
20	0.05
30	0.16
40	0.35
50	0.60
60	0.73

4.3 Use your knowledge of the structure of cell membranes to explain these results.

....

....

....

....

....

(4 marks)

4.4 A second investigation found that membrane permeability increased as the pH was decreased. Suggest an explanation for this.

....

....

....

(3 marks)

Examiners love a good practical question, so you'll need to brush up on terms like 'negative control'. When it comes to explaining results, be clear about what any table or graph is showing you — if the results for a colorimetry experiment show transmission of light rather than absorbance, the numbers will be the opposite way round to the ones above.

Score

30

Cell Membranes — 2

1   Plants contain a mixture of solutes. Depending on the relative concentrations of solutes inside a plant cell and its environment, water will move into or out of the cell by osmosis.

Some students wanted to investigate the water potential of white potato cells. To do so they incubated samples of white potato in different concentrations of sucrose solution. The mass of each sample was measured before and after the incubation. The change in mass was then calculated. **Figure 1** shows a calibration curve of the results.

Figure 1

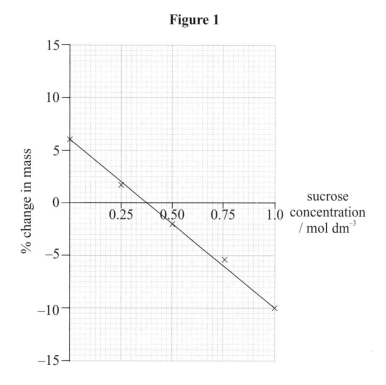

1.1   The students prepared the different concentrations of sucrose solution for their investigation using a stock solution of 1 mol dm⁻³ sucrose solution and distilled water.
Complete **Table 1** to show the volumes of stock solution and water used to make up each concentration.

Table 1

Concentration of sucrose solution to be made up / mol dm⁻³	Volume of 1 mol dm⁻³ sucrose solution used / cm³	Volume of water used / cm³	Final volume of solution to be made up / cm³
1	20	0	20
0.75	15		20
0.5			20
0.25			20
0			20

(2 marks)

1.2   Give **two** control variables for this investigation.

1. ....

2. ....

(2 marks)

Table 2 shows the relationship between sucrose concentration and water potential.

Table 2

Sucrose concentration / mol dm^{-3}	0.1	0.2	0.3	0.4	0.5	0.6	0.7	0.8	0.9	1.0
Water potential / kPa	−270	−540	−850	−1130	−1460	−1810	−2190	−2590	−3030	−3530

1.3 Use **Table 2** and **Figure 1** to estimate the water potential of the potato tissue.
Show your working.

water potential = ... kPa
(2 marks)

1.4 Suggest how the water potential of sweet potato tissue is likely to differ from the water potential of the white potato tissue used in the students' investigation. Explain your answer.

....

....

....
(2 marks)

2   Ca^{2+} ATPases are carrier proteins that transport Ca^{2+} ions across cell-surface membranes.
Each Ca^{2+} ATPase has one subunit that has an ATP binding site and acts as an enzyme.

2.1 Ca^{2+} ATPase spans the width of the cell-surface membrane.
The ATP binding site is always on the cytoplasm side of the membrane. Suggest why.

....

....
(1 mark)

2.2 Suggest and explain why Ca^{2+} ATPase has a subunit that acts as an enzyme.

....

....

....
(2 marks)

2.3 Explain why Ca^{2+} ions are always transported across cell-surface membranes
via carrier or channel proteins.

....

....
(2 marks)

EXAM TIP

'Estimate' means you need to give an approximate value rather than calculate an exact answer.
It needs to be a sensible estimate though, not just a stab in the dark guess, so you need to
think about the best method to use to obtain your estimate.

Score

13

Cells and the Immune System — 1

Not all cells are as nice as the ones you've just seen — some are out to cause trouble. The following questions are all about disease and the immune response. I know, your primary response is going to want you to turn away from this page, but make sure you stick at it. You want to get those memory cells activated, ready for your exam.

1   **Figure 1** shows an antibody.

Figure 1

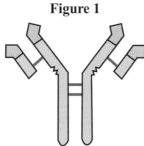

1.1   What is an antibody?

   ....
   (1 mark)

1.2   Name a type of cell that produces antibodies.

   ....
   (1 mark)

1.3   Explain how the structure of the antibody shown in **Figure 1** makes it adapted to its function.

   ....

   ....

   ....

   ....
   (3 marks)

Some antibodies have a more complex structure, made up of several monomers joined together.
This is shown in **Figure 2**.

Figure 2

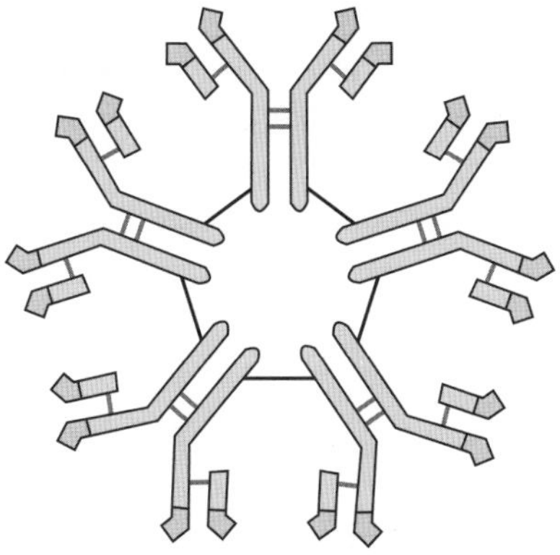

1.4   Suggest and explain **one** advantage of the structure in **Figure 2**, compared to that in **Figure 1**.

   ....

   ....
   (2 marks)

1.5 Some cells can produce antibodies at a rate of 2000 molecules per second.
Calculate how many antibodies would be produced by one of these cells in one hour.
Give your answer in standard form.

number of antibodies = ...
(2 marks)

2 Scientists are developing a vaccine against a viral disease that is often fatal in young children.

The vaccine has been tested on animals and is ready for human trials.
Initially, the vaccine is being tested on adults.

2.1 Suggest **two** factors the scientists should consider when selecting adult volunteers for this trial.

1. ....

2. ....
(2 marks)

Scientists conducting the trial compared the mean antibody concentration in males and females before and after the vaccine was administered. The results are shown in **Figure 3**.

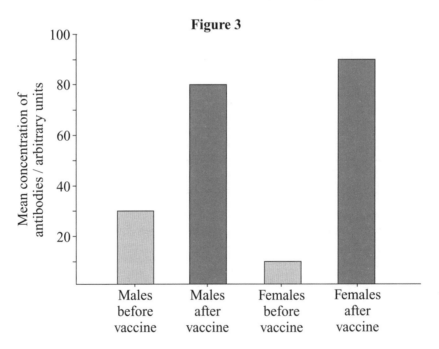

Figure 3

2.2 Using the data in **Figure 3**, calculate the percentage change in mean antibody concentration for females after they received the vaccine.

percentage change = ...%
(1 mark)

2.3 Statistical tests on the difference between the mean antibody concentration in males and females showed a result of P > 0.05. Explain what this information tells you about the results.

....

....
(2 marks)

The scientists are aiming to protect all children who are vulnerable to this disease by 2040.

2.4 Explain why it is possible to protect all children in a population without vaccinating them all.

....

....

(2 marks)

Vaccination programmes are not always completely effective.
One possible cause for this lack of success is antigen variability.

2.5 Explain how antigen variability could prevent a vaccination programme from being entirely successful.

....

....

....

(3 marks)

3   **Figure 4** shows the structure of the human immunodeficiency virus (HIV).

Figure 4

3.1 On **Figure 4**, name and label the part of the virus which allows it to gain access to a host cell.

(1 mark)

3.2 HIV can only infect cells that express the CD4 cell-surface receptor, such as T-cells. Explain why.

....

....

....

(3 marks)

HTLV-I is another virus that infects T-cells. It has the same structure as HIV and replicates the same way.
The HTLV-I genetic material contains a gene called Tax. When T-cells express the Tax protein, they begin
to divide uncontrollably.

3.3 Using this information, explain how a T-cell begins to express the Tax protein once the HTLV-I
genetic material has gained access to the cell.

....

....

....

....

(4 marks)

34

4   Leishmaniasis is a parasitic disease spread through the bites of sandflies.
    Figure 5 shows a method used for detecting the presence of *Leishmania* parasites in the blood.

Figure 5

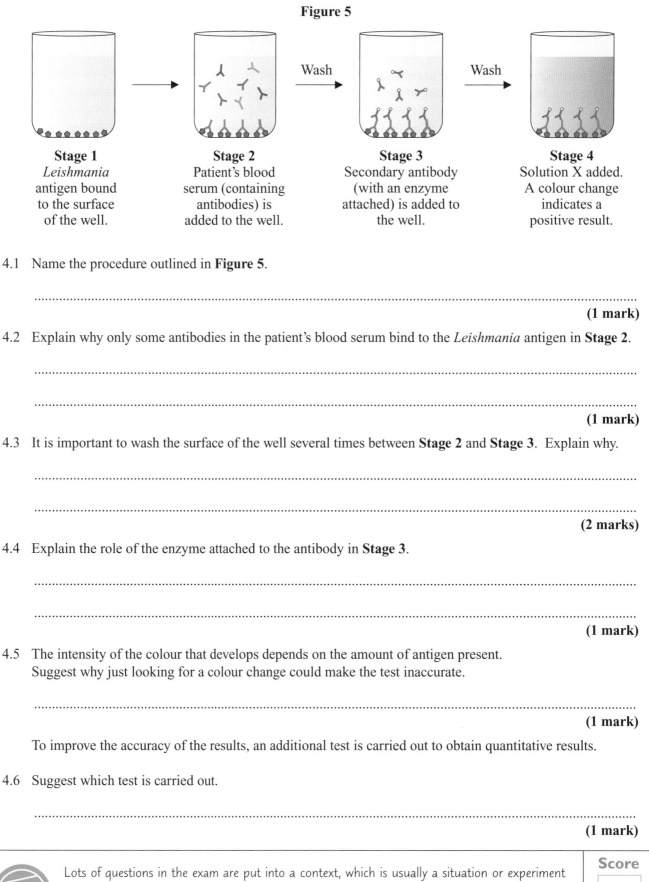

Stage 1	Stage 2	Stage 3	Stage 4
Leishmania antigen bound to the surface of the well.	Patient's blood serum (containing antibodies) is added to the well.	Secondary antibody (with an enzyme attached) is added to the well.	Solution X added. A colour change indicates a positive result.

4.1 Name the procedure outlined in **Figure 5**.

   ....
                                                                                                              (1 mark)

4.2 Explain why only some antibodies in the patient's blood serum bind to the *Leishmania* antigen in **Stage 2**.

   ....

   ....
                                                                                                              (1 mark)

4.3 It is important to wash the surface of the well several times between **Stage 2** and **Stage 3**. Explain why.

   ....

   ....
                                                                                                              (2 marks)

4.4 Explain the role of the enzyme attached to the antibody in **Stage 3**.

   ....

   ....
                                                                                                              (1 mark)

4.5 The intensity of the colour that develops depends on the amount of antigen present.
     Suggest why just looking for a colour change could make the test inaccurate.

   ....
                                                                                                              (1 mark)

   To improve the accuracy of the results, an additional test is carried out to obtain quantitative results.

4.6 Suggest which test is carried out.

   ....
                                                                                                              (1 mark)

Lots of questions in the exam are put into a context, which is usually a situation or experiment you've not come across before. Don't panic. You just need to break down the question, using the knowledge you do have, and apply it to the context. So it doesn't matter if you've never heard of Leishmaniasis before, just use what you know about how monoclonal antibodies work.

Score

34

Cells and the Immune System — 2

1   **Figure 1** shows the primary immune response following a bacterial infection.

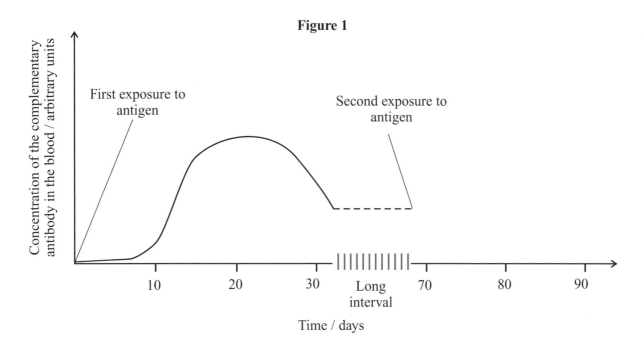

Figure 1

1.1 On **Figure 1**, sketch a line to represent the secondary immune response.

(1 mark)

1.2 Explain the shape of the curve for the primary immune response.

....

....

....

....

....

....

(4 marks)

2   Group B streptococcus (GBS) is a bacterium that can be carried, without harm, in a healthy human body. However, if a newborn baby becomes infected with GBS, it can lead to meningitis or other serious diseases.

GBS is typically passed on from a carrier mother to her baby during birth. Scientists are currently working to develop a vaccine against GBS, which will be given to pregnant women.

2.1 Suggest why a pregnant woman would be vaccinated against GBS when she is not at risk from infection.

....

....

(1 mark)

2.2 Describe how a vaccine could lead to immunity against a GBS infection.

....

....

....

....

....

....

....

(5 marks)

When a baby breastfeeds, it receives some of its mother's antibodies.
This gives the baby immunity against the diseases its mother is immune to.

2.3 Describe **two** differences between the immunity obtained from
breastfeeding with the immunity obtained from a vaccine.

1. ....

....

2. ....

....

(2 marks)

Meningitis occurs when the protective layers around the brain and spinal cord become infected.
It can be caused by bacteria, such as GBS, or certain viruses.

2.4 Meningitis caused by GBS bacteria can be treated with the antibiotic cefotaxime.
Cefotaxime intereferes with cell wall synthesis.
Using this information, explain why viral meningitis cannot be treated with cefotaxime.

....

....

(1 mark)

3   Alzheimer's disease is a brain disorder characterised by symptoms such as memory loss and
confusion. Scientists think that Alzheimer's disease may be the result of structures called amyloid
plaques developing in the brain. Several monoclonal antibodies are being trialled as drugs to treat
those diagnosed with Alzheimer's disease. One such drug, gantenerumab, is a monoclonal antibody
that targets a protein called beta-amyloid, which is the main component of amyloid plaques.

3.1 Using your knowledge of the immune response, suggest how a monoclonal antibody
that targets beta-amyloid might work to destroy plaques.

....

....

....

(2 marks)

A group of scientists investigated how well gantenerumab cleared beta-amyloid plaques in the hippocampus area of mice brains. Some of their results are shown in **Figure 2**.

Figure 2

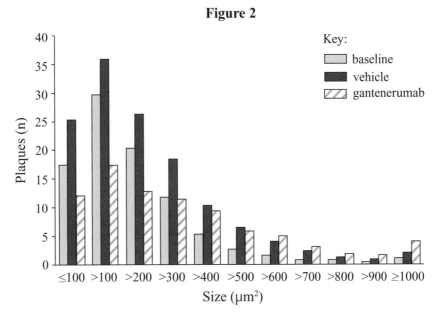

- The baseline data in **Figure 2** shows the size and number of plaques in untreated mice at the start of the investigation.

- The vehicle data shows the size and number of plaques in mice treated only with the vehicle used to deliver the gantenerumab and not with the drug itself.

- Treatment with both the vehicle and gantenerumab lasted 5 months.
  Results were recorded at the end of this time period.

3.2 Explain why some mice were treated with the vehicle only.

....

....

....

(2 marks)

3.3 Give **one** conclusion that can be drawn from the results shown in **Figure 2**.

....

....

(1 mark)

3.4 A student looking at the data in **Figure 2** concluded that gantenerumab will be a useful treatment for Alzheimer's disease in humans.

Explain why this is not a valid conclusion.

....

....

....

....

....

....

(4 marks)

38

4   **Figure 3** shows a simplified model of the different antigens present on red blood cells from different blood types.

Figure 3

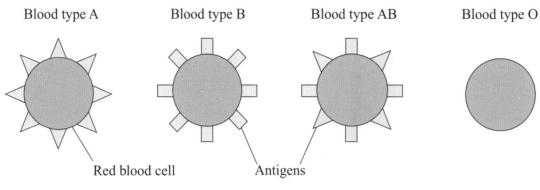

Blood type A   Blood type B   Blood type AB   Blood type O

Red blood cell   Antigens

4.1 Use the information in **Figure 3** to explain why it is important that people are given the correct blood type when receiving a blood transfusion.

....

....

....
(3 marks)

4.2 Describe the sequence of events that would occur if **blood type B** was given to someone with **blood type A**.

....

....

....

....

....

....
(6 marks)

4.3 Explain why anyone can receive **type O** blood.

....

....
(1 mark)

4.4 Monoclonal antibodies can be used to determine a person's blood type. Suggest how.

....

....
(2 marks)

Exchange and Transport Systems — 1

If you read 'Exchange and Transport Systems' and got excited about answering questions on the rail network, prepare to be disappointed. If you read 'Exchange and Transport Systems' and got excited about answering questions on how gases are exchanged in fish, insects, plants and humans... well, it's your lucky day.

1 **Figure 1** shows a gill filament of a fish.

Figure 1

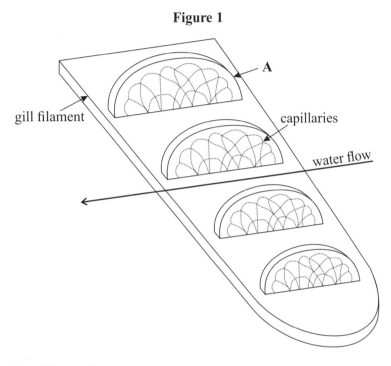

1.1 Name structure **A** on **Figure 1**.

....
(1 mark)

1.2 Draw an arrow on structure **A** to show the direction of blood flow.
(1 mark)

1.3 Label structure **A** to show where the highest and lowest concentrations of oxygen are found in the blood.
(1 mark)

1.4 Explain **one** way in which the structure of the gill filament is adapted to its function.

....

....

....
(2 marks)

2 A student dissected a grasshopper. As part of the dissection, she removed a piece of the grasshopper's exoskeleton.

2.1 Suggest a tool that the student could have used to cut through the exoskeleton.

....
(1 mark)

Figure 2 shows a diagram of the grasshopper's gas exchange system.

Figure 2

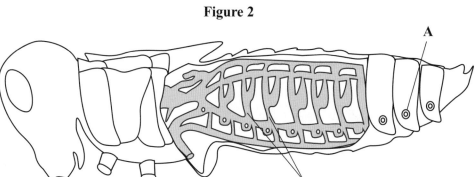

2.2 Identify the structures labelled **A** and **B** in **Figure 2**.

A ....

B ....

(2 marks)

2.3 The student wants to examine the structures labelled **B** more closely, with the use of a temporary mount.
A stain is **not** needed to view these structures.
Using this information, describe how the student would prepare the mount.

....

....

....

....

(3 marks)

2.4 In insects, the need for efficient gas exchange can conflict with the need to limit water loss.
Give **two** ways that the grasshopper is adapted to limit water loss.

1. ....

2. ....

(2 marks)

3 A student investigated the stomatal density of a non-xerophytic plant's leaves. She studied ten samples of lower epidermis under a microscope. The samples were taken from different leaves of the same plant.

Table 1 shows the number of stomata the student counted within the microscope's field of view for each sample. The field of view measured 0.025 mm² in each case.

Table 1

	Sample									
	1	2	3	4	5	6	7	8	9	10
Number of stomata	5	6	7	4	3	8	5	5	3	4

3.1 Using **Table 1** and the information provided, estimate the number of stomata you would expect to find on a leaf with a surface area of 150 mm². Show your working.

Number of stomata: ....

(2 marks)

3.2 Give **two** reasons why your answer to question **3.1** might not be an accurate estimate of the number of stomata present on the leaf.

1. ....

2. ....

(2 marks)

3.3 Name the cells that are the site of gas exchange in a leaf.

....

(1 mark)

Figure 3 shows an electron micrograph image of part of a xerophyte leaf.

Figure 3

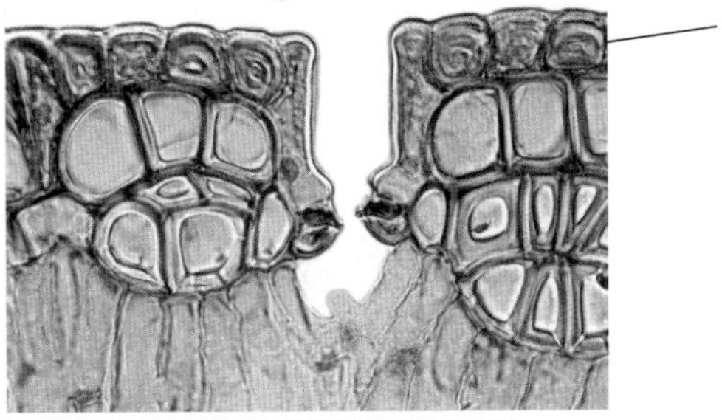

epidermis

Remember, a xerophyte is a plant that is adapted to life in warm, dry or windy habitats.

DR KEITH WHEELER/SCIENCE PHOTO LIBRARY

3.4 Describe and explain the xerophytic adaptation shown in **Figure 3**.

....

....

....

....

(3 marks)

4 *Lepus capensis* and *Lepus othus* are two species of hare.
Lepus othus has relatively short ears compared to *Lepus capensis*.

4.1 Which of these two hare species would you expect to find in Alaska, where the climate is cold? Explain your answer.

....

....

....

....

(3 marks)

4.2 Alaskan hares are hunted by larger mammals, such as polar bears. Explain how you would expect the metabolic rate of an Alaskan hare to differ from the metabolic rate of a polar bear.

....

....

....

....

(3 marks)

5   Sharks exchange oxygen across their gill lamellae using a counter-current
    gas exchange system. **Figure 4** shows how the relative oxygen concentration
    of water changes with distance along a shark's lamella.

Figure 4

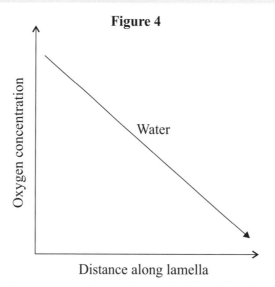

5.1 On **Figure 4**, sketch the relative oxygen concentration of the blood flowing through the lamella.

(1 mark)

Figure 5 shows how the relative oxygen concentrations of water and blood would change with distance
along a shark's lamella if gas exchange took place via a parallel flow system.

Figure 5

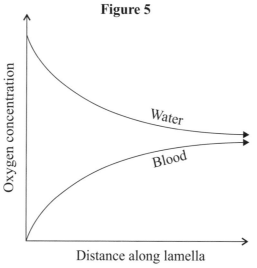

5.2 Use **Figure 5** to explain why a parallel flow gas exchange system would be less efficient than a
     counter-current gas exchange system.

....

....

....

....

....

(3 marks)

Make sure your working is clear in calculation questions that are worth multiple marks. Even if
you get the final answer wrong, you could pick up some marks from your working — but only
if the marker can tell what you were trying to do and where you got your numbers from.

Score

31

Exchange and Transport Systems — 2

1 Bacterium **A** has a surface area to volume ratio of 5 : 1. Bacterium **B** has a surface area to volume ratio of 84 : 22. Bacterium **C** has a surface area of 15.75 μm² and a volume of 3.5 μm³.

Use the information above to determine which **one** of the bacteria (**A**, **B** or **C**) is likely to be able to carry out gas exchange at the fastest rate. Show your working.

Bacterium: ....

(2 marks)

2 Intrapulmonary pressure is the pressure inside the lungs.
Figure 1 shows how intrapulmonary pressure changes during breathing.

Figure 1

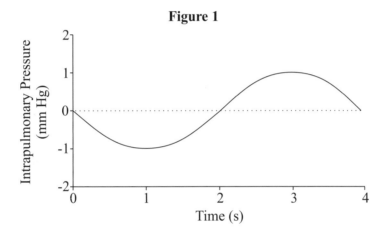

2.1 Name **two** muscles that contract when a person inspires.

1. ....

2. ....

(2 marks)

2.2 State the time period in **Figure 1** during which air is being taken into the lungs.
Explain your answer.

....

....

....

(3 marks)

2.3 State the time in **Figure 1** at which the lung volume is at its smallest.

....

(1 mark)

3 Emphysema is a lung disease that leads to the breakdown of the alveoli walls.

3.1 Give **two** ways that healthy alveoli are adapted for gas exchange.

1. ....

....

2. ....

....

(2 marks)

Flow-volume loops show air flow during expiration and inspiration, plotted against the volume of air in the lungs. **Figure 2** shows a flow-volume loop for a healthy person and one for a patient with emphysema.

Figure 2

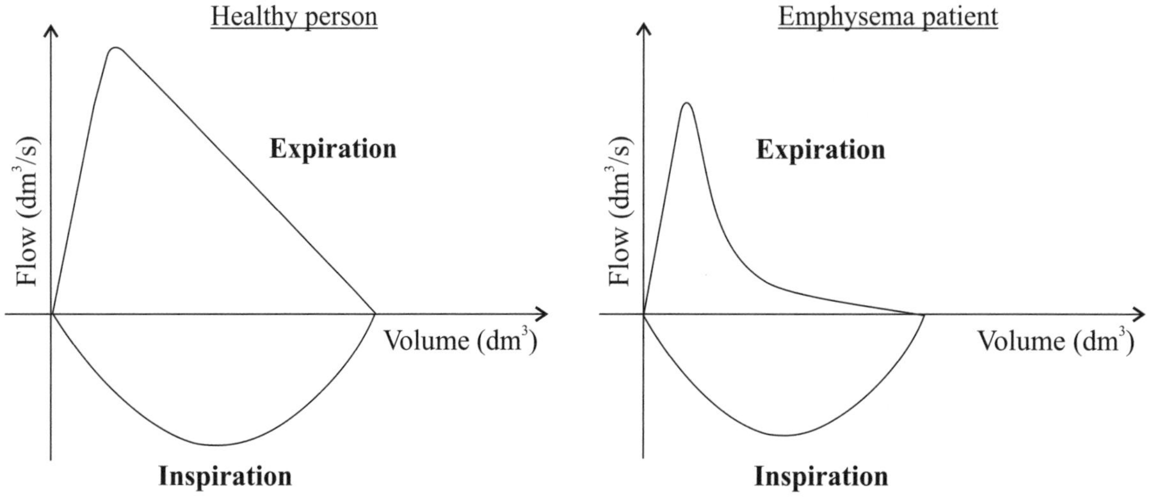

3.2 Suggest why the inspiration section of the emphysema patient's flow-volume loop is similar to that of the healthy person's, but the expiration section of the loop is not.

....

....

....

....

....

(3 marks)

3.3 The pulmonary ventilation rate (PVR) is the volume of air inspired or expired in one minute.
A patient has a PVR of 7.60 dm^3 $minute^{-1}$ and takes 16 breaths per minute.
Calculate the volume of air in each breath in cm^3.

.... cm^3

(2 marks)

4   Asbestos is a fibrous material that was commonly used in construction work in Britain until it was banned in 1999. Long-term exposure to asbestos fibres can lead to a lung condition called asbestosis.

Asbestosis involves the build up of inelastic scar tissue in the lungs.

4.1 Suggest why people with asbestosis may have a faster ventilation rate than normal.

....

....

....

(2 marks)

Figure 3 shows the number of death certificates per year in Great Britain, which identified asbestosis as the underlying cause, from 1978 to 2014.

Figure 3

4.2 A student concludes from **Figure 3** that the asbestos ban has been unsuccessful at protecting people against asbestosis. Evaluate this conclusion.

....

....

....

....

....

....

....

....

(4 marks)

EXAM TIP If you're asked to evaluate something, you need to make a judgement based on the evidence you've been given. Make sure you consider both sides of the argument in your answer — think about all the possible factors that might have affected the data you're looking at.

Score

21

More Exchange and Transport Systems — 1

That's right — you're not done with exchange and transport systems just yet. Here's another great big section full of questions about them. You can't exchange them for something nicer, I'm afraid — get cracking.

1   Trypsin is an endopeptidase. It breaks down proteins into smaller peptides.

Figure 1 shows a protein.

Figure 1

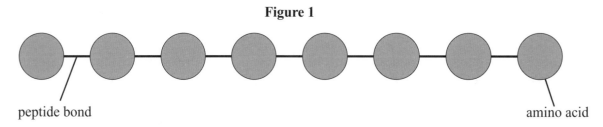

peptide bond   amino acid

1.1 On **Figure 1**, draw an arrow to indicate **one** place where trypsin could cleave the protein.

(1 mark)

1.2 In addition to endopeptidases, there are **two** other types of enzymes that digest proteins.

Name these enzymes and describe how they work.

Name:..

Function:..

Name:..

Function:..

(4 marks)

1.3 The amino acids released by protein digestion are absorbed by the ileum epithelial cells.
Explain how these amino acids are absorbed.

....

....

....

....

....

....

....

....

....

....

(5 marks)

1.4 Enteropeptidase is an enzyme produced by the cells lining the small intestine when food is ingested.
The role of enteropeptidase is to convert trypsinogen, an inactive enzyme, into trypsin, its active form.
A mutation in one of the genes needed to make enteropeptidase can cause enteropeptidase deficiency,
which can be life-threatening.

Explain why enteropeptidase deficiency could be life-threatening.

....

....

....

....

....

....

(3 marks)

2 Scientists investigated the breakdown of different types of commonly used
oils by Lipase A in the small intestine. The results can be seen in **Figure 2**.

Figure 2

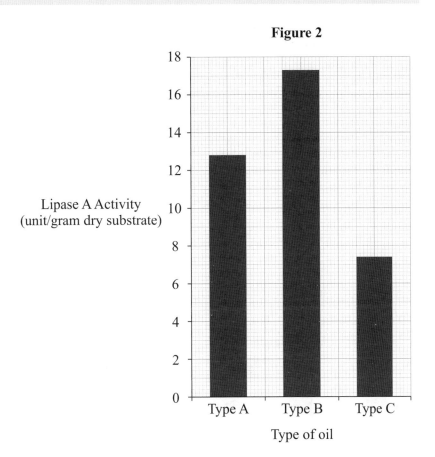

2.1 Lipase A is more effective at hydrolysing oil Type B than oil types A or C. Suggest an explanation for this.

....

....

....

(2 marks)

2.2   Calculate the ratio of Lipase A activity for oils Type B : Type C, shown in **Figure 2**.

Ratio: .... : 1
(1 mark)

2.3   Name **one** substance other than lipase that aids lipid digestion.

....
(1 mark)

2.4   Give **two** substances that lipids are hydrolysed into.

1. ....

2. ....
(2 marks)

2.5   Describe how the products of lipid digestion are absorbed into the ileum epithelial cells.

....

....

....

....

....
(3 marks)

3   **Figure 3** shows a model gut set up by a student to investigate the digestion and absorption of starch.

Figure 3

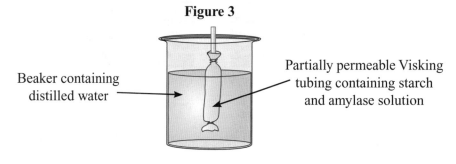

Beaker containing
distilled water

Partially permeable Visking
tubing containing starch
and amylase solution

3.1   Describe how the student would set up a control for this investigation.

....

....
(1 mark)

3.2 Suggest **two** reasons why this model is not wholly representative of absorption in the gut.

1. ....

....

2. ....

....

(2 marks)

The contents of the Visking tubing and the beaker were tested with iodine and Benedict's reagent at the start of the experiment, and after they had been left for 20 minutes. **Table 1** shows the results of these tests.

Table 1

	Iodine test result	Benedict's test result
Visking tubing contents at start	Positive	Negative
Beaker contents at start	Negative	Negative
Visking tubing contents after 20 minutes	Negative	Positive
Beaker contents after 20 minutes	Negative	Positive

3.3 Explain the iodine test results.

....

....

....

....

....

....

(4 marks)

3.4 Explain the Benedict's test results.

....

....

....

....

....

....

(4 marks)

Score

33

More Exchange and Transport Systems — 2

1   **Figure 1** shows the oxygen dissociation curves for
     humans and llamas, a mammal that lives at high altitudes.

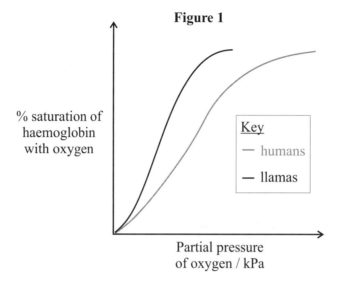

Figure 1

% saturation of
haemoglobin
with oxygen

Partial pressure
of oxygen / kPa

Key
— humans
— llamas

1.1 Describe and explain the shape of the oxygen dissociation curve for humans.

....

....

....

....

....

....

....

....

....
(5 marks)

1.2 Explain the differences between the oxygen dissociation curves for llamas and humans.

....

....

....

....

....

....
(3 marks)

Figure 2 shows the oxygen dissociation curve for a person who is exercising, alongside a person who is not exercising.

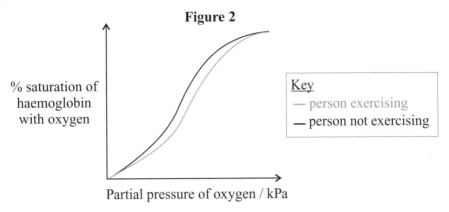

Figure 2

% saturation of haemoglobin with oxygen

Key
— person exercising
— person not exercising

Partial pressure of oxygen / kPa

1.3 Explain why the oxygen dissociation curve for the person exercising is to the right of the oxygen dissociation curve for the person who is not exercising.

....

....

....

(3 marks)

2   **Figure 3** shows a diagram of a mammalian heart.

Figure 3

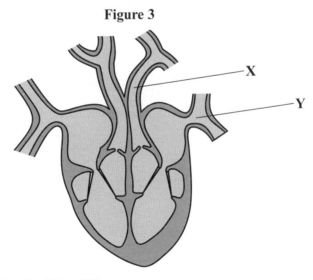

X

Y

2.1 Name the parts of the heart labelled **X** and **Y**.

Name of **X** ....

Name of **Y** ....

(2 marks)

A student carried out a dissection of a mammalian heart.

2.2 State **three** precautions that must be taken in order to safely carry out a dissection.

1. ....

2. ....

3. ....

(3 marks)

The student produced a biological drawing of the heart.

2.3 Give **one** instruction that the student would need to follow in order to produce a clear and useful drawing.

....

(1 mark)

3 Buerger's disease is a type of cardiovascular disease. It causes the small and medium arteries and veins in the hands and feet to experience thrombosis (blood clotting) and become inflamed.

3.1 People with Buerger's disease may eventually need to have fingers or toes amputated. Suggest why.

....

....

....

....

(2 marks)

Buerger's disease causes a reduction in the volume of tissue fluid that passes through capillary beds.

3.2 Describe how tissue fluid is formed in healthy tissues, and how it is returned to the circulatory system.

....

....

....

....

....

....

....

....

(5 marks)

Capillary beds are important exchange surfaces.

3.3 Explain **one** way in which the structure of capillaries helps them carry out their function.

....

....

(1 mark)

Don't forget that you should also revise the practicals you did in class — the exam will test you on your practical skills as well as the theory. By the time you're sitting the exam, it might have been a while since you did some of the practicals, so make sure you've reminded yourself of what you did, the equipment you used, and the safety precautions you had to take.

Score

25

More Exchange and Transport Systems — 3

1   **Figure 1** shows a cross-section of the human heart.

Figure 1

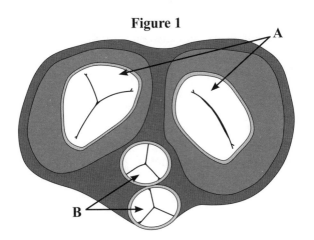

1.1   What is the role of the valves labelled **A** in **Figure 1**?

    ....

    ....

    ....

                                                                                                          (2 marks)

1.2   In terms of pressure changes in the heart, explain what causes the valves labelled **B** in **Figure 1** to open.

    ....

    ....

                                                                                                          (1 mark)

Cardiac output is the volume of blood pumped out of the left ventricle in one minute.
Scientists investigated the effect of body position on heart rate and cardiac output.
Table 1 shows their results.

Table 1

	Standing up	Lying down
Mean heart rate / bpm	74	57
Mean cardiac output / $cm^3\ min^{-1}$	4700	4700
Mean stroke volume / cm^3		

1.3   The stroke volume is the volume of blood that is pumped out by the left ventricle in one cardiac cycle.
Use the information in **Table 1** to complete the table to show the mean stroke volume.

                                                                                                          (1 mark)

> Use the information you've been given in the question to come
> up with a formula linking stroke volume, cardiac output and
> heart rate. Then substitute in the numbers from the table.

Topic Three — Exchange and Transport

1.4 The scientists ensured that the participants of the investigation had been in the required position for five minutes before they recorded these measurements. Suggest why.

....

....

(1 mark)

1.5 Suggest why there is a difference in heart rate between standing up and lying down in **Table 1**.

....

....

(1 mark)

1.6 Explain why the scientists used 'mean' measurements.

....

....

(1 mark)

2   **Figure 2** shows the pressure changes in an individual's heart during the cardiac cycle.

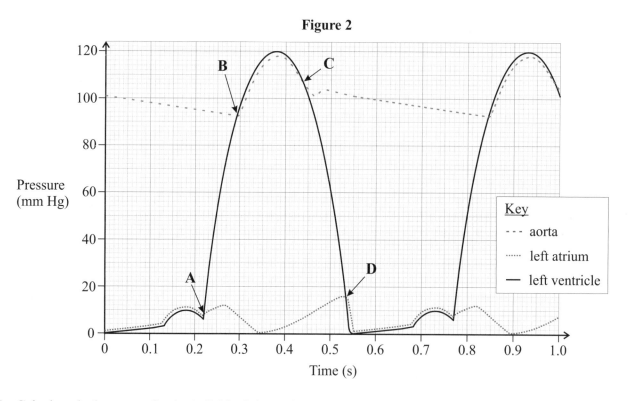

Figure 2

2.1 Calculate the heart rate for the individual shown in **Figure 2**.

.... beats per minute
(1 mark)

2.2 When on **Figure 2** does the left atrium start to contract?

> Hint: when a chamber contracts, there's a
> sudden rise in pressure inside the chamber.

.... seconds

(1 mark)

2.3 Describe and explain the events that are occurring at points **A** to **D** on **Figure 2**.

....

....

....

....

....

....

....

....

....

....

....

....

(6 marks)

2.4 Explain the difference between the maximum pressures of the left atrium and the left ventricle of the heart.

....

....

....

(1 mark)

2.5 Using your own knowledge and information from **Figure 2**, explain **one** way in which the aorta is adapted for its function.

....

....

....

(2 marks)

Score

18

More Exchange and Transport Systems — 4

1 A student used a potometer to investigate transpiration in a plant. **Figure 1** shows how the potometer was set up. The student closed the tap, then took the capillary tube out of the beaker of water long enough for an air bubble to form. She then recorded the amount of time it took for the air bubble to move between the two markers, and used it to calculate the transpiration rate.

Figure 1

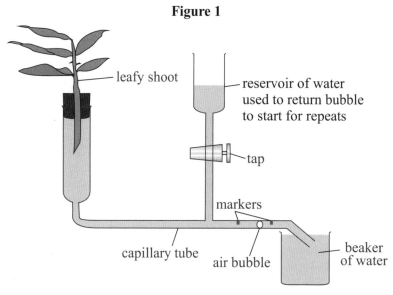

1.1 When setting up this experiment, it is important that water does not touch the leaves. Using your knowledge of water transport in plants, explain why.

....

....

....

(2 marks)

The student used the potometer to investigate the effect of temperature on the transpiration rate. The results are shown in **Table 1**.

Table 1

Temperature / °C	Mean transpiration rate / cm³ per minute
20	0.20
30	0.34
40	0.85
50	1.24
60	1.36

1.2 Describe and explain the relationship between the temperature and the transpiration rate in **Table 1**.

....

....

....

....

....

(3 marks)

2   Xylem vessels are found running from the roots to the leaves in plants.
Scientists measured the rate of water flow through the xylem of a plant in its natural
environment at different times of the day. The results are presented in **Table 2**.

Table 2

Time of day	Rate of water flow in xylem / mm^3 second^{-1}
00:00	0.8
06:00	2.8
12:00	4.5
18:00	3.0

2.1   Using your knowledge of water transport in the xylem, explain the difference in the results between
00:00 and 12:00 in **Table 2**.

....

....

....

....

(3 marks)

In order to investigate the structure of the xylem, the scientists also carried out a dissection
on a leaf of the plant.

2.2   Suggest why the scientists kept the dissected plant tissue in water until they were ready to view the cells.

....

....

(1 mark)

2.3   Suggest a step in the dissection that the scientists would have carried out in order to observe the xylem
vessels under a microscope.

....

....

(1 mark)

3   Translocation in a plant describes the movement of solutes to where they are needed within the plant.

3.1   When treated with metabolic inhibitors, translocation in a plant stops.
Explain why.

....

....

....

(2 marks)

Figure 2 represents the flow of solutes in the phloem of a tree, according to the mass flow hypothesis.

Figure 2

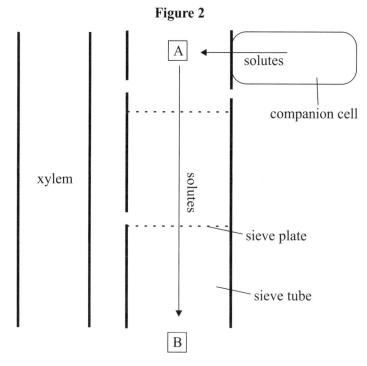

3.2 Describe and explain how the level of pressure at point **A** in **Figure 2** differs to that at point **B**.

....

....

....

....
(3 marks)

A ring of bark is removed from the tree at point **B**.

3.3 Explain how this would affect the concentration of solutes at point **A**, according to the mass flow hypothesis.

....

....
(2 marks)

3.4 Other than a ringing experiment, describe **one** other type of experiment that could be carried out to monitor translocation in trees.

....

....

....

....
(3 marks)

EXAM TIP

If a question asks you to 'describe and explain' something, make sure you do both. 'Describing' means giving an account of something, e.g. saying <u>how</u> a variable changes in a table or graph, whereas 'explaining' means setting out reasons, e.g. saying <u>why</u> the variable changes. Doing just one or the other will mean you miss out on marks.

Score

20

DNA, RNA and Protein Synthesis

Protein synthesis isn't easy, but imagine the warm, glowing feeling you'll get once you've worked your way through all these questions on it. Can't imagine it? Never mind, give the questions a go and you'll soon feel it.

1   The average human cell contains around 2 m of DNA.
       The average human cell nucleus is only 10 μm in diameter.

1.1   Describe how the DNA in a eukaryotic cell is arranged so that it can fit into the nucleus.

....

....
(2 marks)

1.2   Prokaryotic DNA is not stored in a nucleus.
       Give **one** other difference between the way that DNA is arranged in eukaryotic cells and prokaryotic cells.

....

....
(1 mark)

It is estimated that the DNA in a human cell contains around 20 000 protein-encoding genes.
These genes correspond to only 1.5% of the DNA sequence.

1.3   Using the information provided above, calculate the average length of a human gene in metres.

Length of gene = ... m
(2 marks)

1.4   What name is given to the complete set of genes present in a cell?

....
(1 mark)

1.5   What name is given to the complete set of proteins that a cell is able to produce?

....
(1 mark)

In prokaryotes, around 90% of the DNA is protein-encoding.

1.6   Suggest **two** reasons why prokaryotes have a much greater percentage of protein-encoding DNA
       than humans.

1. ....

2. ....
(2 marks)

1.7   Protein-encoding DNA leads to the production of mRNA.
       Other parts of the DNA encode functional RNA. Give **two** examples of functional RNA.

1. ....

2. ....
(2 marks)

2 Leigh syndrome is a metabolic disorder that affects the central nervous system. It can be caused by a mutation in the MT-ATP6 gene, which is located in the mitochondrial DNA.

2.1 Give **two** differences between the structure of DNA found in the mitochondria and the structure of DNA found in the nucleus.

1. ....

2. ....

(2 marks)

2.2 What name is given to the location that a gene occupies on a particular DNA molecule?

A Intron ☐

B Exon ☐

C Allele ☐

D Locus ☐

(1 mark)

Table 1 contains some of the DNA codons that code for particular amino acids.

Table 1

Amino acid	DNA codon
Isoleucine	ATT, ATC, ATA
Glutamic acid	GAA, GAG
Leucine	CTG, TTA, TTG
Methionine	ATG
Valine	GTT, GTC, GTA, GTG
Arginine	CGG, AGA
Alanine	GCT, GCC, GCA, GCG

2.3 Give **one** piece of evidence from **Table 1** that shows the genetic code is degenerate.

....

....

(1 mark)

Figure 1 shows **one** of the mutations in the MT-ATP6 gene that can cause Leigh syndrome.

Figure 1

Original gene: CAA CCA ATA GCC CTG GCC GTA

Mutated gene: CAA CCA ATA GCC CGG GCC GTA

Codon position: 152   153   154   155   156   157   158

2.4 Describe the effect that the mutation shown in **Figure 1** will have on the mRNA sequence produced from the MT-ATP6 gene.

....

....

(1 mark)

2.5 Using **Table 1** for reference, describe the effect that the mutation shown in **Figure 1** will have on the amino acid sequence produced from the MT-ATP6 gene.

....

....

(1 mark)

2.6 MT-ATP6 codes for a subunit of ATP synthase, an enzyme involved in respiration.
Explain how a change in its amino acid sequence could affect the function of ATP synthase.

....

....

....

(3 marks)

2.7 Describe how the mRNA produced from the MT-ATP6 gene is translated into a protein.

....

....

....

....

....

....

....

(5 marks)

3   Transcriptomics involves studying the RNA present in a cell.
One technique involved in transcriptomics is described in **Figure 2**.

Figure 2

| All of the mRNA is extracted from a cell. | → | An enzyme is used to convert the mRNA into complementary DNA (cDNA). | → | The sequence of the cDNA molecules is determined. This allows the mRNA molecules to be identified. | → | The data is analysed to determine the level of mRNA expression. |

3.1 Describe how mRNA is produced from DNA by RNA polymerase.

....

....

....

....

....

....

(4 marks)

A team of scientists have developed a new drug. The team used the method in **Figure 2** to investigate how the levels of three different mRNA molecules changed when eukaryotic cells were treated with the drug.

Figure 3 shows two images. One represents the cDNA for one of the mRNA molecules.
The other represents the original DNA strand from which the mRNA was produced in the nucleus.

Figure 3

cDNA   Original DNA

3.2   Explain why the cDNA and the original DNA shown in **Figure 3** are different.

....

....

....

(2 marks)

The results of the scientists' experiment are shown in **Figure 4**.

Figure 4

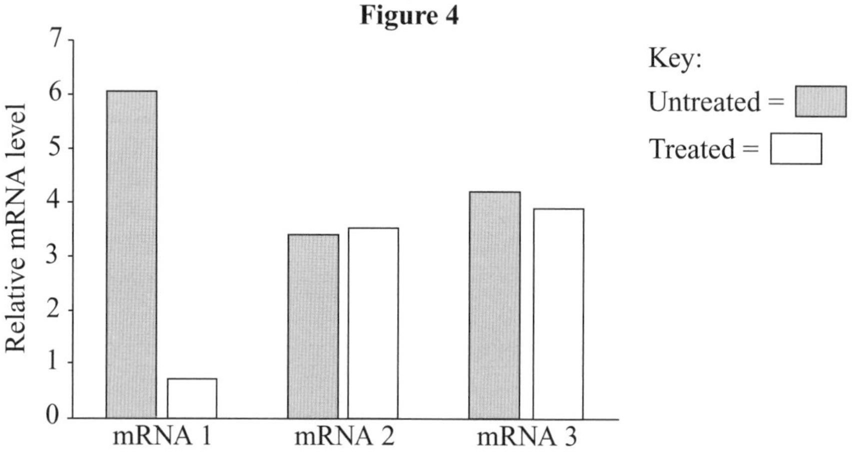

Key:
Untreated =
Treated =

The scientists hypothesised that the new drug had two possible methods of action:
Method 1:   By preventing RNA polymerase from working.
Method 2:   By destroying particular mRNA sequences.

3.3   With reference to **Figure 4**, explain why the drug cannot be acting via Method 1.

....

....

....

(2 marks)

3.4   Explain how the results shown in **Figure 4** can be explained if the drug acts via Method 2.

....

....

....

(2 marks)

EXAM TIP Make sure you know the basics of DNA and RNA structure, as well as the relationship between the base sequence in DNA, mRNA and tRNA. If you do, questions like 2.4 will be easy marks in the exam. It's important to remember that U replaces T in RNA too.

Score

35

Diversity, Classification and Variation — 1

It is due to variations in the genetic code that there is such a great diversity of life on Earth. And because there's so much diversity, scientists find it easier to classify organisms into groups. There's a lot to remember for this section, but don't worry — these questions are here to help you make sure you're all set for your exams.

1   **Figure 1** is a phylogenetic tree. It shows how different species from the order Carnivora are related.

Figure 1

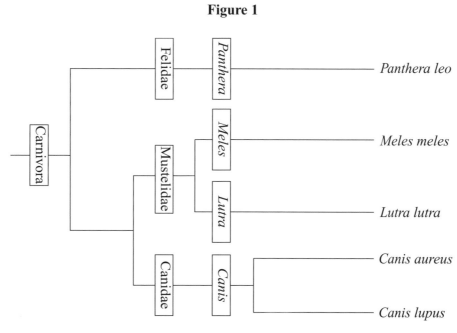

1.1 What is the definition of a species?

....

....

(1 mark)

1.2 The plural of genus is genera.
How many different genera are represented in **Figure 1**?

....

(1 mark)

1.3 Which **two** species in **Figure 1** are most closely related? Give a reason for your answer.

....

....

(1 mark)

1.4 What taxon is represented by the groups Felidae, Mustelidae and Canidae in **Figure 1**?

    A   Kingdom   ☐

    B   Phylum   ☐

    C   Class   ☐

    D   Family   ☐

(1 mark)

2 Species become better adapted to their environment via the process of natural selection.

Figure 2 shows two populations (**A** and **B**) experiencing natural selection.

Figure 2

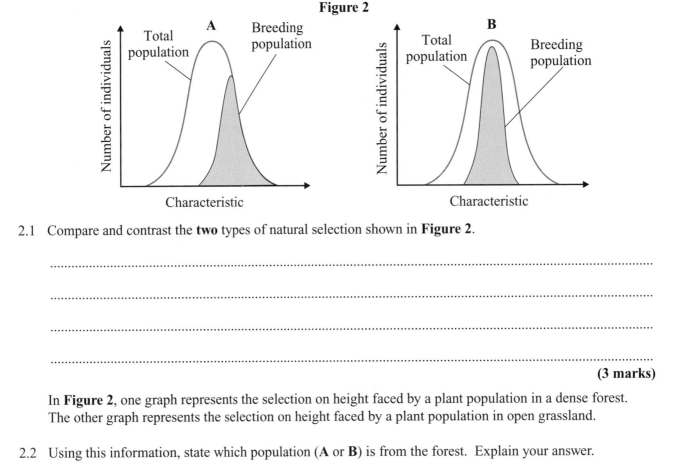

2.1 Compare and contrast the **two** types of natural selection shown in **Figure 2**.

....

....

....

....
(3 marks)

In **Figure 2**, one graph represents the selection on height faced by a plant population in a dense forest. The other graph represents the selection on height faced by a plant population in open grassland.

2.2 Using this information, state which population (**A** or **B**) is from the forest. Explain your answer.

....

....
(2 marks)

2.3 Suggest why the plant population in open grassland is undergoing a different type of selection to the one in the dense forest.

....

....
(1 mark)

Clutch size is the number of eggs laid by a female bird during one breeding season.
Figure 3 shows the mean number of eggs in a clutch over several years for a bird population.
The error bars indicate standard deviation.

Figure 3

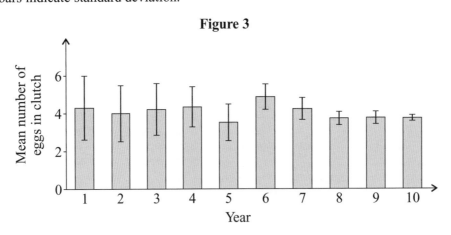

2.4 Suggest an explanation for the changes shown in **Figure 3**.

....

....

....

....

(3 marks)

3 When classifying organisms, scientists often look at the proteins found within the organisms.

3.1 Explain why proteins can be analysed to help classify organisms.

....

....

....

(3 marks)

Scientists compared the amino acid sequence of a protein in four species, to that in humans.
They counted the differences in each amino acid sequence, compared to the sequence in humans.
The data obtained is presented in **Table 1**.

Table 1

Species	Number of differences in amino acid sequence compared to human protein
A	25
B	7
C	1
D	7

3.2 Using the information in **Table 1**, discuss the scientists' results.

....

....

....

(2 marks)

3.3 It was concluded that species **B** and **D** were more closely related to each other than they were to humans.
Explain why this is not a valid conclusion for this data.

....

....

(1 mark)

EXAM TIP

Standard deviation is a measure of the variation around the mean. Error bars can be used to show standard deviation in graphs. Put simply — the shorter the bar, the smaller the standard deviation and the less spread out the data is. Not all error bars represent standard deviation though, so make sure you read the question carefully to figure out what they mean.

Score

19

Diversity, Classification and Variation — 2

1   Scientists investigated the diversity of plants in an ungrazed field. The data obtained is shown in **Table 1**.

Table 1

Species	Number of individual plants counted in different quadrats					Mean number counted
Rapeseed	24	46	32	28	32	
Common sunflower	1	0	2	1	1	
Common poppy	8	12	6	10	8	
Creeping thistle	13	14	7	15	13	

1.1   Complete **Table 1** to show the mean number of each species counted.

(1 mark)

1.2   Using the mean values you added to **Table 1** and the formula provided below, calculate the index of diversity for plants in this field. Show your working.

$$d = \frac{N(N-1)}{\Sigma n(n-1)}$$

where N = total number of organisms of all species
and n = total number of organisms of one species

$d =$ ....

(2 marks)

The scientists then gathered data in a second field on which farm animals were allowed to graze. The mean number of creeping thistle was much lower in the second field than in the first.

1.3   The scientists wanted to determine if the difference in means between the two fields was significant. State which statistical test they could have used to determine this. Explain your choice.

....

....

(2 marks)

1.4   Further investigations in both fields showed the overall biodiversity of the grazed field to be lower than that of the ungrazed field. Suggest an explanation for this.

....

....

....

(2 marks)

2 Scientists wanted to investigate the impact of different farming practices on ladybird biodiversity. To do so, they counted the number of different ladybird species on organic and conventional farms. This allowed them to compare the species richness of the ladybirds in the different types of farm.

2.1 Explain why it may have been more useful for the scientists to compare indexes of diversity for their investigation.

....

....

....

(2 marks)

The scientists' data can be seen in **Figure 1**. The error bars indicate standard deviation.

Figure 1

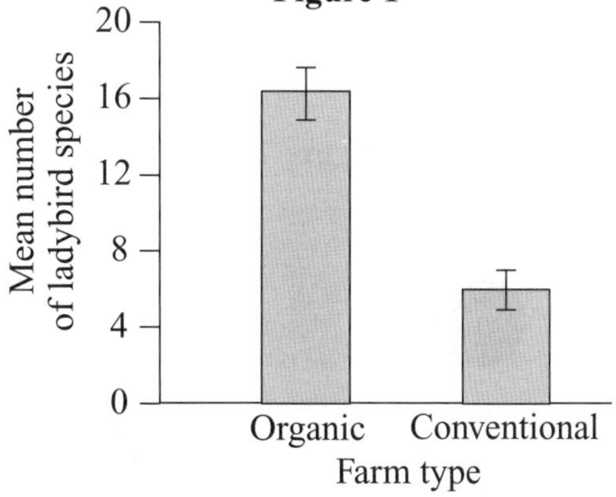

2.2 The scientists concluded that conventional farming had a much greater impact on the number of ladybird species than organic farming. Use the data in **Figure 1** to evaluate this claim.

....

....

....

....

....

(3 marks)

2.3 Describe and explain **two** ways in which the scientists could have ensured that the results they obtained were representative of the farms sampled.

1. ....

2. ....

(2 marks)

3 A student wanted to investigate the effectiveness of different types of antibacterial hand sanitiser against a type of bacteria found on the surface of the skin. She was provided with paper discs, three different types of hand sanitiser, a bottle of bacterial broth culture and an agar plate.

3.1 The agar plate that the student used would have first been autoclaved. Explain why.

....

....

(2 marks)

68

3.2 Describe a method that the student could use for her investigation.
Include details of the aseptic techniques she should carry out.

....

....

....

....

....

....

....
(5 marks)

Figure 2 shows the student's results.

Figure 2

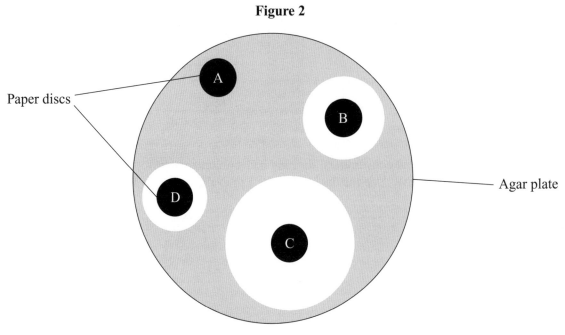

Paper discs

Agar plate

3.3 Disc **A** did not contain any antibacterial hand sanitiser. Explain why it was used.

....

....
(2 marks)

The area of the inhibition zone surrounding each paper disc indicates the effectiveness of the
antibacterial hand sanitiser.

3.4 Complete **Table 2** by calculating the areas of the inhibition zones in **Figure 2**.

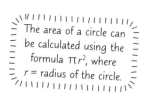
The area of a circle can be calculated using the formula πr^2, where r = radius of the circle.

Table 2

Disc	Area of Inhibition Zone / mm²
B	
C	
D	

(1 mark)

4   Gametes are produced by meiosis. Errors occurring in meiosis can lead to significant health problems.

4.1   Explain how meiosis gives rise to genetic variation.

....

....

....

....

....

(4 marks)

4.2   The diploid number for human cells is 46. Using the formula provided below, calculate the possible
number of different combinations of chromosomes following meiosis in humans.

number of combinations = 2^n
where n = the number of homologous chromosome pairs

number of different combinations of chromosomes = ...

(1 mark)

Patau syndrome is a rare chromosomal disorder.
Figure 3 shows the chromosomes of a male with Patau syndrome.

Figure 3

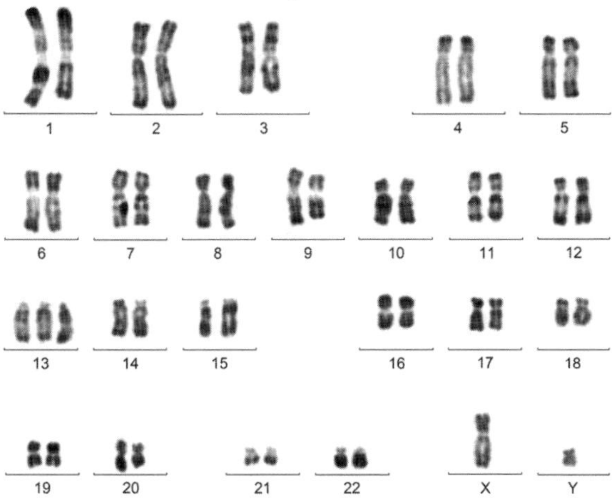

Pr Philippe VAGO, ISM/SCIENCE PHOTO LIBRARY

4.3   Using **Figure 3**, suggest and explain how events in meiosis can cause Patau syndrome.

....

....

....

....

....

(4 marks)

Phew. There's a lot of maths on these pages. The question might seem simple if you're given
the formula, but it's still easy to make mistakes. You need to make sure that you're substituting
the correct numbers into the formula. For example, with the index of diversity formula, make
sure you don't get 'N' (number of all organisms) and 'n' (number of one species) mixed up.

Score

33

Diversity, Classification and Variation — 3

1 Scientists investigated whether different fish species showed any preference for slow- or fast-moving water in a river. The scientists set up a trap in an area of slow-moving water and another in an area of fast-moving water in the same river. They then counted the number of each fish species caught.

The scientists analysed the results for each species using a Student's t-test. This allowed them to determine whether any difference in the mean number of each species caught in each area of water was due to chance. **Table 1** shows their results.

Table 1

Fish species	Mean number of fish		t-test statistic > critical value at $P \leq 0.05$
	Slow-moving water	Fast-moving water	
A	22	7	Yes
B	21	44	Yes
C	32	22	No
D	96	15	Yes
E	10	28	Yes

1.1 Describe what the results of the t-test show.

....

....

....

(2 marks)

The scientists wanted to determine if the fish's preferences for slow- or fast-flowing water were due to genetic differences between the species.

1.2 Suggest **two** factors that the scientists would have had to control in their investigation in order to determine this.

1. ....

2. ....

(2 marks)

Another team of scientists estimated the genetic diversity of one of the fish populations.

1.3 Describe and explain **one** technique they could have used to do this.

....

....

....

(2 marks)

1.4 Give **one** reason why genetic diversity is important for a population.

....

(1 mark)

2   Ampicillin is an antibiotic used to treat bacterial infections. It acts as an irreversible competitive inhibitor of transpeptidase, an enzyme required in bacterial cell wall synthesis.

Figure 1 shows the survival rate of **two** different strains of bacteria in the presence of increasing concentrations of ampicillin.

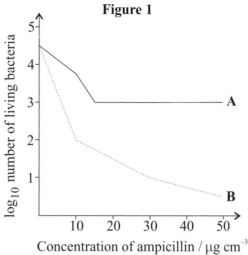

Figure 1

2.1   Describe **two** differences between the effect of increasing ampicillin concentration on **strain A** and the effect on **strain B**.

1. ....

....

2. ....

....

(2 marks)

2.2   Strain **A** was isolated from an area where high levels of ionising radiation were detected. Suggest and explain how this may have contributed to the results shown in **Figure 1**.

....

....

....

....

....

(4 marks)

3   In agriculture, sheep are selectively bred for desired characteristics. This means that humans decide which sheep will breed and which will not. As a result, agricultural sheep do not always exhibit the same courtship behaviours as wild sheep.

3.1   Explain how courtship behaviour enables successful mating.

....

....

....

(3 marks)

Male wild bighorn sheep have large horns, which they use to fight other males for access to females.

3.2 Describe how male wild bighorn sheep may have evolved large horns through natural selection.

....

....

....

....

....

....

(4 marks)

Some populations of wild bighorn sheep are hunted for their horns.
There is evidence to suggest that the average horn size of male bighorn sheep is reducing in some areas.

3.3 What type of selection could be acting on male horn size in areas where hunting occurs?
Explain your answer.

....

....

....

(3 marks)

Figure 2 shows the percentage mortality in populations of wild and agricultural sheep, following the outbreak of a new disease.

Figure 2

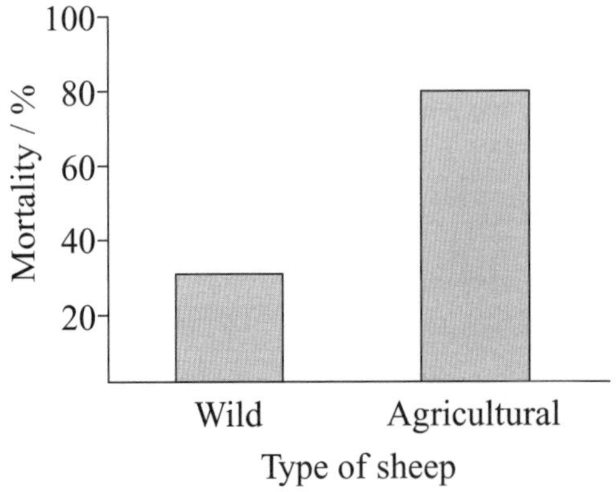

3.4 Suggest an explanation for the difference in mortality shown in **Figure 2**.

....

....

....

(2 marks)

EXAM TIP — If you get a question like 3.2 in the exams, you must make sure your answer relates to the specific context in the question. In other words, don't just write about how natural selection works in general — you need to relate it to the evolution of large horns in male bighorn sheep in particular. Think about how having larger horns might make the males better adapted.

Score

25

Diversity, Classification and Variation — 4

1   Cystic Fibrosis (CF) is a genetic condition caused by a mutation in the CFTR gene.
CFTR is a channel protein present in the respiratory, digestive and reproductive tracts.
It allows the movement of chloride ions across cell membranes.

Many different mutations are known to cause CF. The most common is referred to as DeltaF508.
It results in the loss of an amino acid at position 508 in the CFTR protein.

1.1   State **one** way in which a mutation could result in the loss of an amino acid from a protein.

....

(1 mark)

One of the effects of cystic fibrosis is increased water absorption by the cells in the lungs.
This means that mucus in the lungs is unusually thick and difficult to clear.

1.2   Explain how the DeltaF508 mutation could lead to increased water absorption by the cells in the lungs.

....

....

Hint: think about the function of the CFTR protein and how it might affect osmosis.

....

....

(3 marks)

1.3   Rarely, individuals with mutations in both of their CFTR alleles do not display all the symptoms of
cystic fibrosis or their symptoms are unusually mild. Suggest an explanation for this.

....

....

(2 marks)

2   Scientists are investigating the courtship behaviour of an island bird species.

Figure 1 shows the courtship sequence of males in a single population of these birds, along with the
probability that one element of the courtship behaviour leads to another element taking place.

Figure 1

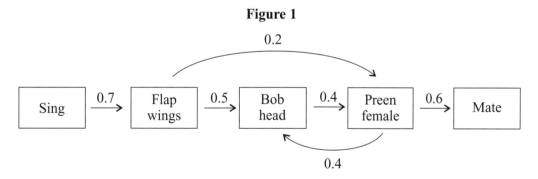

2.1   Calculate the probability that a successful mating will occur when each behaviour is carried out once.

Probability = ...

(1 mark)

2.2 Male birds sing to attract females to them. Each bird species has a unique song.
Explain why this difference in song is important.

....

....

....
(2 marks)

Figure 2 shows the courtship sequence in what was thought to be another population of the same species.

Figure 2

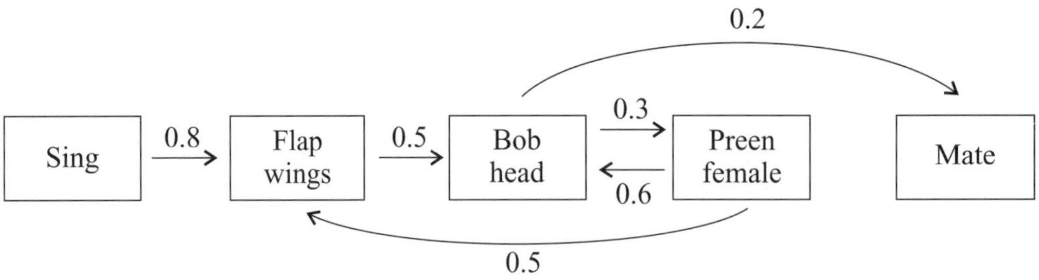

Scientists now believe that the two populations are in fact two separate species of bird.

2.3 Using the information in **Figures 1** and **2**, discuss the extent to which the two bird populations can be classified as two separate species.

....

....

....

....

....

....
(4 marks)

DNA evidence confirms that the two populations are separate species.

It also suggests that the population whose courtship behaviour is shown in **Figure 1** is much less genetically diverse than the population whose behaviour is shown in **Figure 2**.

Researchers think this may be due to strong competition for mates between males in the first population.

2.4 Suggest how strong competition between males would reduce the genetic diversity of a population.

....

....

....
(2 marks)

EXAM TIP — Remember, a mutation affects the DNA base sequence, which may alter which amino acid is coded for. A change to the amino acid sequence can alter the final structure of the protein. Imagine using rectangular bricks to build a house and then suddenly switching to round bricks.

Score

15

Photosynthesis and Respiration — 1

All organisms require energy for life processes. Plants and other organisms have the ability to gain energy through photosynthesis, and release energy through respiration, both of which are really important processes that you need to know — that's why I've included plenty of exam-style questions for you to try.

1   All plants contain several different photosynthetic pigments in their leaves.

Figure 1 shows the absorption spectra for the pigments chlorophyll a, chlorophyll b and carotene.

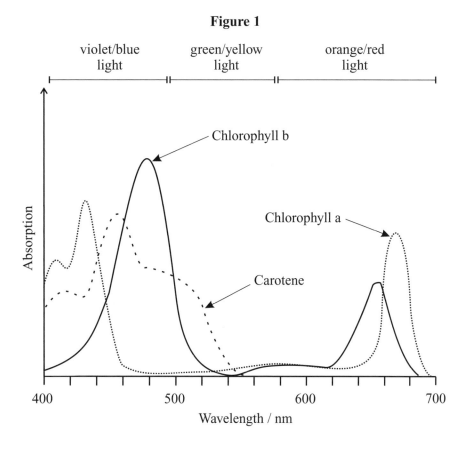

Figure 1

1.1   Use **Figure 1** to describe the absorption of light by chlorophyll a.

       ....

       ....
                                                                                                              (2 marks)

1.2   Describe the role of chlorophyll in the light-dependent reaction of photosynthesis.

       ....

       ....

       ....
                                                                                                              (2 marks)

In a typical forest, smaller plant species have light as a limiting factor because larger trees restrict the amount of light that reaches the forest floor.

1.3   Suggest **one** limiting factor for photosynthesis in larger trees.

       ....
                                                                                                              (1 mark)

76

2　A scientist carried out an experiment to investigate the effect of different light intensities on the rate of photosynthesis in an aquatic plant.

The experiment was conducted under two different concentrations of carbon dioxide (low and high). Light intensity was varied by placing a lamp at different distances from a beaker which contained the aquatic plant. Temperature was controlled throughout the experiment. Photosynthetic rate was calculated by measuring the rate at which oxygen was released.

2.1　Suggest **one** other way in which photosynthetic rate could have been measured.

....
(1 mark)

2.2　Explain how the scientist could have made sure his results were valid.

....

....
(1 mark)

Table 1 shows the results of the experiment.

Table 1

Distance of lamp from plant / m	Rate of O_2 release with low CO_2 concentration / arbitrary units	Rate of O_2 release with high CO_2 concentration / arbitrary units
1.75	0.2	0.2
1.50	0.4	0.4
1.25	0.6	1.1
1.00	0.8	1.4
0.75	1.0	1.6
0.50	1.2	1.8
0.25	1.2	1.8

2.3　Explain the results of the experiment.

....

....

....

....

....

....
(4 marks)

2.4　Suggest **one** way that the scientist could improve this experiment.

....

....
(1 mark)

2.5 Describe how you would present the results in **Table 1** as a graph.
Explain why you have chosen a certain type of graph.

....

....

....
(3 marks)

2.6 The following equation can be used as a measure of light intensity, where d represents the distance of the light source from the plant.

$$\text{light intensity (arbitrary units)} = \frac{1}{d^2}$$

Using the results in **Table 1**, calculate the light intensity at which photosynthesis has become limited for the aquatic plant exposed to a low CO_2 concentration.

light intensity = ... arbitrary units
(1 mark)

3 A student wanted to find out whether the leaves of shade-tolerant plants and the leaves of shade-intolerant plants contain similar pigments.

3.1 Describe how the student could carry out a chromatography experiment to determine this.

....

....

....

....

....

....

....

....

....
(5 marks)

3.2 Explain **two** safety precautions that the student should take during their experiment.

1. ....

....

2. ....

....
(2 marks)

3.3 Explain how the chromatography experiment separates out the pigments.

....

....

....

....

(3 marks)

3.4 Describe how the student could demonstrate that their results are repeatable and reproducible.

....

....

....

(2 marks)

Figure 2 shows the chromatography results obtained from the investigation for leaves of shade-intolerant plants. **Table 2** shows the reference R_f values for some common pigments.

Figure 2

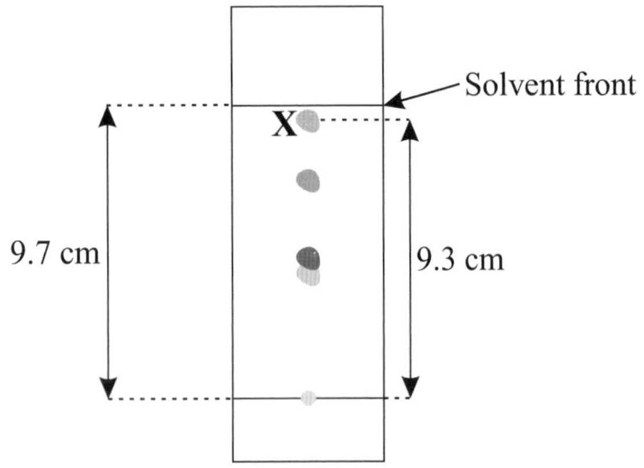

Solvent front
X
9.7 cm
9.3 cm

Table 2

Pigment	R_f Value
carotene	0.95
chlorophyll a	0.43
chlorophyll b	0.35
xanthophyll 1	0.30
xanthophyll 2	0.10

3.5 Use the information in **Figure 2** and **Table 2** to identify pigment **X**.

Pigment X = ...

(1 mark)

3.6 The results of the student's investigation showed that there was a different proportion of pigments in the leaves of shade-tolerant plants than in the leaves of shade-intolerant plants. Explain why.

....

....

....

(1 mark)

EXAM TIP

If you're asked to interpret data from a table or graph, make sure you take some time to study the experiment in detail, so you know exactly what the investigation was trying to find out. Getting your head around what the results should be showing you will make the questions easier to answer. Okay folks, we haven't quite finished Photosynthesis and Respiration yet...

Score

30

Photosynthesis and Respiration — 2

1 Electrons play an important role in the light-dependent reaction of photosynthesis.

1.1 Describe the role of electrons in the production of ATP in the light-dependent reaction, after photoionisation has taken place.

....

....

....

....

....

....

....

(4 marks)

The movement of electrons involves the use of a dehydrogenase enzyme. The activity of this enzyme can be investigated using a redox indicator dye known as DCPIP, which undergoes a colour change from blue to colourless when it is reduced.

1.2 Describe how DCPIP can be used to determine whether dehydrogenase activity is taking place.

....

....

(1 mark)

A student carried out an experiment to investigate the effect of light intensity on dehydrogenase activity in extracts of chloroplasts.

The student selected a few leaves and removed the midribs. They then blended the leaves with chilled isolation solution, and filtered the liquid using a funnel and muslin cloth to remove large pieces of leaf.

The filtered liquid was then added to centrifuge tubes and centrifuged at a high speed for 10 minutes to make the chloroplasts gather at the bottom of each tube, in a pellet. The pellets were re-suspended in fresh, chilled isolation solution to form the chloroplast extract. A set volume of chloroplast extract and DCPIP were then added to three separate test tubes.

1.3 Suggest why each of the following stages were carried out during the experiment.

1. The midribs were removed from the leaves ....

....

2. The mixture was blended ....

....

3. The isolation solution was chilled ....

....

(3 marks)

The three test tubes set up by the student were as follows:

- **Tube 1** – 1 cm^3 of isolation solution without chloroplast extract and 4 cm^3 of DCPIP exposed to light
- **Tube 2** – 1 cm^3 of isolation solution with chloroplast extract and 4 cm^3 of DCPIP covered by foil
- **Tube 3** – 1 cm^3 of isolation solution with chloroplast extract and 4 cm^3 of DCPIP exposed to light

1.4 Explain why the student set up **Tube 1**.

....

....

(1 mark)

1.5 Complete **Table 1** by filling in the three blank spaces with the expected results.

Table 1

Tube	Colour of solution at the beginning of the experiment	Colour of solution at the end of the experiment
1	blue	
2	blue	
3	blue	

(2 marks)

1.6 Suggest how the student could adapt this experiment to investigate the effect of light intensity on the rate of dehydrogenase activity.

....

....

....

....

....

(3 marks)

2 Rotenone is a broad-spectrum insecticide. It's a respiratory inhibitor that works by inhibiting an enzyme known as NADH:ubiquinone oxidoreductase, a membrane protein in the electron transport chain.

2.1 The use of rotenone on farms could result in the pollution of nearby water courses.
Explain why this may cause the fish in the water course to die.

....

....

....

(2 marks)

2.2 Scientists investigating the role of rotenone used isolated mitochondria.
Suggest which substrate they used in this investigation and explain why.

....

....

(2 marks)

3 **Figure 1** shows part of aerobic respiration in animal cells.

Figure 1

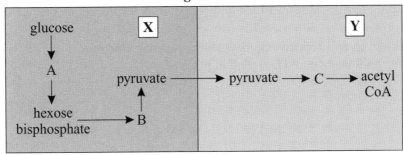

3.1 Name the locations in the cell represented by **X** and **Y** in **Figure 1**.

X ....   Y ....
(1 mark)

3.2 Describe the reaction between glucose and substance A.

....

....
(3 marks)

3.3 Describe the process that converts pyruvate into acetyl CoA.

....

....

....

....

....
(5 marks)

3.4 With reference to **Figure 1**, explain how glycolysis can be maintained during anaerobic respiration.

....

....

....

....
(4 marks)

3.5 Root cells of over-watered plants can only carry out glycolysis. Suggest why.

....

....
(2 marks)

3.6 Describe the process of anaerobic respiration in plant cells.

....

....

....
(4 marks)

4 A scientist investigated the rate of respiration in yeast cells. She set up several test tubes which each contained a mixture of yeast cells, and a different concentration of glucose solution. To each of the test tubes she added an indicator known as methylene blue, which changes from blue to colourless when it is reduced. The scientist measured how long it took for the colour change to occur.

4.1 Methylene blue acts as an alternative coenzyme by accepting electrons.
Name **two** coenzymes that it could be acting in place of.

1. ....

2. ....

(2 marks)

4.2 Describe how the scientist could have set up a control for the experiment.

....

....

....

(2 marks)

4.3 Name **two** variables that the scientist would have needed to keep constant.
Suggest how they could have done so.

1. ....

....

2. ....

....

(4 marks)

4.4 Shaking a test tube of yeast and glucose solution would cause the colourless indicator to return to its blue colour. Explain why.

....

....

....

(2 marks)

4.5 Methylene blue accepts electrons from the electron transport chain during oxidative phosphorylation.
Describe what happens during oxidative phosphorylation.

....

....

....

....

....

(4 marks)

Ah, practicals — fun to carry out, not so fun to answer questions on. For each Required Practical, remember to learn what equipment is required, how the equipment works, what method is used, which controls are used, if any, and which variables need to be controlled. This will stand you in good stead for any questions you need to answer on them. Enjoy.

Score

51

Photosynthesis and Respiration — 3

1   A student was investigating the effect of pH on the rate of anaerobic respiration in yeast.
He set up two conical flasks — one at pH 5 and the other at pH 7. Each conical flask
contained glucose solution and was attached to a gas syringe. The student added 10 g of
yeast to each conical flask and measured the volume of carbon dioxide produced over time.

1.1   Carbon dioxide dissolves in water to form a weakly acidic solution.
Explain how this may affect the validity of the student's results.

....

....

....

(2 marks)

Figure 1 shows the results of the experiment.

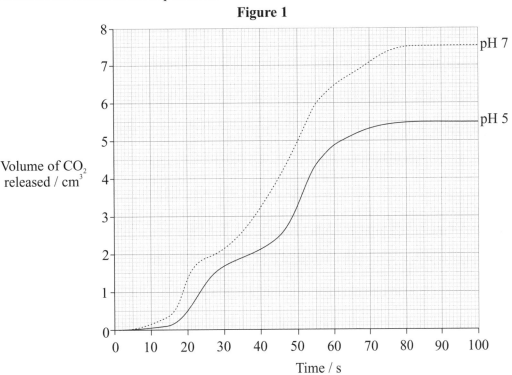

Figure 1

1.2   Describe and explain the shape of the curves after 80 seconds.

....

....

(2 marks)

1.3   Draw a tangent to the curve representing pH 5 to find the rate of reaction at 45 seconds.
Show your working.

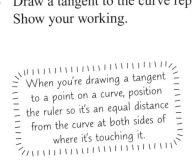

When you're drawing a tangent
to a point on a curve, position
the ruler so it's an equal distance
from the curve at both sides of
where it's touching it.

Rate = ... $cm^3\,s^{-1}$

(1 mark)

1.4 For each molecule of glucose, aerobic respiration in yeast produces four more molecules of carbon dioxide than anaerobic respiration. Explain why.

....

....

....

....

(4 marks)

2   Ribulose bisphosphate (RuBP) and glucose are produced as a result of the light-independent reaction of photosynthesis.

2.1 Name the enzyme that catalyses the reaction of CO_2 with RuBP.

....

(1 mark)

2.2 Explain why it is important that RuBP and glucose are produced as a result of the light-independent reaction.

RuBP ....

....

Glucose ....

....

(2 marks)

Experiments were carried out to see if varying the concentration of carbon dioxide had any effect on the light-independent reaction.

2.3 Using your knowledge of the light-independent reaction, suggest the effects of reducing the carbon dioxide concentration on the formation of GP and RuBP. Explain your answer.

....

....

....

....

(4 marks)

2.4 Suggest what effect lowering the light intensity would have on the formation of GP and RuBP.

....

....

....

(3 marks)

Energy Transfer and Nutrient Cycles — 1

The energy from photosynthesis passes through organisms in a food chain. When an organism dies, nutrient cycles recycle the essential mineral ions for the growth of new organisms. The circle of life — so beautiful. Unfortunately, I couldn't make these questions beautiful too. They're pretty tough, but give them a go anyway.

1   Farmers need to create the best environmental conditions for their crops, to increase their yields.

1.1 Farmers often apply fertilisers to their fields after the crops have been harvested. Explain why.

....

....

(1 mark)

Some fertilisers are made of dead plant material, such as composted vegetables or crop residues.

1.2 Describe how nitrogen in dead plant material is made available to growing plants in the soil.

....

....

....

....

....

(4 marks)

One farmer discovered a population of a fungal species in her field that can form mycorrhizae with crop plants.

1.3 Explain how the presence of this fungal species could affect crop yield.

....

....

....

....

(3 marks)

Another farmer's field was flooded and became waterlogged.
Waterlogging creates anaerobic conditions in the soil.

1.4 Using your knowledge of the nitrogen cycle, explain how this could affect crop yield.

....

....

....

....

(3 marks)

2 Palm trees are grown in plantations in many countries around the world. The lipids and other products harvested from them are very profitable as they can be used to make fuel and many other useful materials.

2.1 Other than lipids, name **one** group of biological molecules that are synthesised by plants, using the glucose obtained from photosynthesis.

....

(1 mark)

The net primary production of a mature palm plantation was investigated.

2.2 Define 'net primary production'.

....

....

(1 mark)

This palm plantation measured 120 ha in area. Over 3 months, 1.9×10^{10} kJ of energy was produced by the palm tree plantation. In one year, the plantation had respiration losses of 3.0×10^8 kJ ha^{-1}.

2.3 Calculate the net primary productivity of this palm plantation.
Show your working.

Make sure your answer matches the units shown here.

.... kJ ha^{-1} yr^{-1}
(2 marks)

In order to determine the energy produced by this plantation, scientists measured the energy content in a sample of young palm trees.

2.4 Describe a method the scientists would have used to measure the chemical energy content of one sapling.

....

....

....

....

(3 marks)

2.5 Plants including palm trees require a source of phosphorus for healthy growth.
Describe how sources of phosphorus become available for plants to absorb from the soil.

....

....

....

....

(2 marks)

EXAM TIP — If you're having a hard time remembering the nitrogen cycle, try drawing it out... again and again, until it sticks and you can draw it all off by heart. Then when you get a question on the nitrogen cycle in the exam, you can always quickly sketch it out — that way it's easier to pinpoint the part of the cycle that the question is asking about. It's as easy as that...

Score

20

Energy Transfer and Nutrient Cycles — 2

1   A farmer is raising animals on his farm. **Figure 1** shows the energy intake and losses for one of his animals over one day.

Figure 1

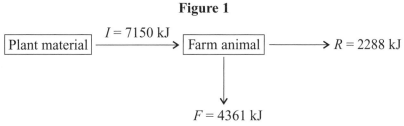

1.1   Calculate the efficiency of energy transfer between the plant material and the farm animal over one day.

....%
(2 marks)

1.2   Suggest and explain **one** difference you would see in **Figure 1** if the farm animal was raised at a higher altitude, where the temperature is lower.

....

....
(2 marks)

1.3   The farmer keeps his animals in outdoor pens in larger numbers to increase the product yield. Describe **one** way that this method increases the product yield.

....

....
(2 marks)

1.4   Keeping farm animals in pens can increase the spread of infectious diseases. Suggest the effect that becoming infected with disease may have on the net production of these farm animals.

....

....
(1 mark)

1.5   In a pond near to the farm, there has been rapid growth of algae. Local fishermen can no longer find any fish to catch in the pond. Suggest an explanation for why this may have happened.

....

....

....

....

....

....
(4 marks)

2   A scientist investigated the effect of artificial fertiliser applied to a crop field. The scientist divided the field into small plots and applied different masses of fertiliser to each one. After several months, the dry mass of crop plants in each plot was measured. The scientist's results are shown in **Table 1**.

Table 1

Mass of fertiliser added to plot / kg ha^{-1}	Dry mass of crop yield / tonnes ha^{-1}
0	4.5
40	5.4
80	6.3
120	6.9
160	7.3
200	6.6
240	5.9
280	5.6

2.1   Describe the results shown in **Table 1**.

....

....
                                                                                                              (2 marks)

2.2   Calculate the maximum percentage increase in dry mass of crop yield seen when fertiliser is added, compared to when no fertiliser is added.

                                                                                          ....%
                                                                                                              (1 mark)

2.3   The dry mass of crop plants, rather than the mass of freshly harvested crops, was measured. Explain why.

....

....
                                                                                                              (1 mark)

2.4   The scientist hopes to use this experiment to advise all farmers on the optimum amount of fertiliser to use. Suggest **one** change the scientist would need to make to the experiment in order to be able to do this.

....

....
                                                                                                              (1 mark)

2.5   Artificial fertilisers contain water-soluble minerals that plants need for growth. Applications of very high concentrations of fertiliser can cause a reduction in the yield of crops, especially when the soil is dry. Suggest why.

....

....

....
                                                                                                              (2 marks)

2.6 Leaching is less likely to occur after using a natural fertiliser than after using an artificial fertiliser. Suggest why.

....

....

....

....

(3 marks)

3 **Figure 2** shows a simplified food web for a farm growing crops, that is infested with pests. Primary consumer 1 and primary consumer 2 are the pest species. The food web shows the net primary productivity of producers, net productivity of consumers and percentage efficiency of energy transfer between some of its trophic levels.

Figure 2

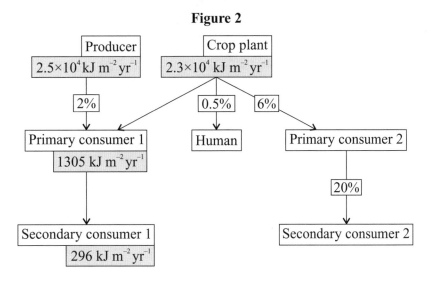

3.1 The chemical energy in food ingested by secondary consumer 1 is less than the net production of primary consumer 1. Suggest why.

....

(1 mark)

Humans could increase the amount of energy available for themselves by eliminating the two pest species.

3.2 Calculate the amount of energy that humans could obtain from the crop if they eliminate these species. Assume that all the energy consumed by the pests would be available to humans.

.... kJ m^{-2} yr^{-1}
(2 marks)

EXAM TIP

To work out the net production of consumers, you use the equation $N = I - (F + R)$ — the energy from ingested food, minus the energy lost through faeces and urine, and respiration. Don't get this confused with the equation for net primary production (NPP) which is $GPP - R$, i.e. the energy produced by photosynthesis (GPP) minus that lost by respiration (R).

Score

24

Stimuli and Responses — 1

A stimulus is a change in the internal or external environment that triggers a response in an organism. Like how seeing another page of questions triggers a response to go take a nap. You should really keep going though.

1   Electrical impulses in the heart are generated by the sinoatrial node (SAN)
     and conducted across the muscle tissue in a highly coordinated sequence.

Figure 1 shows a diagram of the heart. The SAN and atrioventricular node (AVN) are labelled.

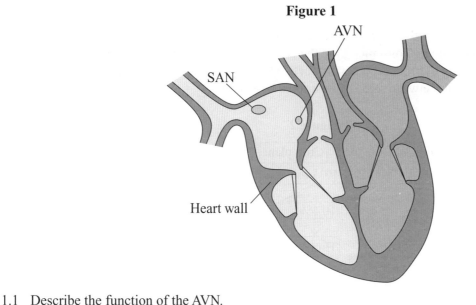

Figure 1

1.1   Describe the function of the AVN.

     ....
     (1 mark)

The heart wall contains muscle tissue and collagen, which acts as a structural support.
Collagen does not conduct electricity.

1.2   Explain why the collagen in the heart wall also has a role in helping to ensure that the ventricles
       contract at the right time.

     ....

     ....

     ....
     (2 marks)

2   The autonomic nervous system can affect heart rate. It has two branches, called
     the sympathetic and parasympathetic nervous systems. The sympathetic nervous
     system prepares the body for action in the form of a 'fight or flight' response.

2.1   Sympathetic neurones secrete the neurotransmitter noradrenaline onto receptors at the sinoatrial node.
       Suggest the effect this will have on heart rate. Explain your answer.

     ....

     ....

     ....
     (2 marks)

After a 'fight or flight' response, blood pressure is high.

2.2 Describe how blood pressure is brought back to normal following a 'fight or flight' response.

....

....

....

....

....

(4 marks)

3   A Pacinian corpuscle is a mechanoreceptor found in the skin, which detects pressure stimuli.
Figure 2 shows a simplified diagram of a Pacinian corpuscle at rest.

Figure 2

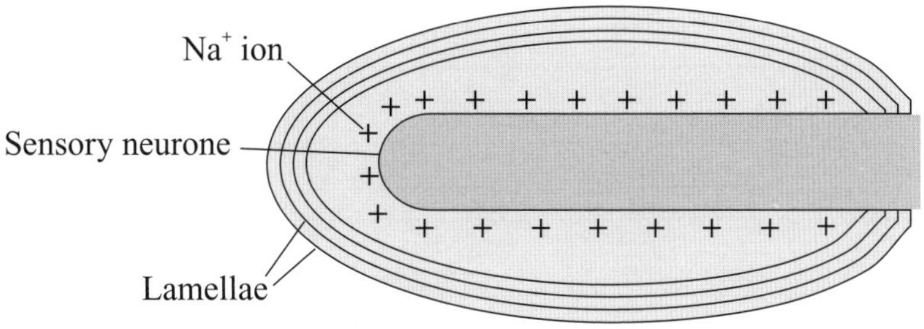

3.1 Describe how the Pacinian corpuscle shown in **Figure 2** will change when exposed to a pressure stimulus.

....

....

....

....

(3 marks)

3.2 Give **one** reason why the change you explained in **3.1** may not lead to the generation of an action potential.

....

....

(1 mark)

3.3 Suggest an explanation for why there are several different types of mechanoreceptor in the skin.

....

....

....

(2 marks)

4   Photoreceptors in the eye (rods and cones) are found in the retina. **Figure 3** shows
     the distribution of photoreceptors in two different areas of a human retina.

Figure 3

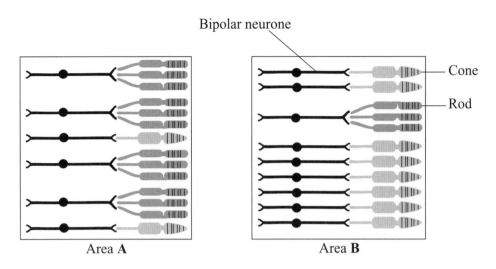

4.1 Which area of the retina shown in **Figure 3** (**A** or **B**) is better adapted to dim light conditions?
     Explain your answer.

     ....

     ....

     ....

     ....

                                                                                                            (3 marks)

4.2 An individual looks at a coloured image.
     Explain why the image would be seen in greater detail if processed by area **B**.

     ....

     ....

     ....

     ....

     ....

                                                                                                            (4 marks)

4.3 People with red-green colour blindness have difficulty distinguishing certain shades of red and green.
     This can be due to faulty photoreceptors.
     Suggest which photoreceptors may be faulty in a person with red-green colour blindness.

     ....

     ....

                                                                                                            (1 mark)

Stimuli and Responses — 2

1   A student carries out an experiment on plant growth responses. The student grows four seedlings in identical conditions for two weeks. She then places each seedling in a separate covered box, with a light source pointed at an angle of 90° towards the seedling, as shown in **Figure 1**.

Figure 1

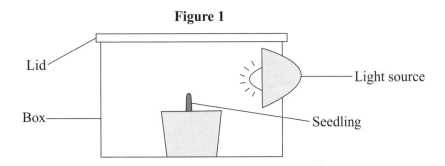

The student labels the seedlings **A** to **D**. She applies the following treatments to each seedling:

*   The shoot tip of seedling **A** is covered with tin foil.
*   The shoot tip of seedling **B** is cut off.
*   The shoot tip of seedling **C** is cut off. Indoleacetic acid (IAA) is added to the top of the shoot on the side nearest to the light source only. It is reapplied at regular intervals.
*   Seedling **D** is not treated.

The degree of curvature of each seedling after one week is shown in **Table 1**.

Table 1

Seedling	Degree of curvature / °
A	0
B	0
C	40 (towards light source)
D	40 (towards light source)

1.1   Name the growth response shown by seedling **D**.

....
(1 mark)

1.2   What do the results of the experiment suggest about where indoleacetic acid is produced in a plant? Explain your answer.

....

....
(2 marks)

1.3 Explain why no curvature was observed in seedlings **A** and **B**.

A: ....

....

B: ....

....

(2 marks)

1.4 Explain why there was no difference in results for seedlings **C** and **D**.

....

....

(1 mark)

2 Female mosquitoes obtain some of their nutrients by feeding on the blood of humans or other animals. They use their sense of smell to move towards or away from stimuli in order to find a blood meal. A scientist set up a choice chamber experiment to see how different odours influenced this movement response in female mosquitoes. **Figure 2** shows a diagram of the experimental setup.

Figure 2

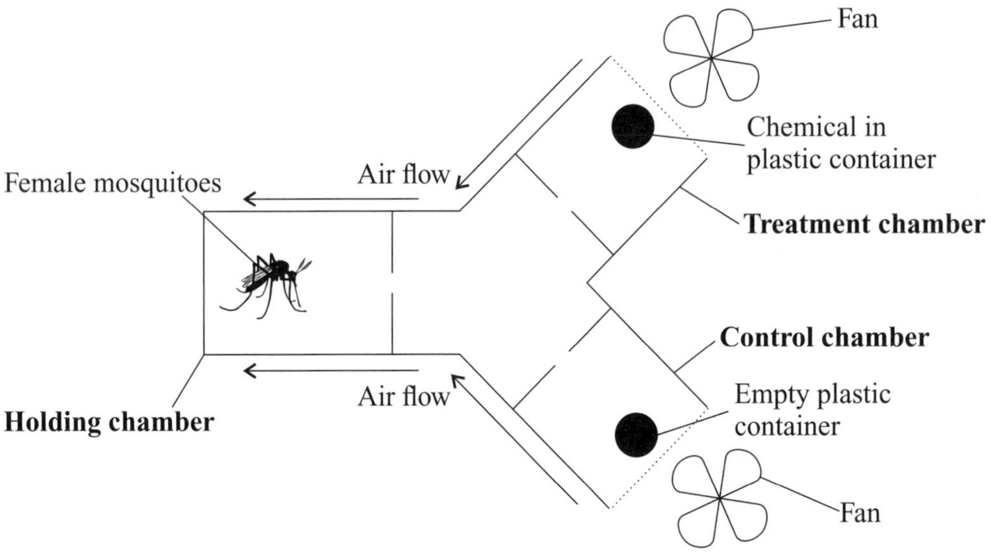

The scientist carried out trials with four different chemicals (**A** to **D**). Each chemical had a different odour.

At the beginning of each trial, the scientist placed a different chemical in the treatment chamber, having allowed time for the chemical from any previous trials to disperse.

He then released the mosquitoes from the holding chamber and recorded how many flew into the treatment chamber and how many flew into the control chamber.

2.1 Give **two** variables that the scientist should have controlled in the experiment.

1. ....

2. ....

(2 marks)

Table 2 shows the results of the scientist's experiment.

Table 2

Chemical	Number of mosquitoes at end of experiment		
	In the treatment chamber	In the control chamber	Total
A	54	6	60
B	49	13	62
C	4	58	62
D	25	35	60

2.2 Explain what type of simple response was shown by the mosquitoes to chemical **A**.

....

....

....

(2 marks)

2.3 One of the chemicals tested was carbon dioxide. Suggest an explanation for why an attraction to increased concentrations of carbon dioxide is beneficial to female mosquitoes.

....

....

....

....

(3 marks)

2.4 The scientist thought that **one** of the chemicals showed potential to be used as a mosquito repellant.
Suggest which chemical (**A**, **B**, **C** or **D**) could be used as a mosquito repellent. Explain your answer.

....

....

....

(2 marks)

2.5 The scientist expected 50% of the mosquitoes to move into the treatment chamber and 50% to move into the control chamber if a chemical had no effect on their movement.
Suggest a statistical test that the scientist could use to analyse his data. Explain your choice.

....

....

....

(2 marks)

> **EXAM TIP**
> Questions about statistics could pop up anywhere in the exams — and probably where you least expect them to. You need to know when to use the Student's t-test, the chi-squared test and a correlation coefficient. You need to be able to explain why you'd use them too.

Score

17

Nervous Coordination — 1

Nervous impulses are the electrical charges transmitted along a neurone. Without them your body can't function properly — e.g. muscle movement is coordinated by nervous impulses. Right, neurones at the ready...

1   **Figure 1** shows a cross section through a neurone cell membrane while it is at rest.

Figure 1

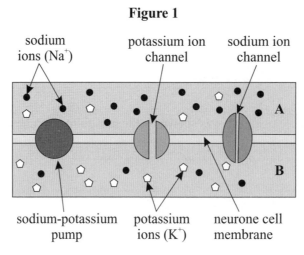

1.1   When a neurone is at rest, the outside of the cell membrane is positively charged compared to the inside. State why.

....

....
(1 mark)

1.2   Explain why there is a greater concentration of sodium ions on side **A** of the cell membrane shown in **Figure 1**.

....

....
(2 marks)

1.3   State why sodium ions on the outside of the cell do not move across the cell membrane shown in **Figure 1**.

....
(1 mark)

1.4   Describe the movement of potassium ions across a neurone cell membrane that is required to establish a resting potential.

....

....

....
(3 marks)

1.5   Explain why sodium ion channels are not evenly distributed across the surface of a myelinated neurone.

....

....

....
(3 marks)

2   The calf and tibialis anterior muscles are located in the legs. The calf muscle attaches to the heel bone, and the tibialis anterior muscle attaches to the metatarsal bones.

Figure 2 shows a diagram of the interaction of these two muscles during a movement of the foot.

Figure 2

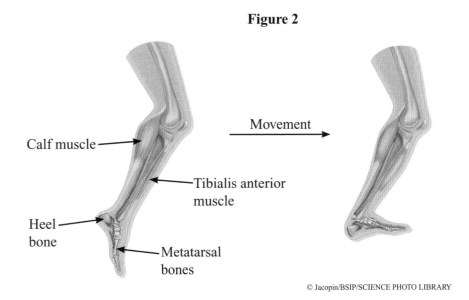

© Jacopin/BSIP/SCIENCE PHOTO LIBRARY

2.1   Explain how the interaction between the muscles and bones labelled in **Figure 2** leads to the movement of the foot.

....

....

....
(2 marks)

2.2   Explain why it is important that the bones involved in the movement of the foot are incompressible.

....

....
(1 mark)

2.3   The erector spinae muscles are found along the length of the spine.
These muscles are involved in maintaining posture over long periods of time.
Suggest and explain how the composition and properties of the erector spinae muscles might differ from the calf muscle.

....

....

....

....

....

....

....
(5 marks)

3 **Figure 3** shows a neuromuscular junction.

Figure 3

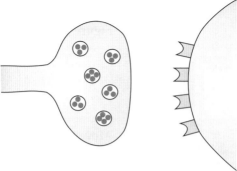

3.1 Draw an arrow on **Figure 3** to show the direction that a nerve impulse would travel across this neuromuscular junction.

(1 mark)

3.2 Explain why the transmission of nervous impulses only occurs in one direction across a neuromuscular junction.

....

....

(2 marks)

3.3 An action potential arrives at a neuromuscular junction.
Describe how the action potential stimulates the release of calcium ions throughout the muscle fibre.

....

....

....

(3 marks)

3.4 Explain **two** ways in which the release of calcium ions following an action potential is important for muscle contraction.

1. ....

....

2. ....

....

(4 marks)

3.5 Curare is a poison which binds to acetylcholine receptors and inhibits them.
Suggest and explain what effect a high dose of curare would have on the contraction of muscles.

....

....

....

....

....

(4 marks)

4   **Figure 4** shows a section of muscle tissue.

Figure 4

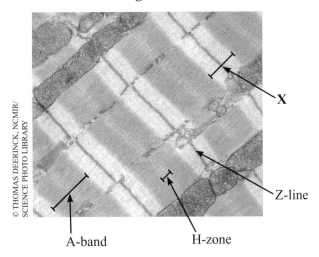

4.1   Name the part of the myofibril labelled **X** on **Figure 4**.

....
                                                                                          (1 mark)

4.2   Which part of a sarcomere labelled on **Figure 4** contains the lowest concentration of actin filaments?
      Give a reason for your answer.

....

....
                                                                                          (2 marks)

4.3   During muscle contraction the lengths of the sarcomeres shorten.
      Name the parts of the sarcomere that shorten.

....
                                                                                          (1 mark)

4.4   Describe how the myosin and actin filaments interact to shorten the length of the sarcomeres during
      muscle contraction.

....

....

....

....

....

....

....
                                                                                          (5 marks)

This isn't an easy topic. Practice makes perfect though, so keep going until you can answer all these questions correctly. One thing to remember is that neurotransmitters (such as acetylcholine) can transmit action potentials across both cholinergic synapses and neuromuscular junctions — the mechanisms involved are similar but there are a few differences too.

Score

41

Nervous Coordination — 2

1   A group of scientists investigated how the diameter of different myelinated neurones affected the speed of nerve impulse conductance along them. Their results are shown in **Table 1**.

Table 1

Axon diameter / μm	Speed of conductance / m s⁻¹
2	10
4	22
6	35
8	46
10	58
12	70

1.1   Name the process by which nervous impulses are conducted along myelinated neurones.

....

(1 mark)

1.2   Draw a suitable graph to show the results in **Table 1**. Include a line of best fit.

(2 marks)

1.3   Use the graph you have drawn to predict the speed of conductance in a myelinated neurone with a diameter of 7 μm.

.... m s⁻¹

(1 mark)

1.4 Explain the relationship between axon diameter and speed of conductance shown by the results in **Table 1**.

....

....

....

....

(3 marks)

1.5 The scientists repeated the investigation in non-myelinated neurones.
Suggest how their results may have been different to the results shown in **Table 1**.

....

....

(1 mark)

1.6 Apart from myelination of the neurones used, give **one** other variable that the scientists should have kept constant during the investigation. Explain your answer.

....

....

....

(2 marks)

2   Disopyramide is a drug that can be used to treat people that have an irregular heartbeat.
The drug works by blocking some sodium and potassium ion channels on neurone cell membranes.
Overall the action of disopyramide can increase the duration of an action potential.

2.1 Describe the importance of a refractory period during an action potential.

....

....

....

....

....

(4 marks)

2.2 Explain how blocking potassium ion channels increases the duration of an action potential.

....

....

....

(3 marks)

2.3 Suggest why people with a heartbeat that is too fast might be prescribed disopyramide.

....

....

....

(1 mark)

3   **Figure 1** shows the interaction between a group of neurones. Neurones A and B release the excitatory neurotransmitter acetylcholine. Neurone C releases the inhibitory neurotransmitter GABA.

Figure 1

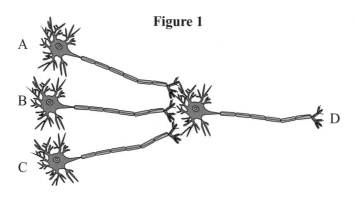

Table 2 shows what happens when a nervous impulse arrives at the end of each neurone in **Figure 1**.

Table 2

Neurones activated by an impulse	Action potential initiated in neurone D
A + B	Yes
B + C	No
A + C	No
A + B + C	Yes

3.1   Explain how **Table 2** shows that acetylcholine is an excitatory neurotransmitter and GABA is an inhibitory neurotransmitter.

....

....

....

....

(2 marks)

3.2   Suggest and explain why an action potential is initiated in neurone **D** when neurones **A**, **B** and **C** are activated by an impulse, but not when neurones **A** and **C** are activated by an impulse.

....

....

....

(2 marks)

Acetylcholinesterase (AChE) is an enzyme found at cholinergic synapses, which breaks down acetylcholine. Metrifonate is a drug which inhibits AChE.

3.3   At another synapse, neurone **X** is activated and triggers an action potential in neurone **Y** by releasing acetylcholine. Explain what might happen at the synapse if metrifonate was present in the synaptic cleft between neurones **X** and **Y**.

....

....

....

(2 marks)

4 Creatine is a dietary supplement often used by weightlifters — it affects the levels of phosphocreatine in the muscles. A team of scientists investigated the use of a creatine supplement. They measured the amount of phosphocreatine present in the muscles of four weightlifters at the beginning of an experiment and after taking a creatine supplement for five days. Their results are shown in **Table 3**.

Table 3

| Individual | Concentration of phosphocreatine in muscle / mmol kg⁻¹ dry mass | | |
	Before creatine supplement	After creatine supplement	Percentage difference / %
1	66	81	22.7
2	84	90.6	7.9
3	81	96	
4	69	85.8	

4.1 Complete **Table 3** to show the percentage difference in the concentration of phosphocreatine before and after taking a creatine supplement.

(2 marks)

4.2 Calculate the mean percentage difference in phosphocreatine concentration of all the individuals after taking a creatine supplement.

....%
(1 mark)

The scientists also investigated the effect of creatine on weightlifting performance using a different group of weightlifters over a 10-day period.

Each day they recorded the maximum weight each individual could lift, and immediately after this each individual was given a supplement. Half of the individuals were given a creatine supplement and the other half of individuals were given a placebo supplement that did not contain any creatine. Three hours later the maximum weight each individual could lift was recorded again.

4.3 Explain why using creatine supplements might improve a weightlifter's performance.

....

....

....
(3 marks)

4.4 The scientists found no significant difference in the performance of the weightlifters taking creatine and those taking a placebo. They concluded that the creatine supplement had no effect on the performance of a weightlifter. Suggest **two** reasons why their conclusion may be flawed. Explain your answer.

1. ....

....

2. ....

....
(4 marks)

If you're asked to draw a graph in the exams or plot data of any kind, remember that the independent variable goes on the *x*-axis and the dependent variable (the thing you're measuring) on the *y*-axis. Be careful to plot your points accurately too — there's usually only 1 plotting mark up for grabs and if you put just one of the points in the wrong place, you won't get it.

Score

34

Homeostasis — 1

Homeostasis — just the title makes this topic sound tricky, but don't worry, I've got lots of exam-style questions for you. When you're done with these you'll know this topic backwards... and forwards...

1 During exercise, the body experiences changes in blood pH and core body temperature.

1.1 Explain why it is necessary for homeostatic mechanisms to resist these changes.

....

....

....

(2 marks)

1.2 Negative feedback mechanisms enable the body to maintain its core temperature and blood pH during exercise. What is meant by negative feedback?

....

....

(1 mark)

1.3 Multiple negative feedback mechanisms are involved in controlling blood pH. Explain why.

....

....

(2 marks)

1.4 Other than blood pH and body temperature, name **two** levels in the body that are controlled as part of homeostasis.

1. ....

2. ....

(2 marks)

Intense exercise under hot conditions can cause body temperature to increase above 37.5 °C. The resulting condition is referred to as hyperthermia. When body temperature rises above 40 °C, a person is classed as having severe hyperthermia.

1.5 Suggest how severe hyperthermia can cause life-threatening disruption to metabolic processes.

....

....

....

....

(2 marks)

People with severe hyperthermia often stop sweating, which causes their body temperature to continue to rise.

1.6 What type of feedback mechanism is happening at this point? Explain your answer.

....

....

(2 marks)

2   Insulin, glucagon and adrenaline all have an effect on blood glucose concentration.
Insulin increases the transport of glucose into cells.

2.1   Explain why glucose can only enter cells through glucose transporters.

....

....

(1 mark)

2.2   Describe how insulin increases the transport of glucose into cells.

....

....

(2 marks)

2.3   Describe **one** other mechanism of insulin action that helps to regulate blood glucose concentration.

....

....

(1 mark)

The action of glucagon is said to be antagonistic to that of insulin.

2.4   Describe the role of glucagon in the regulation of blood glucose concentration.

....

(1 mark)

2.5   Describe **two** mechanisms of glucagon action.

1.   ....

....

2.   ....

....

(2 marks)

2.6   Describe how glucagon acts via a second messenger.

....

....

....

....

....

(4 marks)

Athletes often experience a large increase in their adrenaline levels before they compete.

2.7   Explain how the action of adrenaline might increase the performance of an athlete.

....

....

....

(2 marks)

3 The glycaemic index (GI) of a food is a value that indicates how quickly the food increases blood glucose concentration, compared with pure glucose.

Scientists conducted an experiment with two groups of people, to investigate the effect of taking a supplement with a high GI food. One group was given a high GI food and a supplement, and the other group were given the same high GI food without a supplement. The results can be seen in **Figure 1**.

Figure 1

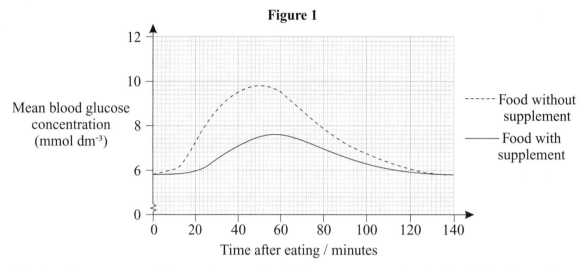

3.1 Calculate the percentage difference in mean blood glucose concentration for the food with supplement, compared to the food without supplement, when the blood glucose concentration has reached its peak.

....

(1 mark)

3.2 Describe the impact of the high GI food with the supplement on blood glucose concentration, as shown in **Figure 1**.

....

....

....

(2 marks)

The food supplement is being considered for use in patients with Type II diabetes.

3.3 Suggest and explain why this food supplement might be considered useful for people with Type II diabetes.

....

....

....

....

....

(3 marks)

3.4 State **two** ways that Type II diabetes is usually managed.

1. ....

2. ....

(2 marks)

4 A student wanted to investigate the concentration of glucose in urine samples from different people.

The student first produced four glucose solutions of different, known concentrations in different test tubes, using serial dilutions from a 4.0 mM glucose solution. He did this by adding 5 cm³ of distilled water to four test tubes, labelled 2-5. He then transferred 5 cm³ of 4.0 mM glucose solution (in test tube 1) into test tube 2, mixed the solution and transferred 5 cm³ from test tube 2 into the test tube 3. He repeated this step for test tubes 3-5. **Table 1** is designed to show the final concentration of glucose solution in each test tube.

Table 1

Test tube	Final concentration of glucose / mM
1	4.0
2	
3	
4	
5	

4.1 Complete **Table 1** by filling in the four blank spaces with the correct concentrations of glucose solution.

(1 mark)

4.2 Describe how the student could use the glucose solutions he had prepared to identify the concentration of glucose in each urine sample.

....

....

....

....

....

(4 marks)

4.3 The student set up another test tube to act as a control. Suggest what this test tube contained.

....

(1 mark)

4.4 Explain why a control would be used in this experiment.

....

....

(1 mark)

4.5 Suggest why urine testing is not commonly used to determine the blood concentration of a person with diabetes.

....

....

(2 marks)

Homeostasis — 2

1   **Figure 1** shows the structure of a nephron.

Figure 1

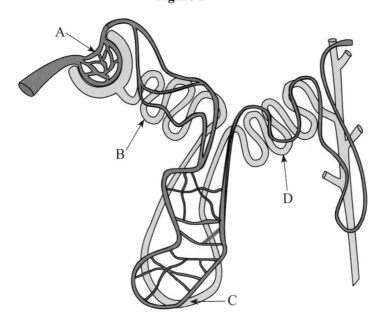

1.1   Explain **one** way in which the structure at point **B** in **Figure 1** is adapted for selective reabsorption.

   ....

   ....

   ....
                                                                                                                                (2 marks)

1.2   In a normal functioning kidney, how would you expect the concentration of glucose present in the glomerular filtrate to differ between points **A** and **D** in **Figure 1**? Explain your answer.

   ....

   ....

   ....
                                                                                                                                (2 marks)

1.3   Name the structure at point **C** in **Figure 1**.

   ....
                                                                                                                                (1 mark)

1.4   Describe the role of the structure at point **C** in **Figure 1** in controlling blood water potential.

   ....

   ....

   ....

   ....

   ....
                                                                                                                                (4 marks)

1.5 Suggest why frogs and toads do not have the structure found at point **C** in **Figure 1**.

....

....

(1 mark)

1.6 Suggest how the structure found at point **C** in **Figure 1** may be adapted to aid survival in desert animals.

....

....

(2 marks)

2   The kidneys filter the blood to remove waste products from the body in the form of urine.

2.1 Explain how the kidneys filter the blood.

....

....

....

....

....

(4 marks)

2.2 Name **two** substances present in the glomerular filtrate.

1. ....

2. ....

(2 marks)

The average blood volume of an adult is 70 cm^3 per kg of body weight.
An individual weighing 65 kg had an average glomerular filtration rate of 110 cm^3 min^{-1}.

2.3 Calculate how many times the blood of this individual was filtered during the course of one day.
Show your working.

....

(2 marks)

2.4 Over the course of a day, the average amount of urine released from the kidneys is only about 1 cm^3 min^{-1}.
Explain why this value is much lower than the glomerular filtration rate.

....

....

(2 marks)

2.5 Chronic kidney disease can result from a number of different causes, such as consistent high blood pressure.
Suggest why patients with chronic kidney disease often have plasma proteins present in their urine.

....

....

(2 marks)

2.6 A person with diabetes may have glucose in their urine. They may also produce large volumes of urine. Suggest why a person with diabetes would have these symptoms.

....

....

....

....

....

(3 marks)

3 The kidneys play a key role in controlling the water potential of the blood. Antidiuretic hormone (ADH) is an important hormone in this process.

3.1 What name is given to the process of maintaining the water potential of the blood?

....

(1 mark)

Different factors affect the level of antidiuretic hormone (ADH) in a person's body.

3.2 Drinking alcohol decreases the body's secretion of ADH.
Explain how this leads to dehydration.

....

....

....

....

(3 marks)

3.3 Explain how the body detects dehydration and increases ADH secretion.

....

....

....

....

(3 marks)

Some people have a condition called SIADH, where they continuously secrete ADH.
This can lead to an abnormally low blood sodium level.

3.4 Explain how SIADH can lead to an abnormally low blood sodium level.

Think about the effect that too much ADH would have on the kidneys and therefore the volume of blood.

....

....

....

....

(3 marks)

4 Scientists measured the concentration of glucose in the blood of a group of people with Type I diabetes. They compared the results to a control group without diabetes. Prior to the blood test, each person had fasted for eight hours. The results can be seen in **Table 1**.

Table 1

	Mean value (± standard deviation)	
	People with Type I diabetes	People without diabetes
Glucose / mg per 100 cm³	148.68 (± 13.89)	73.29 (± 8.13)

4.1 Suggest why each person had to fast for eight hours prior to the blood test.

....

....

(1 mark)

4.2 Explain the results shown in **Table 1**.

....

....

....

(3 marks)

4.3 The scientists conducted a statistical test to determine whether the difference in the results for patients with Type I diabetes and individuals without diabetes was significant. Name the statistical test that was carried out and explain your choice.

Statistical test: ....

Reason: ....

(2 marks)

4.4 The probability value of the statistical test was found to be less than 0.05. Explain what this shows.

....

....

....

(2 marks)

4.5 Explain why it is important to maintain a stable blood glucose concentration.

....

....

....

....

(3 marks)

 You really need to know the structure of a nephron and all the processes it is involved in back to front. Then it'll be much easier to apply your knowledge to new scenarios, like question 4.5 about frogs and toads. Better put that cuppa on hold then and get back to the notes...

Score

48

Genetics — 1

Organisms pass on their genes to their offspring. There can be one or more different versions of a gene, called alleles, which are represented using letters. Hopefully this sounds familiar because I've got plenty to test you on...

1   Duchenne Muscular Dystrophy (DMD) is a genetic disorder that causes progressive muscle weakening.
     It is caused by a recessive allele of the dystrophin gene, which is located on the X-chromosome.

Figure 1 represents one family where two unaffected parents have an unaffected daughter,
an unaffected son, and a son with DMD.

Figure 1

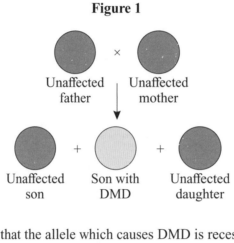

1.1   Explain how **Figure 1** shows that the allele which causes DMD is recessive.

     ....

     ....

     ....
                                                                                                                      (2 marks)

1.2   Using the notation X^m to represent an X chromosome containing the DMD mutation,
      give the genotypes of both parents shown in **Figure 1**.

      Mother's genotype: ....

      Father's genotype: ....
                                                                                                                      (1 mark)

      The daughter in **Figure 1** is thinking about having children.
      She decides to undergo genetic testing to find out if she is a carrier of the DMD mutation.

1.3   Give the probability that the daughter is a carrier of the DMD mutation.

                                                      Probability = ...
                                                                                                                      (1 mark)

1.4   If the daughter did turn out to be carrier of the DMD mutation, calculate the probability of her having a
      child with DMD, assuming that the father was unaffected.

                                                      Probability = ...
                                                                                                                      (1 mark)

1.5 Explain why if either of the sons in **Figure 1** decided to have children, they may choose not to undergo genetic testing for DMD.

....

....

....

....

(3 marks)

A scientist collected data from a large number of families, all of which had an unaffected father and an unaffected mother who was a carrier of the DMD mutation.

Table 1 shows a summary of the data the scientist collected.

Table 1

	Unaffected sons	Sons with DMD	Unaffected daughters	Carrier daughters
Number of individuals	1106	984	1057	1422

1.6 Give the expected ratio of offspring without DMD to offspring with DMD in this study.

....

(1 mark)

1.7 Suggest a suitable statistical test that could be used to analyse whether the observed results are significantly different from the expected results.

....

(1 mark)

2 Scientists are investigating the inheritance of cuticle colour in a new species of insect.

The scientists find that cuticle colour is controlled by a single gene with three different alleles.

- The red allele (P^R) results in the production of a red pigment.
- The purple allele (P^P) results in the production of a purple pigment.
- The yellow allele (P^y) results in the production of a yellow pigment.

The P^P and P^R alleles are codominant. The P^y allele is recessive.

The phenotypes corresponding to each possible genotype are shown in **Table 2**.

Table 2

Phenotype	Genotype
Red cuticle	$P^R P^R$ or $P^R P^y$
Purple cuticle	$P^P P^P$ or $P^P P^y$
Yellow cuticle	$P^y P^y$
Red cuticle with purple spots	$P^P P^R$

2.1 Explain why the P^P and P^R alleles can be said to be codominant.

....

....

....

(2 marks)

2.2 Describe the difference between a homozygous genotype and a heterozygous genotype, giving an example of each from **Table 2**.

....

....

....

(2 marks)

As part of the scientists' investigation, insects with the genotype P^{R}P^y were crossed with red and purple spotted insects.

2.3 Draw a genetic diagram to show the expected phenotypic ratio in the offspring of this cross.

Expected phenotypic ratio: ....

(3 marks)

The results of the scientists' cross are shown in **Table 3**.

Table 3

	Red cuticle	Purple cuticle	Red cuticle with purple spots	Total
Number of offspring	48	19	21	88

2.4 Use **Table 3** and your answer to **2.3** to calculate how many offspring from this cross would be expected to have a red cuticle.

Number of offspring with a red cuticle: ....

(1 mark)

The scientists used a chi-squared test to compare the observed and expected results.

2.5 State the null hypothesis for this statistical test.

....

....

(1 mark)

2.6 The chi-squared value was calculated to be 0.82 and the critical value for the chi-squared test was determined to be 5.99. Using this information, explain whether or not the null hypothesis can be rejected.

....

....

(1 mark)

2.7 The statistical test was performed at the 5% probability level. Explain what this tells you about the results.

....

....

(1 mark)

3   In maize plants, different genes control seed colour and shape. The allele for coloured seeds (C) is dominant over the allele for colourless seeds (c). The allele for a full seed shape (S) is dominant over the allele for shrunken seeds (s).

A scientist crossed a maize plant that was heterozygous for both genes with a maize plant that was homozygous recessive for both genes.

3.1 Give the phenotypes of the parent plants.

....

(1 mark)

The phenotypes of the offspring produced by the cross are shown in **Figure 2**.

Figure 2

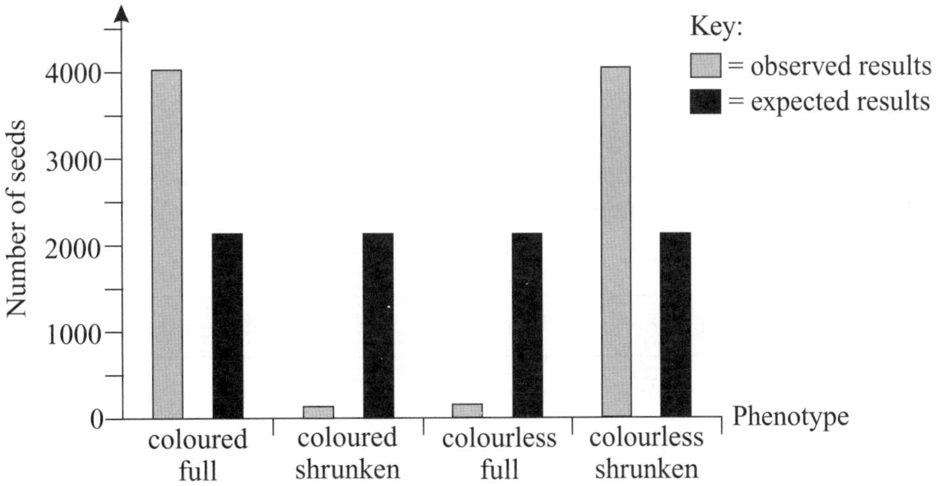

3.2 Explain why the results in **Figure 2** suggest that the genes that control seed colour and shape are autosomally linked.

....

....

....

....

(3 marks)

EXAM TIP: Genetic crosses can get quite complex, especially when they involve multiple alleles. You should always label any genetic diagrams you are asked to draw in the exams. That way it'll be clear to the examiner what you're trying to show and, most importantly, what to award the marks for. Punnett squares are usually the simplest type of diagram to draw and to follow.

Score

25

Genetics — 2

1   Coat colour in horses is influenced by a variety of autosomal genes.

The dominant allele for the grey gene (G) results in coat colour turning progressively grey.
The recessive allele (g) results in the normal coat colour being maintained (non-grey phenotype).

1.1   A non-grey female is crossed with a heterozygous male.
Draw a genetic diagram in the space below to show the expected ratio of phenotypes of the offspring.

Expected phenotypic ratio: ....

(3 marks)

The extension gene also influences coat colour. The dominant allele (E) results in the production of
black pigment, while the recessive allele (e) results in the production of red pigment.

The dominant allele of the white gene (W) blocks pigment production.
A horse with the W allele will have a white coat irrespective of what extension alleles they have.

1.2   Name the term used to describe the interaction between the extension and white genes described above.

....

(1 mark)

1.3   Complete **Table 1** by filling in the pigment produced as a result of each genotype.
If no pigment is produced, write 'none'.

Table 1

Genotype	Pigment produced
EeWw	
Eeww	
eeww	

(1 mark)

1.4   If a male that is heterozygous for both the extension and white coat colour genes is crossed with a
red-pigment producing female, what is the probability that their offspring will produce a black pigment?
Show your working.

Probability of offspring producing black pigment = ...

(3 marks)

1.5 The white gene and extension gene are both located on chromosome 3.
Explain how this could affect the expected results of the cross described in **1.4**.

....

....

....

(3 marks)

2   A scientist is investigating the inheritance of two genes in a particular species of flowering plant.

A single gene controls flower colour. The dominant allele (R) results in red flowers,
and the recessive allele (r) results in yellow flowers.

A second gene controls the number of flowers on each stem. The dominant allele (M) results in multiple
flowers on each stem, and the recessive allele (m) results in only a single flower on each stem.

The scientist initially crosses a plant that is homozygous dominant for both genes with a plant that is
homozygous recessive for both genes. He then observes the phenotypes of the offspring.

2.1 Describe the difference between the genotype and the phenotype of an organism.

....

....

(1 mark)

2.2 Give the genotypes of all possible gametes that could be produced in this cross.

....

(1 mark)

2.3 Describe the expected phenotype(s) of the offspring.

....

....

(1 mark)

The offspring from the cross described above were subsequently crossed with each other
and the phenotypes of the offspring in the next generation were observed and recorded.
The expected results of this cross are shown in **Table 2**.

Table 2

	RM	Rm	rM	rm
RM	RRMM	RRMm	RrMM	RrMm
Rm	RRMm	RRmm	RrMm	Rrmm
rM	RrMM	RrMm	rrMM	rrMm
rm	RrMm	Rrmm	rrMm	rrmm

2.4 Using the results shown in **Table 2**, complete **Table 3** with the expected phenotypic ratios of the offspring.

Table 3

	Multiple red flowers	Single red flower	Multiple yellow flowers	Single yellow flower
Expected number of offspring				

(1 mark)

The scientist decides to use a chi-squared test to determine whether there is a significant difference between his observed results and the expected results.

Table 4 shows some critical values for the chi-squared test.

Table 4

	Probability level					
	0.5	0.2	0.1	0.05	0.01	0.001
Degrees of freedom	Critical values					
1	0.46	1.64	2.71	3.84	6.64	10.83
2	1.39	3.22	4.61	5.99	9.21	13.82
3	2.37	4.64	6.25	7.82	11.34	16.27
4	3.36	5.99	7.78	9.49	13.28	18.47

Abridged from Statistical Tables for Biological, Agricultural and Medical Research (6th ed.) © 1963 R.A Fisher and F. Yates.
Reprinted with permission of Pearson Education

2.5   The scientist calculates the chi-squared value to be 11.67 and chooses a probability level of 0.05.
Use **Table 4** to determine the critical value for the scientist's results.

You'll need to work out the degrees of freedom first. Here, it's the number of classes minus 1.

critical value =...
(1 mark)

2.6   Use your answer to question **2.5** to explain whether there is a significant difference
between the observed and expected results.

....

....
(1 mark)

2.7   Explain **two** reasons why the observed results of a genetic cross could be different from the expected results.

1. ....

....

....

2. ....

....

....
(4 marks)

EXAM TIP — Unfortunately you need to understand a bit about statistics for this topic — the chi-squared test to be precise. Now, this can be a bit tricky to get your head around, but take your time when working through the questions and I'm sure you'll be fine. Remembering how to work out degrees of freedom is the key to finding the critical value.

Score

21

Populations and Evolution

Evolution is responsible for the huge diversity of species on Earth. There are some complex processes involved, so the next few pages won't be easy — but you'll be glad you've done them if this topic comes up in your exams.

1   The distribution of a species of flightless bird was studied by a scientist. **Figure 1** shows the distributions of three populations of this species. The species cannot survive in a mountain habitat so the populations are distributed in a ring around the base of a mountain range. The arrows show gene flow between them.

Figure 1

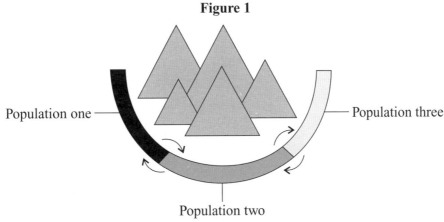

Population one

Population three

Population two

1.1   The Hardy-Weinberg principle does **not** apply to these populations.
Using **Figure 1**, suggest **one** reason why.

....

....
                                                                (1 mark)

1.2   Genetic variation in the populations can be maintained by the gene flow between them.
Give **one** other source of genetic variation in a population.

....
                                                                 (1 mark)

1.3   Population **one** and population **three** are geographically isolated from one another by the mountain range.
Explain why this could lead to speciation of these two populations.

....

....

....

....

....
                                                            (4 marks)

1.4   The scientist observed that population **two** was beginning to show different courtship behaviours to population **one**. Suggest what may happen to the gene flow between these two populations as a result. Explain your answer.

> Courtship behaviour is carried out to attract a mate of the right species. You should remember it from Topic 4.

....

....

....
                                                                 (3 marks)

2   In a species of small rodent, fur colour is controlled by a single gene with two alleles.
The dominant 'W' allele results in a white fur phenotype. Two copies of the recessive 'w' allele
result in a brown fur phenotype. Fur colour provides the rodents with camouflage from predators.

Scientists measured the frequency of these two alleles in populations of the rodent and recorded this against
the latitude at which the populations were found. When measured in degrees north (° N), latitude is a
measure of how far north a location is from the equator. The higher the number, the further north it is.
Table 1 shows the frequencies of the two fur colour alleles in populations living at different latitudes.

Table 1

Latitude / ° N	Allele frequency 'W'	Allele frequency 'w'
64	0.62	
66		0.33
68		0.17
70	0.92	0.08

2.1   Complete the table by calculating the missing allele frequencies.

(1 mark)

2.2   Use the Hardy-Weinberg equation(s) to calculate the frequency of the white fur phenotype at latitude 70° N.
Show your working.

frequency = ...

(2 marks)

2.3   As the latitude increases, the frequency of snowy weather increases. Using this information, explain how
natural selection has led to the differences in allele frequencies between the populations in **Table 1**.

....

....

....

....

....

....

(4 marks)

2.4   Another group of scientists studied a population of the same rodent species at 62° N.
They found the allele frequency of 'W' to be 0.58 and the allele frequency of 'w' to be 0.35.
The scientists hypothesised that this population showed a mutation, resulting in a third allele for fur colour.
Using the information provided, suggest why they made this hypothesis.

....

....

(1 mark)

3 A team of scientists discovered a new species of tree frog in a forest. The species showed two different colour phenotypes, green and yellow. The green allele is dominant and the yellow allele is recessive. The scientists recorded the phenotype frequencies present in the frog population over several years.

The scientists' results are shown in **Figure 2**.

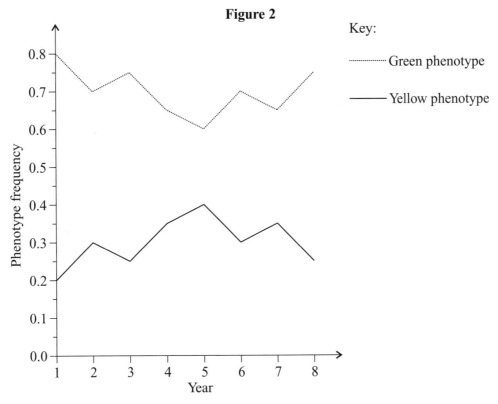

Figure 2

Key:

.... Green phenotype

———— Yellow phenotype

3.1 Using **Figure 2** and the Hardy-Weinberg equations, calculate the expected frequency of heterozygous individuals in the population in **Year 3**. Show your working.

frequency = ...
(3 marks)

3.2 Using **Figure 2**, explain how you know selection is not acting on this phenotypic trait.

....

....

....

....
(3 marks)

3.3 Suggest **one** reason why the phenotype frequencies are changing over time.

....
(1 mark)

3.4 The scientists discovered that the same frog species was also present in another forest on an isolated island. Explain why this second group of frogs is not considered to be in the same population as the first group.

....

....
(1 mark)

4   There are about 15 different species of finch across the Galapagos Islands. It is believed that they all evolved from a common ancestor. **Figure 3** shows two species of Galapagos finch.

Figure 3

Species **A**   Species **B**

© GARY HINCKS/SCIENCE PHOTO LIBRARY

The common ancestor that species **A** and **B** evolved from may have had a medium-sized beak for feeding on small seeds. Species **A** can feed on larger, tougher seeds and species **B** feeds on nectar from flowers.

4.1   Suggest an explanation for how disruptive selection may have acted on the population of the common ancestor to produce species **A** and **B**.

....

....

....

....

....

(4 marks)

In 2004, a severe drought caused a reduction in the number of large seeds produced. The year following the drought, scientists observed that not only had the population size of species **A** fallen, but the average beak size for this species was now significantly smaller.

4.2   Explain how this change in average beak size would have occurred.

....

....

....

....

(3 marks)

4.3   The Galapagos Islands are off the coast of South America. Suggest **one** reason why genetic drift may have a greater effect on a population of Galapagos finches than a population on the South American mainland.

....

....

(1 mark)

Populations in Ecosystems — 1

Ecosystems can be pretty complicated — there are a lot of factors affecting the populations within them. This stuff might not be your niche, but having a go at these questions will get you much better prepared for the exam.

1   **Figure 1** shows the types of vegetation present at each stage of primary succession in a sand dune ecosystem.

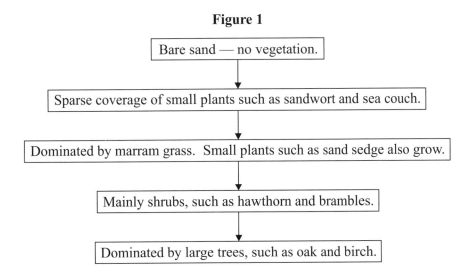

Figure 1

Bare sand — no vegetation.

Sparse coverage of small plants such as sandwort and sea couch.

Dominated by marram grass. Small plants such as sand sedge also grow.

Mainly shrubs, such as hawthorn and brambles.

Dominated by large trees, such as oak and birch.

1.1 Which **two** of the species named in **Figure 1** are pioneer species?

....
(1 mark)

1.2 Describe the role of pioneer species in primary succession.

....

....

....
(2 marks)

1.3 Woodland is the climax community for the ecosystem in **Figure 1**. Explain what this means.

....

....
(1 mark)

1.4 Suggest why marram grass was only dominant in the third stage in **Figure 1**.

....

....

....

....

....
(4 marks)

2 A student was investigating a forest ecosystem. He noticed that different areas of the forest had varying amounts of ground vegetation. He decided to investigate whether the amount of ground vegetation was affected by the amount of light reaching the forest floor.

2.1 Explain the difference between the terms 'community' and 'ecosystem'.

....

....

....

(2 marks)

2.2 Apart from light, suggest **one** other abiotic factor that might affect the distribution of ground vegetation within a forest.

....

(1 mark)

The student used a random number generator to produce coordinates. He then used these coordinates to place a quadrat at different locations in the forest. The quadrat was divided into 100 squares. Each time the student placed the quadrat, he counted the number of squares that contained plants in order to calculate the percentage cover of ground vegetation. He also used a light meter to record the light intensity.

2.3 Suggest **one** other method that the student could have used to place the quadrats.

....

....

(1 mark)

Table 1 shows the student's results.

Table 1

Quadrat number	Ground vegetation cover / %	Light intensity / lux
1	0	160
2	18	100
3	50	300
4	23	280
5	0	50
6	10	230
7	85	500
8	3	90
9	0	260
10	34	490

2.4 Describe and explain the type of graph the student should use to present the data in **Table 1**.

....

....

....

(2 marks)

2.5 Suggest **one** reason the student's data might not be valid.

....

....

(1 mark)

3 A student grew a bacterial culture in a flask of liquid broth. She measured the amount of light being absorbed by the broth culture every hour over a period of 24 hours, and used the measurements to calculate the number of bacteria present. **Figure 2** shows the growth of the population of bacteria.

Figure 2

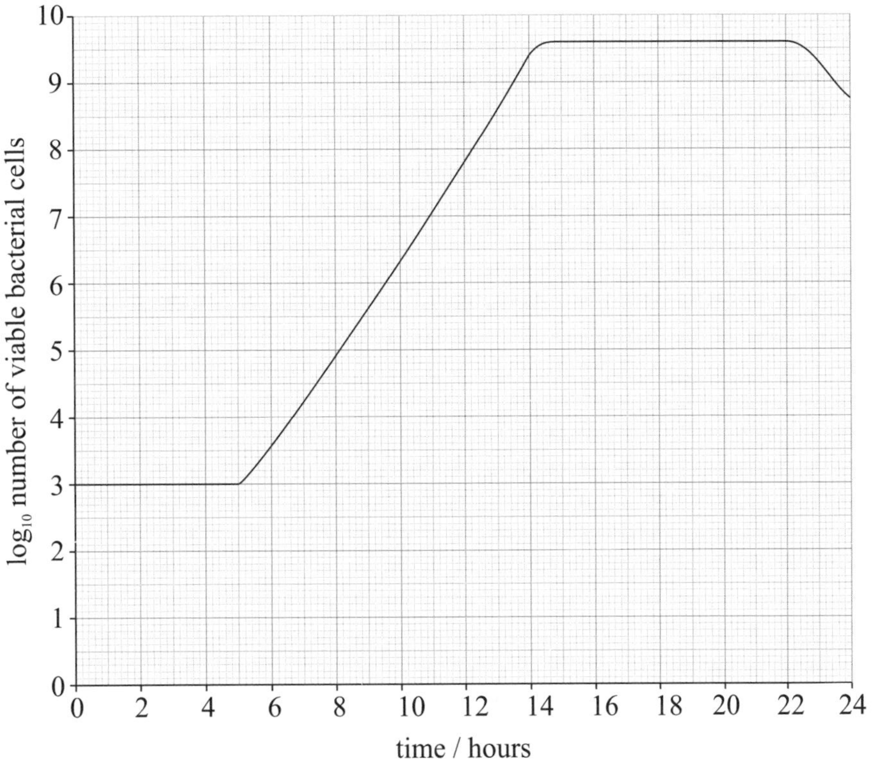

3.1 Calculate the rate of bacterial population growth between 5 hours and 12 hours.
Show your working.

rate = ...cells hour^{-1}

(2 marks)

3.2 Suggest an explanation for why the line on the graph levels off after around 14 hours.

....

....

....

(3 marks)

EXAM TIP

Make sure you know your stuff when it comes to processing and presenting data. You might have to name a suitable graph type for a data set, so make sure you learn what the different types are for. You might also have to read a less familiar scale — logarithms are easy to work out, but you do need to know where the log and antilog (10^x) buttons are on your calculator.

Score

20

Populations in Ecosystems — 2

1   Fens are low-lying, marshy areas of land that are dominated by reeds, rushes and sedge. Over time, they can naturally develop into an ecosystem known as carr woodland, which is dominated by shrubs and trees.

There are large areas of fen in the east of England, which form the habitat of many rare species of plant, insect and bird. Many tourists visit the area every year to enjoy the scenery and wildlife, and to go boating on a network of waterways that run through the fens.

These fens are carefully managed to maintain the sustainability of the natural resources they provide. As a conservation strategy, grazing ponies and cattle have been introduced to some of these fens.

1.1   Explain what is meant by the term 'sustainability'.

....

....
(1 mark)

1.2   Explain why grazing animals have been introduced to some parts of the fen ecosystem.

....

....

....

....

....
(3 marks)

1.3   Suggest **one** other conservation strategy, with a similar outcome to grazing, that might also be carried out in the fens.

....
(1 mark)

1.4   Suggest **one** reason why there might be conflicts between human needs and conservation in the fens in the east of England.

....

....
(1 mark)

2   Ecologists were investigating the size of a population of sand martins in a nature reserve. They captured a sample of 24 sand martins and placed a ring on the leg of each individual bird. One week later, the group captured another sample of sand martins. There were 23 in this sample, 7 of which were already ringed.

2.1   Use the information above to calculate an estimate of the total population size of sand martins in the nature reserve. Show your working.

total population size = ...
(2 marks)

2.2 Explain why the ecologists waited a week before capturing a second sample.

....

....
(1 mark)

2.3 Suggest why the accuracy of the results might have been affected if the ecologists had waited several months before capturing a second sample.

....

....
(1 mark)

3 The golden spiny mouse is a species of small mammal found in the Middle East, often living in rocky habitats. It has spiny fur, which is thought to provide some protection against predation. It is also able to concentrate its urine to conserve water. Its diet consists mainly of grains, grasses, insects and snails.

3.1 Give **one** way that golden spiny mice are adapted to the biotic conditions in their ecosystem.

....
(1 mark)

Figure 1 shows how a population of golden spiny mice changed over time.

Figure 1

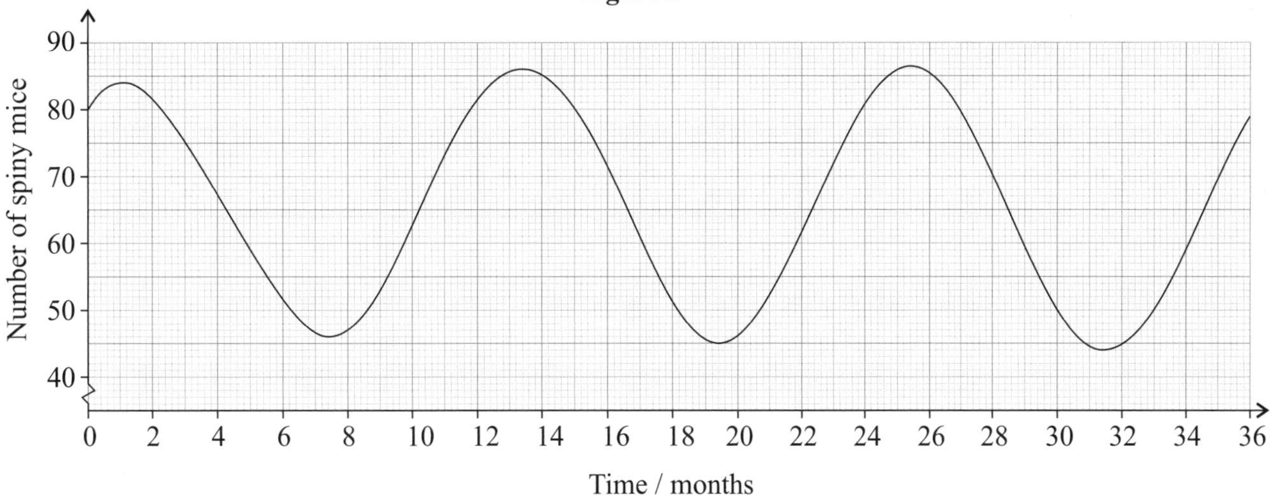

3.2 Explain how intraspecific competition could have caused the shape of the curve in **Figure 1**.

....

....

....

....

....
(3 marks)

3.3 Using **Figure 1**, estimate the carrying capacity of the golden spiny mouse population.

carrying capacity = ...
(1 mark)

128

3.4 Suggest how a change in air temperature could cause a fall in the size of the golden spiny mice population.

....

....

....

(2 marks)

The Cairo spiny mouse is found in rocky areas, and feeds on insects, snails, seeds and some green vegetation. It is native to northern Africa and the Middle East, and lives in some of the same ecosystems as golden spiny mice.

Cairo spiny mice are mainly active during the night, whereas golden spiny mice are mainly active during the day. However, studies have shown that, when Cairo spiny mice are removed from the environment, golden spiny mice are active during both the day and night.

3.5 Suggest and explain why Cairo spiny mice and golden spiny mice living in the same areas are active at different times of day.

....

....

....

....

....

(3 marks)

3.6 Describe a method that could be used to estimate the spiny mouse population at a particular point in time.

....

....

....

....

....

....

(4 marks)

4   The Marsh Fritillary and High Brown Fritillary are two species of butterfly. Their populations have declined in the UK in recent decades, partly because of a reduction in the availability of suitable habitats. The Two Moors Threatened Butterfly Project was a conservation project that took place on Dartmoor and Exmoor, national parks in the southwest of England, between 2005 and 2016. The project's aim was to reverse the decline of some butterfly species, including the Marsh Fritillary and the High Brown Fritillary.

The project involved working with landowners to improve the condition of the habitat. Methods included the introduction of grazing animals and the removal of invading plant species to encourage the growth of the plant species that the butterfly larvae feed on.

Figure 2 shows the population index of the Marsh Fritillary on Dartmoor compared to its population index in the UK from 2005 to 2016. A population index shows relative population sizes and trends.

Figure 2

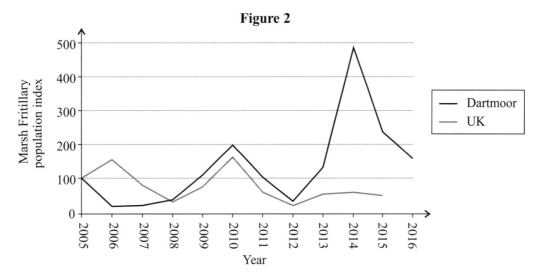

Figure 3 shows the population index of the High Brown Fritillary on Dartmoor and Exmoor compared to the index in the UK from 2005 to 2016.

Figure 3

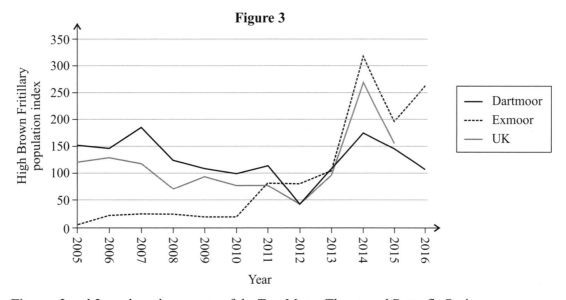

Using **Figures 2** and **3**, analyse the success of the Two Moors Threatened Butterfly Project.

....

....

....

....

....

....

....

....

....

(5 marks)

Score

29

Mutations and Gene Expression — 1

Gene expression is an interesting topic. Unfortunately 'interesting' doesn't mean 'easy', but there's no need to panic — these questions will help you to get on top form for your exams. Just keep working at them.

1   Lactose is a sugar found in milk. It is broken down by the enzyme lactase. Lactase production usually decreases after infancy, so adults in many parts of the world are unable to digest lactose. This is known as lactose intolerance. Thousands of years ago, mutations arose in European populations which led to the continued production of high levels of lactase in adulthood. This is known as lactase persistence.

One mutation that leads to lactase persistence is a substitution mutation.
It does not occur in the lactase gene, so it does not change the amino acid sequence of lactase.

1.1   The lactase persistence mutation leads to more transcription factors being attracted to the lactase gene during adulthood. Explain how this could lead to continued high levels of lactase production.

....

....

....
(2 marks)

1.2   Explain why a substitution mutation that occurs in a gene may not change the amino acid sequence of the protein it codes for.

....

....

....
(2 marks)

Doctors can diagnose lactose intolerance by performing a milk tolerance test. This is where they give the patient a known volume of milk and record the blood glucose level following ingestion. If the blood glucose level does not rise, then the patient may have not produced any lactase to break down the lactose. **Table 1** shows the results of milk tolerance tests in a group of patients from the UK.

Table 1

	Lactose intolerance	Lactose tolerance
Number of patients	11	196

1.3   Using the results shown in **Table 1**, calculate the percentage of patients that were lactose intolerant.

Percentage of patients = ...%
(1 mark)

1.4   Suggest **one** reason why the milk tolerance test alone cannot confirm lactose intolerance.

....

....
(1 mark)

2 The *PTEN* gene is a tumour suppressor gene that has been linked to a number of cancers, including lung cancer. This gene codes for an enzyme involved in the regulation of the cell cycle.

2.1 Give **one** function of a tumour suppressor gene.

....
(1 mark)

2.2 Explain how a mutation in the *PTEN* gene could lead to the development of a tumour in the lungs.

....

....

....

....
(4 marks)

2.3 Other than a mutation, suggest and explain **one** change that could occur in the *PTEN* gene and which may lead to lung cancer.

....

....
(2 marks)

The incidence of lung cancer is higher in individuals who regularly smoke cigarettes than those who do not. A scientist is analysing a sample taken from an abnormal mass of cells found in the lungs of a smoker. The scientist suspects that the mass is a malignant tumour.

2.4 Suggest and explain why regularly smoking cigarettes increases the likelihood of developing lung cancer.

....

....

....

....
(3 marks)

2.5 Explain why malignant tumours are described as cancerous but benign tumours are not.

....

....
(2 marks)

3 A team of scientists is attempting to improve the yield of a crop plant, by introducing random mutations into the crop plant's DNA. The scientists expose seeds from the crop plant to gamma radiation. They then leave the seeds to grow and record the characteristics of the resulting mature plants.

3.1 Suggest why the scientists expose the seeds to gamma radiation.

....

....
(2 marks)

3.2 The majority of mutations that arise in the seeds do not lead to an improvement in crop yield. Suggest **two** reasons for this.

1. ....

....

2. ....

....

(2 marks)

The scientists used DNA sequencing to identify the mutations in one of the plants grown from seed.

Figure 1 shows part of the sequence of a wild-type plant gene and the corresponding sequence in the mutated plant.

Here, 'wild-type' just means the version of the gene that occurs in the population of plants that weren't irradiated.

Figure 1

Wild-type gene: ... **TTA** TTT CTT ACG CCA GAA CGT ...

Mutant gene: ... **ATT** TTT CTT ACG CGC AGA ACG ...

1st mutation   2nd mutation

3.3 Describe the **two** mutations shown in **Figure 1**.

1st mutation: ....

2nd mutation: ....

(2 marks)

3.4 Explain why the second mutation could have a much larger effect on the structure of the protein than the first mutation.

....

....

....

....

(3 marks)

The scientists predicted that the way to increase crop yield might be to introduce a mutation into a gene involved in photosynthesis.

3.5 Suggest how a mutation in a gene that codes for a photosynthetic enzyme might lead to an increase in the rate of photosynthesis.

....

....

....

(2 marks)

EXAM TIP

When analysing the likely effects of a mutation on the structure of a protein, think about the number of amino acids that may be affected. You should remember that a protein's structure has a huge effect on its function, and that any change could be positive, negative or neutral.

Score

29

Mutations and Gene Expression — 2

1 Oestrogen is a steroid hormone that is known to have a role in regulating the expression of certain genes. Some studies have suggested that increased levels of oestrogen may be related to the development of some types of cancer, including breast cancer.

1.1 Explain **one** way in which increased levels of oestrogen could contribute to the development of breast cancer.

....

....

....

(2 marks)

1.2 Suggest **one** reason why knowing that a particular cancer has been caused by increased levels of oestrogen could help to improve the treatment plan for that cancer.

....

....

(1 mark)

The age of onset of menstruation affects how long a woman is exposed to oestrogen for. Scientists wanted to know whether the age at which menstruation begins in adolescent females is primarily influenced by environmental or genetic factors. The scientists performed a study looking at identical and non-identical twins that were raised together and those that were raised apart from one another. They recorded the age at which each twin in a pair began menstruation and calculated the number of years difference in this age.

1.3 Suggest why studies on identical twins are useful for investigating whether a particular phenotype is caused by genetic or environmental factors.

....

....

(2 marks)

Figure 1 shows some of the results of the scientists' study.

Figure 1

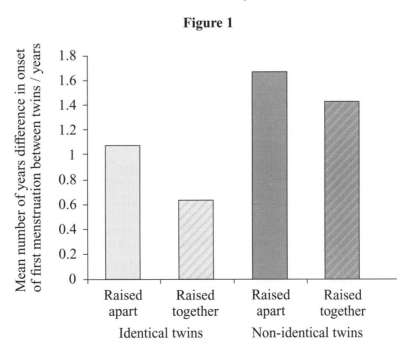

1.4 Explain what the results in **Figure 1** suggest about the influence of environmental and genetic factors on the age of onset of first menstruation.

....

....

....

....

....

....

(4 marks)

2 Many scientists are investigating novel therapies for the treatment of cancer. Their research has indicated that the *MYC* gene is a proto-oncogene that is closely linked to the development of a wide variety of cancers. The *MYC* gene codes for the MYC protein, a transcription factor that activates the expression of a number of genes related to the progression of the cell cycle.

2.1 Explain the role of proto-oncogenes in the development of cancer.

....

....

....

(3 marks)

2.2 Explain how transcription factors, like the MYC protein, regulate gene expression.

....

....

....

....

....

(4 marks)

Scientists have hypothesised that it may be possible to develop a drug that binds to the MYC protein and causes it to change shape.

2.3 Explain why this drug might be effective in the treatment of cancer.

....

....

....

(3 marks)

2.4 Suggest why this drug is likely to have negative side-effects when used in cancer therapy.

....

....

(1 mark)

2.5 Explain why this drug would not be suitable for the treatment of all cancers.

....

....

....

(2 marks)

3 Mutations in the *BRCA1* tumour suppressor gene are a known cause of hereditary breast cancer. Scientists have also found a link between increased methylation of the *BRCA1* promoter region and decreased *BRCA1* expression in patients with non-hereditary breast cancer. A promoter region is a DNA sequence that RNA polymerase must bind to in order to initiate transcription.

3.1 Explain the difference between a DNA mutation and DNA methylation.

....

....

....

(2 marks)

3.2 Using the information provided above, explain how increased methylation of the *BRCA1* promoter region could contribute to the development of breast cancer.

....

....

....

....

(4 marks)

3.3 Explain why drugs that affect DNA methylation need to be specifically targeted to tumour cells, rather than being applied throughout the whole body.

....

....

....

(2 marks)

3.4 Suggest and explain how **one** other epigenetic change, besides DNA methylation, may contribute to the development of cancer.

....

....

....

(2 marks)

You need to be able to explain the roles of both proto-oncogenes and tumour suppressor genes in cancer development. A tumour suppressor gene's role is pretty self-explanatory (it suppresses tumours, i.e. cell growth) and a proto-oncogene has the opposite effect.

Score

32

Topic Eight — Gene Expression

Mutations and Gene Expression — 3

1   Signals from the environment trigger the specialisation of stem cells.
A team of scientists carried out an investigation into the effects of different
signalling molecules on the development of stem cells in human embryos.

Their investigation involved exposing pluripotent embryonic stem cells to various signalling molecules and observing the types of cells that were formed. An outline of the method is shown in **Figure 1**.

Figure 1

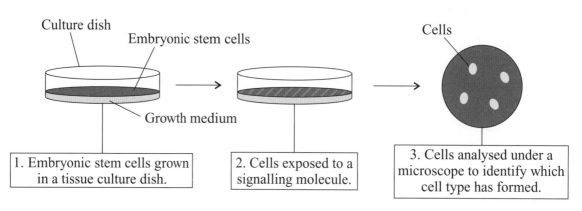

1.1   Explain how the embryonic stem cells in this experiment became specialised to form a specific cell type.

....

....

....

....

....
                                                                                                        (4 marks)

Not all embryonic stem cells are pluripotent. Some are totipotent.

1.2   Explain the difference between totipotent and pluripotent stem cells.

....

....

....
                                                                                                        (2 marks)

One of the scientists in the group suggested that they should consider using induced pluripotent stem cells (iPS cells) in place of embryonic stem cells for their research.

1.3   Describe how induced pluripotent stem cells are produced.

....

....

....
                                                                                                        (2 marks)

1.4 Explain **one** advantage and **one** disadvantage of using induced pluripotent stem cells rather than embryonic stem cells in the investigation shown in **Figure 1**.

Advantage: ....

....

Disadvantage: ....

....

(4 marks)

1.5 Explain why using unipotent stem cells would not have been suitable for this investigation.

....

....

....

(2 marks)

2   siRNA gene silencing is a type of RNAi. It is used in cells to prevent the expression of a particular gene.

siRNA gene silencing works like this:

- In the cytoplasm, a double-stranded siRNA molecule associates with several proteins and unwinds.
- A single strand of siRNA then binds to the target mRNA.
- The proteins associated with the siRNA cut the mRNA into fragments, to be later degraded by the cell.

2.1 Using the information above, explain why siRNAs prevent the expression of the target gene.

....

....

(1 mark)

2.2 Suggest why a mutation in the base sequence of a gene that is targeted by a siRNA molecule could prevent the siRNA from silencing the gene.

....

....

....

....

(3 marks)

A scientist investigated how siRNA silencing affected the expression of a gene, *X*, in a particular cell type.

As part of her investigation, the scientist took cells of a single type and grew them in culture. She then split the cells into two groups, which each received a different treatment.

- The first group was treated with an siRNA sequence targeting gene *X*.
- The second group was treated with 'scramble' siRNA. The scramble siRNA had the same base composition as the siRNA targeting gene *X*, but the order of bases was different.

The results the scientist obtained at an siRNA concentration of 25 nM are shown in **Figure 2** on the next page.

Figure 2

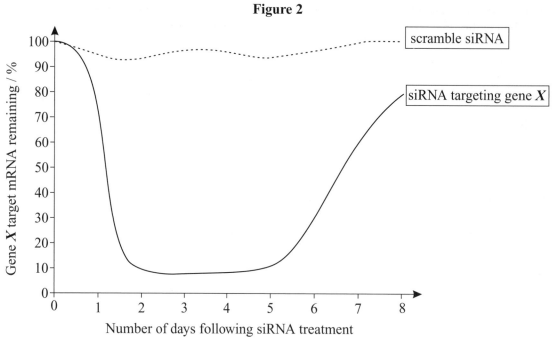

2.3 Explain the purpose of the scramble siRNA in the scientist's investigation.

....

....

....

(2 marks)

2.4 siRNAs are vulnerable to degradation by enzymes in the cell.
    Suggest how this may explain the results shown in **Figure 2** for the siRNA targeting gene *X*.

....

....

....

....

(2 marks)

2.5 The scientist wants to investigate how changing the concentration of siRNA affects expression of gene *X*.
    Describe a method the scientist could use to do this.
    Include details of what she should do to make her investigation valid.

....

....

....

....

....

(3 marks)

Genome Projects and Gene Technologies — 1

You've nearly got through everything you need to know, but there's still the small matter of genome projects and gene technologies to deal with. These questions have all kinds of examples of how scientists can use gene technologies to help out in the real world — it's very impressive. Have a go and see how much you know.

1   Blood has been found at a crime scene. A forensic scientist has been asked to confirm who the blood is from. The forensic scientist takes a sample of the blood, extracts the DNA and then uses the polymerase chain reaction (PCR) to amplify it. The DNA is then analysed using genetic fingerprinting, alongside samples of DNA from the victim of the crime and three potential suspects.

1.1   Describe and explain the process of PCR.

....

....

....

....

....

....

....

(5 marks)

1.2   Explain why it is necessary to amplify the DNA sample using PCR before performing genetic fingerprinting.

....

....

....

(2 marks)

The results of the genetic fingerprint analysis performed by the forensic scientist are shown in **Figure 1**.

Figure 1

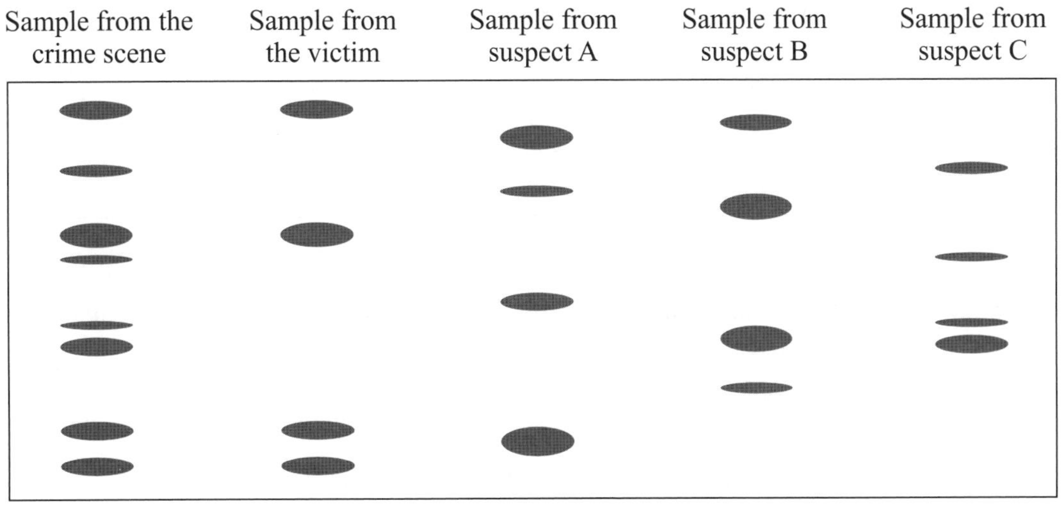

1.3 Explain why DNA samples from different individuals produce different patterns of bands when genetic fingerprinting is performed.

....

....

....

....

....

....

(4 marks)

1.4 On the basis of the results shown in **Figure 1**, what conclusion can be drawn regarding the blood from the crime scene?

....

....

(1 mark)

1.5 Genetic fingerprinting can also be used to determine genetic relationships.
Explain how genetic fingerprinting could be used to determine a child's biological father.

....

....

....

....

....

(3 marks)

2   A genetic counsellor is seeing a 32-year-old woman with a family history of colon cancer. The woman's mother died from colon cancer at the age of 48. The woman's brother has recently been diagnosed with a similar form of colon cancer. After he was diagnosed, he underwent a genetic test which found he had a mutation that had made him more likely to develop colon cancer. The genetic counsellor tells the woman that she is eligible for a genetic test to determine whether she has the same mutation.

2.1 Describe the role of DNA hybridisation in genetic testing.

....

....

....

(2 marks)

2.2 Suggest **one** reason why genetic testing was carried out on the woman's brother, even though he had already been diagnosed with cancer.

....

....

(1 mark)

The genetic counsellor talks to the woman about potential advantages and disadvantages of a genetic test.

2.3 Give **two** ways that knowing the results of a genetic test could be beneficial for the woman.

1. ....

....

2. ....

....

(2 marks)

2.4 Suggest **one** disadvantage for the woman if she were to undergo genetic testing.

....

....

(1 mark)

3   Severe combined immunodeficiency (SCID) is a genetic disorder that affects the functioning of white blood cells. There are a number of different genetic defects that can cause SCID, one of which is a mutation in the IL2RG gene.

A scientist uses a DNA probe to analyse the DNA from three patients with SCID to determine whether their condition is caused by an IL2RG mutation. The scientist's results are shown in **Figure 2**.

Figure 2

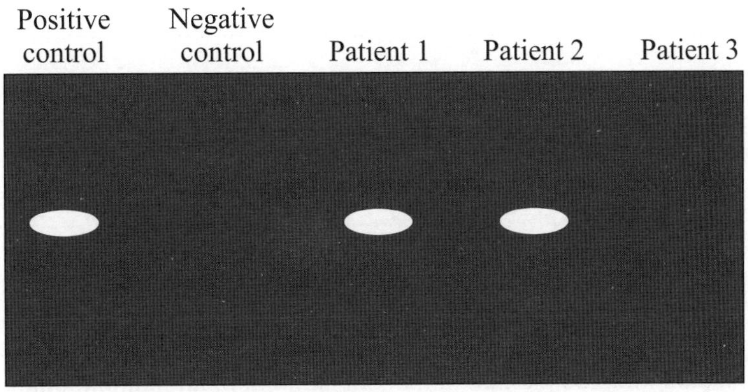

In order to obtain the results shown in **Figure 2**, DNA samples from each individual were cut into fragments using restriction enzymes. The fragments were then separated using gel electrophoresis.

3.1 Describe how the results shown in **Figure 2** were obtained once electrophoresis had taken place.

....

....

....

....

....

(3 marks)

3.2 Explain the purpose of the positive and negative controls in **Figure 2**.

....

....

....

(2 marks)

3.3 Suggest **one** reason why identifying the particular mutation that causes SCID
in an individual might be important.

....

....

(1 mark)

In the future, it is hoped that gene therapy could be used to treat individuals with an IL2RG mutation.
One way this could be achieved is to take a sample of white blood cells from the patient, infect the cells
with a virus containing a functional copy of the IL2RG gene, and then inject the cells back into the patient.

3.4 Describe how a virus containing a functional copy of the IL2RG gene could be produced.

....

....

....

....

....

....

....

(4 marks)

3.5 Explain the role of the virus in gene therapy to treat an IL2RG mutation.

....

....

....

(2 marks)

3.6 Suggest **two** potential disadvantages of using this form of gene therapy to treat a patient with SCID.

1. ....

....

2. ....

....

(2 marks)

> **EXAM TIP**
>
> You need to be able to interpret the results of gel electrophoresis (the technique used to separate
> DNA fragments in genetic fingerprinting) in your exams. Luckily, it's quite straightforward —
> fragments are separated by size, and fragments of the same size (indicating a match) travel
> exactly the same distance in the gel. Use a ruler to compare where bands are located if it helps.

Score

35

Genome Projects and Gene Technologies — 2

1   A group of scientists is experimenting with an enzyme produced by a rare species of plant. In order to produce large amounts of this enzyme quickly and easily, they decide to clone the gene for the enzyme and then produce a strain of *E. coli* that is capable of making the enzyme in large quantities. The process used by the scientists is outlined in **Figure 1**.

Figure 1

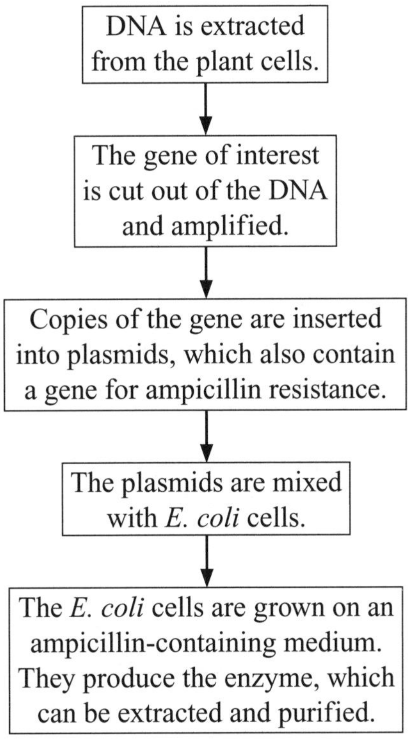

DNA is extracted from the plant cells.

↓

The gene of interest is cut out of the DNA and amplified.

↓

Copies of the gene are inserted into plasmids, which also contain a gene for ampicillin resistance.

↓

The plasmids are mixed with *E. coli* cells.

↓

The *E. coli* cells are grown on an ampicillin-containing medium. They produce the enzyme, which can be extracted and purified.

1.1   Explain why it is possible for the gene from the plant to be expressed in *E. coli* bacteria, despite them being different species.

....

....

(1 mark)

1.2   Suggest **one** reason why the *E. coli* may be able to produce greater quantities of the enzyme more quickly than the plant.

....

....

(1 mark)

1.3   Describe how the gene of interest can be cut out of the plant DNA once it has been extracted from the plant cells.

....

....

....

(2 marks)

1.4 Explain why the scientists chose to insert the gene for ampicillin resistance into the plasmids.

....

....

....

(2 marks)

1.5 As well as adding a gene for ampicillin resistance to the plasmids, the scientists also inserted a promoter region in front of the gene of interest. Explain the purpose of the promoter region.

....

....

....

(2 marks)

2   Some breeds of dog are susceptible to certain inherited genetic conditions that can decrease a dog's quality of life. As a result, dog breeders are encouraged to use genetic testing before mating two dogs together to ensure that the puppies will not inherit any genetic conditions.

A dog breeder wants to breed a new litter of beagle puppies. Beagles are susceptible to a number of inherited genetic conditions, including FVIID, IGS, MLS and NCCD. All of these conditions are recessive, meaning that healthy dogs can be carriers of faulty alleles that cause these conditions.

The breeder has a choice of two females and three males that could potentially be bred together. All of the dogs are healthy. Genetic testing using a series of DNA probes is performed on DNA samples from each of the dogs. The results are shown in **Figure 2**.

Figure 2

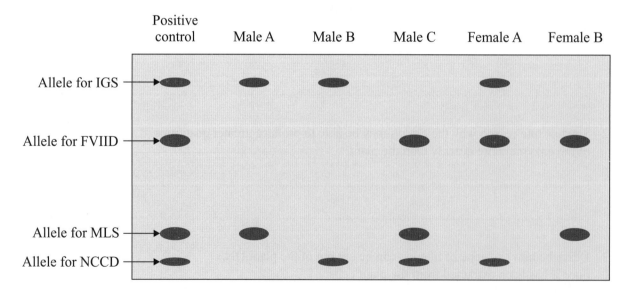

2.1 State the number of different types of DNA probe needed to produce the results seen in **Figure 2**.

....

(1 mark)

2.2 Explain how gel electrophoresis was used to produce the banding pattern shown in **Figure 2**.

....

....

....

....

(3 marks)

2.3 Using **Figure 2**, explain why Male A should not be mated with Female A.

....

....

....

(2 marks)

2.4 Based on the results in **Figure 2**, which pairing should the breeder use? Explain your answer.

....

....

....

(2 marks)

2.5 Many breeders also use genetic fingerprinting when planning to breed a new litter of puppies. Explain why genetic fingerprinting is used in this way.

....

....

....

(2 marks)

2.6 Compare and contrast the processes of genetic fingerprinting and genetic testing using DNA probes.

....

....

....

....

(3 marks)

3   A group of scientists identifies a new strain of bacteria that lives in Antarctic lakes. The scientists sequence the genome of the bacteria. Having done so, they identify a novel version of a gene that codes for an anti-freeze protein. Anti-freeze proteins prevent ice crystals from forming in the cells of organisms that live in sub-freezing conditions.

3.1 Suggest why analysis of the bacterial genome may have more easily led to the discovery of a novel anti-freeze protein than analysis of the genomes of fish found in the same lakes.

....

....

....

(2 marks)

3.2 The genome of the bacteria is 240 000 base pairs in length.
The scientists sequenced the entire genome 6 times in order to ensure that their sequence was accurate.
They used a sequencing technique capable of reading 12 000 base pairs per minute.

Calculate how many hours the team spent sequencing the genome in total.

.... hours
(1 mark)

3.3 Give **one** way that modern sequencing techniques have changed from older sequencing techniques.

....
(1 mark)

A second group of scientists decides to investigate whether the novel anti-freeze gene could be inserted
into maize plants. They hope this will increase the maize plants' resistance to cold. The group obtains
a sample of mRNA extracted from the Antarctic bacteria.

3.4 Describe how a cDNA sequence for the anti-freeze gene could be produced from the mRNA sample.

....

....

....
(2 marks)

3.5 The scientists choose to amplify their cDNA sample *in vivo* before using it to using genetically engineer
maize plants. Explain what is meant by *in vivo* amplification.

....

....
(1 mark)

3.6 Discuss the advantages and disadvantages for society of using genetic engineering to produce a
cold-resistant strain of maize.

....

....

....

....

....

....

....

....
(4 marks)

EXAM
TIP
If a question asks you for two things, e.g. 'advantages and disadvantages', you need to write
about them both. Even if you've described loads of advantages, you wouldn't get full marks
unless you've also written something to balance out the argument on the other side.

Score

32

Mixed Questions — 1

Here we go: a section of juicy Mixed Questions to get your teeth into. These questions draw together different bits of biology from across your A-level course, so they should really get those brain cells firing.

1   A student investigated the effect of pH on the activity of the enzyme lactase, which catalyses the breakdown of lactose into its monomers.

The student used the following method:

1. Add 2 ml of lactose solution and 2 ml of a pH buffer solution to a test tube.
    Swirl the contents of the tube gently for 10 seconds.

2. Add 2 ml of lactase solution to the test tube.
    Swirl the contents of the tube gently for 10 seconds.

3. After 8 minutes, dip a fresh glucose test strip into the solution in the test tube.
    Leave for 2 seconds and then remove.

4. After 1 minute, observe and record the colour of the test strip.
    Any shade of green indicates that glucose is present.
    If the paper remains yellow, no glucose is present.

The student repeated steps 1-4 using buffer solutions of pH 2, 4, 6, 7, 8, 10 and 12.

Table 1 shows the results of the investigation.

Table 1

pH	Glucose test result
2	Green
4	Green
6	Green
7	Green
8	Yellow
10	Yellow
12	Yellow

1.1   What type of biological molecule is lactose?

   A   Nucleotide   ☐

   B   Monosaccharide   ☐

   C   Dipeptide   ☐

   D   Disaccharide   ☐

(1 mark)

1.2   The solution in the test tubes contains water. Explain **one** reason why water may be needed for the reaction occurring in some of the test tubes to take place.

   ....

   ....

   ....

(2 marks)

1.3 What can you conclude about the effect of pH on lactase activity from the results shown in **Table 1**? Explain your answer.

....

....

....

....

(3 marks)

1.4 Describe how enzyme structure is affected by pH.

....

....

....

....

(3 marks)

1.5 The student's method specified that all volumes and timings should have been controlled as part of her investigation. Give **two** other variables that the student should have controlled.

1. ....

2. ....

(2 marks)

1.6 Suggest how the student could continue her investigation to determine a more accurate estimate for the pH at which lactase denatures. Explain your answer.

....

....

....

(2 marks)

1.7 Human lactase is a membrane-bound enzyme found in ileum epithelial cells.
Not all lactase is membrane-bound.
Describe **one** advantage of lactase in the human ileum being membrane-bound.

....

....

....

(1 mark)

1.8 Most young children produce lactase, but the gene that codes for it is switched off as they get older.
In Europe, a mutation over 7000 years ago is thought to have caused this gene to remain active in adults.

Suggest why this mutation became common in Europeans.

....

....

....

....

(3 marks)

2   Mitosis and meiosis are both types of cell division.

Figure 1 represents two cells. One cell is undergoing mitosis. The other is undergoing meiosis I.

Figure 1

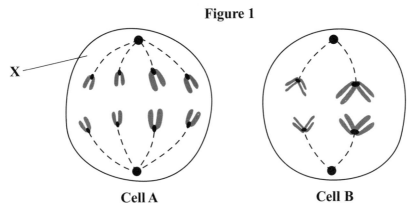

2.1 Identify the structure labelled **X**.

....
(1 mark)

2.2 Which of the cells in **Figure 1** (**A** or **B**) is undergoing meiosis I?
Give a reason for your answer.

....

....
(1 mark)

Figure 2 shows the life cycle of a type of plant called a liverwort. During the life cycle there are haploid (n) and diploid (2n) phases. Four stages of cell division are labelled.

Figure 2

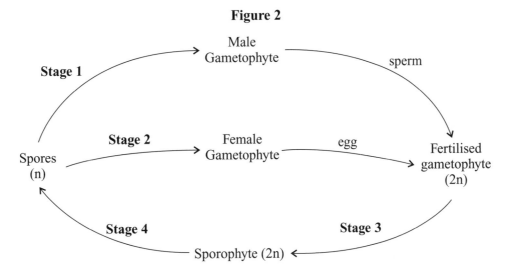

2.3 The diploid number of this liverwort is 40. How many chromosomes are present in the spore?

Number of chromosomes = ...
(1 mark)

2.4 Name the type of cell division occurring at **Stage 4** on **Figure 2**.
Give a reason for your answer.

....

....
(1 mark)

2.5 Spores develop into male or female gametophytes (**Stages 1** and **2**).
A sperm from a male gametophyte then fertilises an egg inside a female gametophyte.
Using this information, explain why **Stages 1** and **2** on **Figure 2** must represent mitosis.

....

....

....

(3 marks)

3 *Vibrio cholerae* are pathogenic bacteria that cause the disease cholera in humans. The bacteria produce a toxin that causes Cl^- channel proteins in the ileum lining to remain open. This can result in the loss of a large volume of water from the blood. **Figure 3** shows a small section of the ileum lining.

Figure 3

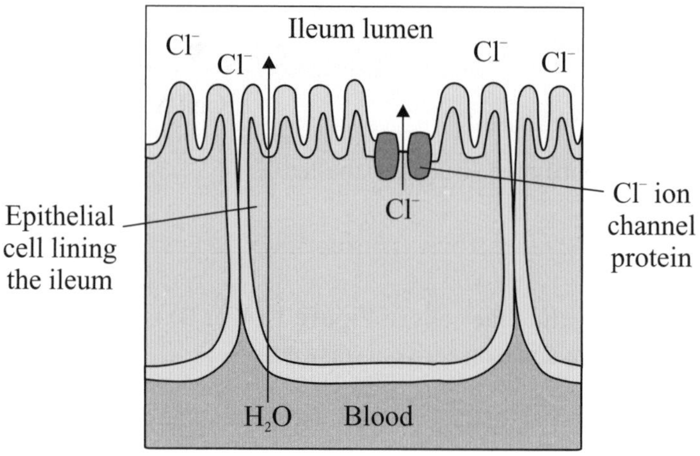

3.1 Use **Figure 3** to explain how cholera causes water to be lost from the blood.

....

....

....

....

....

(4 marks)

3.2 Suggest **one** structural difference between *V. cholerae* and an ileum epithelial cell.

....

....

(1 mark)

3.3 The toxin released by *V. cholerae* is a protein.
It attaches to specific receptor proteins on the surface of the ileum epithelial cells.
Give **one** other example of a pathogen interacting with receptor proteins in the human body.

....

....

(1 mark)

EXAM TIP	Each of these Mixed Questions requires you to apply your knowledge of several different areas of the specification. It shouldn't come as a surprise that you'll get exam questions that require you to do the same thing. What it boils down to is this — you need to know your stuff inside out and back to front. So if you haven't started already, you'd better get revising.	Score 30

Mixed Questions — 2

1 The light-independent reaction is essential for producing useful organic substances in a plant.

Figure 1 shows the light-independent reaction of photosynthesis.

Figure 1

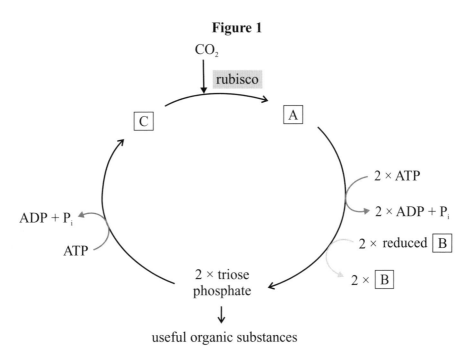

1.1 Name the molecules **A-C** in **Figure 1**.

A ....

B ....

C ....

(3 marks)

1.2 A low temperature can limit the rate of the light-independent reaction. Suggest **one** reason why.

....

....

(1 mark)

1.3 Plant growth can be reduced if the rate of the light-independent reaction is limited.
Explain **one** reason why.

....

....

(2 marks)

1.4 The useful organic substances made by the light-independent reaction can become a plant's biomass. GPP and NPP are measures of the energy in a plant's biomass. Explain the difference between GPP and NPP.

....

....

(2 marks)

2   **Figure 2** shows a single cycle of contraction and relaxation in a slow twitch muscle fibre.

Figure 2

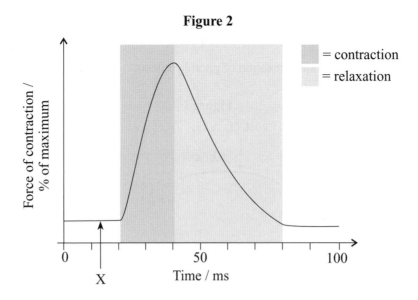

2.1   The muscle fibre is stimulated by an action potential at the point in time marked **X** on **Figure 2**.
Suggest **two** reasons for the delay between receiving the stimulus and contraction of the fibre.

1. ....

....

2. ....

....

(2 marks)

2.2   Explain what is happening to the muscle fibre during the period of relaxation shown on **Figure 2**.

....

....

....

....

....

(3 marks)

2.3   Suggest how **Figure 2** would appear different if it showed a fast twitch muscle fibre.

....

....

(1 mark)

2.4   Slow twitch muscle fibres release more energy than fast twitch muscle fibres. Explain why.

....

....

....

....

(3 marks)

3   The human body acts to keep the blood glucose concentration at around 90 mg per 100 cm³ of blood.

3.1   Name and describe **two** processes that happen in the liver when blood glucose concentration gets too low.

1. ....

....

2. ....

....

(4 marks)

People with Type I diabetes inject insulin to help control their blood glucose concentration.
Gene technology has allowed insulin to be produced by inserting the human gene for insulin into *E. coli*.
The bacteria then produce the hormone as part of their normal protein production.

3.2   First, the DNA fragment containing the human insulin gene is obtained from the mRNA present in human pancreatic cells. Describe how this is done.

....

....

....

(3 marks)

3.3   The DNA fragment is then amplified, before being inserted into vector DNA.
Explain how a DNA fragment would be inserted into vector DNA.

....

....

....

....

....

(3 marks)

3.4   Once present in *E. coli* DNA, the insulin gene is transcribed by the T7 RNA polymerase.
The transcription of T7 RNA polymerase is transcribed by the *lac* promoter region.
The *lac* promoter region is repressed until a molecule called IPTG is added to the *E. coli* culture.

Suggest and explain the importance of this *lac* promoter region in large-scale insulin production.

....

....

....

....

(3 marks)

EXAM TIP   Questions 1.2 and 2.1 ask you to 'suggest' a reason or reasons for something happening. For both of these questions you're not expected to have learned why these things happen. The 'suggest' command word means you need to use your scientific knowledge and the information in the question to work out what the answer might be.

Score

30

Mixed Questions — 3

1   Organisms have a tendency to move into more favourable environments.

1.1   Simple organisms, such as nematodes, move towards or away from heat sources.
Name this type of simple behavioural response.

....
(1 mark)

Some species of deer in the northern hemisphere migrate south during the winter, to warmer climates.
Two populations (**A** and **B**) of a species of deer live in the same area but are separated by a large lake.

During winter, population **A** migrates south-west and population **B** migrates south-east.
The migration of the two populations is shown in **Figure 1**.

Figure 1

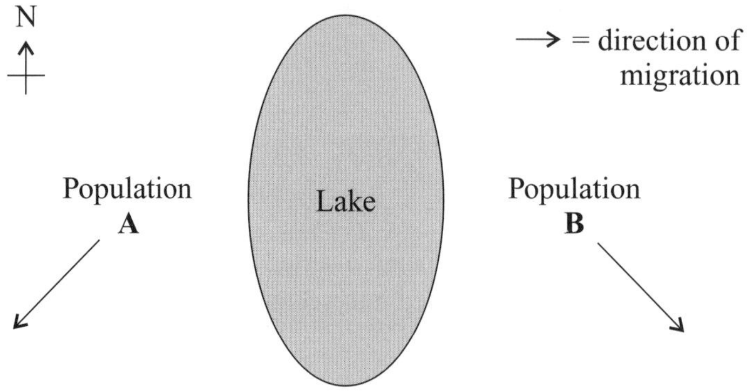

A team of scientists studied the two deer populations to determine how much genetic variation there was between them. The scientists produced a genetic fingerprint for each deer population in order to compare their DNA.

1.2   The scientists extracted a DNA sample from an individual of each population.
State **one** way in which the scientists could have amplified the DNA fragments in these samples, ready to use in genetic fingerprinting.

....
(1 mark)

1.3   Outline the method that the scientists would have used to produce and compare the genetic fingerprints, using the amplified DNA fragments.

....

....

....

....
(3 marks)

1.4   Explain how you might expect the genetic fingerprint of an individual in population **A** to compare with that of an individual in population **B**, if the populations are **not** genetically distinct.

....

....
(1 mark)

1.5 Suggest what may happen to the genetic variation between these two deer populations if they remain physically separated over a long period of time. Explain why.

....

....

....

....

....

(3 marks)

Now for a comprehension question — you'll get one just like it in your Paper 2 A-level exam. In a question like this, it's important to read the passage carefully. Give it a good read through once in full <u>before</u> you tackle any of the question parts. Then, as you answer the question parts, you can recap the relevant bits of the passage.

2 Read the following passage.

1   Petite mutants of the yeast species *Saccharomyces cerevisiae* carry mutations in their nuclear or mitochondrial DNA that result in their mitochondria being inactive. As a result, although petite mutants are able to grow on a substrate containing glucose, they form much smaller colonies than normal cells.

5   Colonies of *Saccharomyces cerevisiae* petite mutants are rarely found in the wild. However, they can be generated in a laboratory using a chemical called ethidium bromide. Ethidium bromide is a DNA intercalator – this means that it can insert itself between strands of DNA. The presence of ethidium bromide between DNA strands can disrupt processes such as DNA replication.

10   Laboratory-generated petite mutants are useful for studying the function of mitochondrial DNA. It is now estimated that only 5% of mitochondrial proteins are encoded for by the mitochondrial genome, with the remainder encoded for by the nuclear genome. One example of a nuclear-encoded gene that is important for mitochondrial function is *NRF-1*. The *NRF-1* gene codes for a transcription factor that
15   activates the expression of other proteins involved in mitochondrial function.

Scientists can also apply the results of studies on petite mutants to more complex organisms. For example, studies on petite mutants have helped to improve understanding of the human mitochondrial proteome.

Using information from the passage and your own knowledge, answer the following questions.

2.1 Petite mutants of the yeast species *Saccharomyces cerevisiae* carry mutations in their nuclear or mitochondrial DNA that result in their mitochondria being inactive (lines 1-2). Suggest how a DNA mutation could lead to the mitochondria being inactive in petite mutants.

....

....

....

....

(3 marks)

156

2.2 Although petite mutants are able to grow on a substrate containing glucose, they form much smaller colonies than normal cells (lines 3-4). Using your knowledge of respiration, explain why:

- Petite mutants are able to grow on a substrate containing glucose, despite lacking functional mitochondria.

- Petite mutants form smaller colonies than normal cells.

....

....

....

....

....

....

(4 marks)

2.3 Colonies of *Saccharomyces cerevisiae* petite mutants are rarely found in the wild (line 5). Explain why this is the case.

....

....

....

(2 marks)

2.4 The presence of ethidium bromide between DNA strands can disrupt processes such as DNA replication (lines 8-9). Suggest how exposing *Saccharomyces cerevisiae* cells to ethidium bromide could result in the production of petite mutants.

....

....

(2 marks)

2.5 The *NRF-1* gene codes for a transcription factor that activates the expression of other proteins involved in mitochondrial function (lines 14-15). Describe how the NRF-1 transcription factor works.

....

....

(2 marks)

2.6 Studies on petite mutants have helped to improve understanding of the human mitochondrial proteome (lines 17-18). Explain why studying the relationship between the genome and proteome of a complex organism, like a human, is difficult.

....

....

....

(2 marks)

EXAM TIP

In the comprehension question in your exam, the passage of text may be on something that you've never heard of before, e.g. petite mutants. Don't worry (and definitely don't run out of the room screaming). This doesn't matter — you just need to use the information from the passage and the knowledge you've gained in your biology course to answer the questions.

Score

24

Mixed Questions — 4

Here's an essay question, just for you. You'll need to use both Year 1 and Year 2 material to answer it.
If you've got a lot to say and you need more space for your answer, you should go onto another sheet of paper.

1   Write an essay on the topic below.

The importance of ATP in living organisms.

....

....

....

....

....

....

....

....

....

....

....

....

....

....

....

....

....

....

....

....

....

....

....

....

....

....

....

....

....

....

....

....

....

....

....

....

....

....

....

....

....

....

....

....

....

....

....

....

....

....

....

(25 marks)

It might be tempting to just fill all these answer lines with absolutely everything you know. But don't. The examiners are looking for you to give information from several different topics, but they also want your answer to be relevant to the question. It's a good idea to write out a short, quick plan of your answer at the top of the paper before you dive in and start your essay.

Score

25

Answers

Topic One — Biological Molecules

Pages 3-4: Biological Molecules — 1

1.1 A molecule made from a large number of monomers joined together *[1 mark]*.

1.2 E.g.

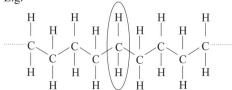

[1 mark]

1.3 E.g. monosaccharides, amino acids and nucleotides *[1 mark]*.

2.1 alpha-glucose/α-glucose *[1 mark]*

You must have specified alpha-glucose to get the mark here. Make sure you know the difference between alpha- and beta-glucose.

2.2 maltose *[1 mark]*

2.3 A water molecule is used *[1 mark]* to break/hydrolyse the glycosidic bond in the disaccharide/maltose *[1 mark]*. This produces the two monomers/alpha-glucose molecules *[1 mark]*.

3.1 alpha helix *[1 mark]*

3.2 Both secondary and tertiary structures contain hydrogen bonds *[1 mark]*. Tertiary structures also contain ionic bonds and disulfide bridges *[1 mark]*.

3.3 Enzymes are proteins that catalyse biological reactions *[1 mark]*. The tertiary structure affects the shape of an enzyme's active site *[1 mark]*. The shape of the active site needs to be specific to the shape of the substrate to catalyse the reaction *[1 mark]*.

3.4 It is made up of several different polypeptide chains *[1 mark]*, held together by bonds *[1 mark]*.

3.5 A low pH interferes with the bonds in the haemoglobin molecule *[1 mark]*. This causes its shape to change, so it can no longer bind to oxygen *[1 mark]*.

Pages 5-8: Biological Molecules — 2

1.1

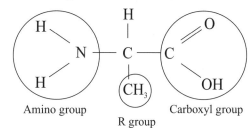

Amino group R group Carboxyl group

[1 mark each]

1.2 It has a different R group *[1 mark]*.

1.3 E.g.

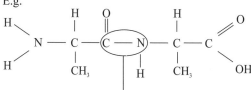

Peptide bond

[1 mark for the correct diagram, 1 mark for correctly labelling the peptide bond]

1.4 water *[1 mark]*

1.5 The human body contains enzymes (which are not present in the laboratory) *[1 mark]*. These catalyse the (hydrolysis) reaction that breaks the bond / increase the rate at which the bond is broken down *[1 mark]*.

2.1 Add Benedict's reagent to the sample and heat in a water bath that has been brought to the boil *[1 mark]*. A positive result gives a coloured, e.g. yellow/orange/brick-red, precipitate *[1 mark]*.

2.2

Sample	Type of carbohydrate present		
	Reducing sugar	Non-reducing sugar	Starch
A		✓	
B			✓
C	✓		

[2 marks for all three correct, otherwise 1 mark for one or two correct answers]

2.3 Any one from: e.g. after testing, they could filter the solutions and weigh the precipitates. / After testing, they could observe the difference in the colour of the precipitates (a green/yellow precipitate indicates less reducing sugar is present than an orange/brick-red precipitate). *[1 mark]*

2.4 glucose and galactose *[1 mark]*

3.1 phospholipid *[1 mark]*

3.2 The phospholipid head is hydrophilic *[1 mark]*, but the phospholipid tail is hydrophobic *[1 mark]*. The molecules arrange themselves in this way to prevent the hydrophobic tails from coming into contact with the water *[1 mark]*.

3.3 E.g. they make up cell membranes *[1 mark]*. The hydrophobic regions act as a barrier to water-soluble substances *[1 mark]*.

4.1 Fatty acid 2 has a double bond between two carbon atoms, whereas fatty acid 1 does not *[1 mark]*. This means that the fatty acid 1 is saturated and fatty acid 2 is unsaturated *[1 mark]*.

4.2 Three fatty acids combine with one glycerol molecule *[1 mark]* in a series of three condensation reactions *[1 mark]*. These form ester bonds between the glycerol and fatty acids *[1 mark]*.

4.3 E.g. triglycerides are used for storage of energy *[1 mark]* because they're insoluble / they contain lots of chemical energy *[1 mark]*.

4.4 Shake some of the sample to be tested with ethanol until it dissolves, then pour into a test tube of water *[1 mark]*. If a lipid is present, a white emulsion will form *[1 mark]*.

4.5 Lipids cannot dissolve in water so if they are present, they form an emulsion *[1 mark]*.

Pages 9-12: Biological Molecules — 3

1.1 E.g. it has lots of side branches *[1 mark]*, meaning stored glucose can be released quickly *[1 mark]*.

Remember, glycogen is the main energy storage molecule in animals.

1.2 E.g.

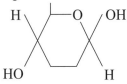

[1 mark]

In alpha-glucose the OH/hydroxyl group and the H/ hydrogen on the right-hand side are reversed *[1 mark]*.

You could have drawn the full skeletal formula for beta-glucose here instead.

1.3 It allows cellulose molecules to form strong fibres/ microfibrils *[1 mark]*, which provide structural support/ support the cell wall *[1 mark]*.

1.4 Advantage: e.g. it is more compact *[1 mark]*. Disadvantage: e.g. it can't be broken down as quickly *[1 mark]*.

2.1 At low temperatures, the rate of the reaction is slow because the kinetic energy of the enzyme and substrate molecules is low *[1 mark]*. As temperature increases to the optimum, the rate increases as there are more successful collisions between enzymes and substrate molecules *[1 mark]*. At temperatures higher than the optimum, the rate decreases as the enzyme is denatured *[1 mark]*.

2.2 Enzyme B because it has the higher optimum temperature *[1 mark]*, which will allow it to function at the higher temperatures found in a tropical climate *[1 mark]*.

2.3 The rate of reaction would be lower across the whole temperature range *[1 mark]*.

2.4 The insecticide molecule is a similar shape to enzyme A's substrate *[1 mark]*. The insecticide molecule occupies enzyme A's active site *[1 mark]* so the substrate cannot fit and the respiration reaction cannot be catalysed *[1 mark]*. This interrupts the respiration process and kills the insect *[1 mark]*.

3.1 Add a few drops of sodium hydroxide to a solution of the sample *[1 mark]*, then a few drops of copper (II) sulfate solution *[1 mark]*. A colour change from blue to purple/ lilac is a positive result *[1 mark]*.

3.2 Its parallel chains and cross linkages make it physically strong *[1 mark]*.

3.3 E.g. Protein B: an enzyme *[1 mark]*. Protein C: an antibody *[1 mark]*.

Enzymes are usually proteins that are roughly spherical, so B could be an enzyme. The two light and two heavy polypeptide chains are typical of an antibody, so C is likely to be an antibody.

3.4 Channel proteins transport molecules and ions across cell membranes *[1 mark]*. The hydrophobic regions are repelled by water and the hydrophilic regions are attracted to it *[1 mark]*. This causes the protein to fold up and form a channel through the membrane (through which water soluble molecules can pass) *[1 mark]*.

4.1 The independent variable is enzyme concentration and the dependent variable is the volume of oxygen produced *[1 mark]*.

4.2 ± 0.5 cm^3 *[1 mark]*

4.3 E.g. collected the gas in a measuring cylinder with a smaller resolution *[1 mark]*.

4.4 Rate = $\dfrac{17}{20}$

= **0.85 cm^3 s^{-1}**

[1 mark for 0.85, 1 mark for the correct units]

4.5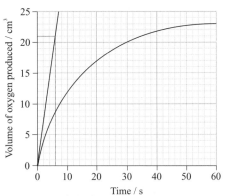

E.g. rate = $\dfrac{21}{6.0}$

= **3.5 cm^3 s^{-1}**

[1 mark, accept anything from 3.2 cm^3 s^{-1} to 3.8 cm^3 s^{-1}]

Tangents can be tricky things to draw accurately so the examiners will usually accept answers that are a bit below or a bit above what they got themselves — even so, try to draw your line as carefully as you can.

4.6 E.g.

[1 mark]

Don't worry if your line's not exactly like this. You just need to make sure it's steeper than the original but still starts and plateaus at the same values.

Pages 13-15: More Biological Molecules

1.1 E.g. it is involved in the co-transport of glucose/amino acids across cell membranes *[1 mark]*.

1.2 E.g. a higher concentration of hydrogen ions lowers the pH *[1 mark]*, so the internal environment becomes more acidic *[1 mark]*.

1.3 Nitrate ions contain nitrogen/N *[1 mark]* which forms part of the organic base in DNA *[1 mark]*.

2.1 Because water has a high latent heat of vaporisation *[1 mark]*, a lot of energy is removed from the kangaroo's body when the water in the saliva evaporates from its forearms *[1 mark]*. This reduces the kangaroo's body temperature *[1 mark]*.

2.2 Water has a high specific heat capacity *[1 mark]*, which means it doesn't heat up as quickly as the air *[1 mark]*.

2.3 There is strong cohesion between water molecules *[1 mark]*. This allows water to travel in a column up the xylem/tube-like transport cells in a tree trunk *[1 mark]*.

3.1 phosphodiester bond *[1 mark]*

3.2 condensation reaction *[1 mark]*

3.3 The molecule contains uracil/U bases (in place of thymine/T bases) *[1 mark]*.

3.4 Complementary/specific base pairing *[1 mark]* means that hydrogen bonds will form between the base pairs A and U, and C and G *[1 mark]*. Because the two halves of the RNA sequence are complementary, it causes the RNA strand to fold into a stem-loop structure *[1 mark]*.

4.1 DNA helicase separates the nucleotide strands / causes the DNA helix to unwind *[1 mark]* by breaking the hydrogen bonds between bases *[1 mark]*. DNA polymerase joins the nucleotides in the new DNA strand together *[1 mark]* by catalysing condensation reactions between the nucleotides *[1 mark]*.

4.2 It is known as a nucleotide derivative because it has a similar structure to a(n) (adenine) nucleotide *[1 mark]* but it has been modified with the addition of two more phosphate groups *[1 mark]*.

4.3 It catalyses the breakdown of ATP *[1 mark]* into ADP and inorganic phosphate *[1 mark]*.

4.4 The results show that DNA replication will not occur in the absence of ATP or when ATP hydrolase is inactive *[1 mark]*. This indicates that the breakdown of ATP (by ATP hydrolase) is essential for DNA replication *[1 mark]*. A possible explanation is that DNA replication requires energy and/or inorganic phosphate released by the breakdown of ATP *[1 mark]*.

Topic Two — Cells

Pages 16-18: Cell Structure and Division — 1

1.1 The student could have placed the root tip on a microscope slide and cut 2 mm/a small section from the very tip of it *[1 mark]*. Then used a mounted needle to break the tip open and spread the cells out thinly *[1 mark]*. Then added a few drops of stain, e.g. ethano-orcein or toluidine blue O, and left it for a few minutes *[1 mark]*. Then placed a cover slip over the cells and pushed down firmly *[1 mark]*.

1.2 Any two from: e.g. worn goggles/gloves / taken care with glass beakers/slides/cover slips / taken care with sharp tools. *[1 mark for each correct answer]*

1.3 Root tips are actively growing so the cells here will be undergoing mitosis/dividing *[1 mark]*.

1.4 E.g. if a cell contains visible chromosomes this indicates that it is dividing *[1 mark]*.

1.5 mitotic index = $\frac{\text{number of cells with visible chromosomes}}{\text{total number of cells observed}}$

80 + 240 = 320 cells in total
240 ÷ 320 = **0.75**
[2 marks for the correct answer, otherwise 1 mark for the correct working]

2.1 E.g. because electron microscopes have a higher resolution *[1 mark]* so they can be used to look at smaller objects (like bacteria) in more detail *[1 mark]*.

2.2 A transmission electron microscope/TEM *[1 mark]*. E.g. transmission electron micrographs show a 2D cross section through a sample as seen in Figure 1 *[1 mark]*.

2.3 Any two from: e.g. a prokaryotic cell is smaller than a eukaryotic cell. / There is no nucleus present in a prokaryotic cell. / A prokaryotic cell contains no membrane-bound organelles. / Ribosomes are smaller in a prokaryotic cell than in a eukaryotic cell. / The DNA in a prokaryotic cell is circular, not linear. / A prokaryotic cell may contain plasmids. *[2 marks]*

2.4 Human cells have no cell wall, so the drugs will have no effect on them *[1 mark]*.

2.5 WNV has an attachment protein on its surface *[1 mark]* which binds to the complementary $\alpha_v\beta_3$ integrin present on human cells *[1 mark]*. If $\alpha_v\beta_3$ integrin isn't functioning on human cells, WNV wouldn't be able to invade and reproduce inside these cells *[1 mark]*.

3.1 Similarities: any one from: e.g. a sperm cell and a bacterial cell can both have a flagellum *[1 mark]*. / A sperm cell and a bacterial cell both have a cell membrane *[1 mark]*.
Differences: any one from: e.g. a sperm cell has a nucleus but a bacterial cell has circular DNA floating freely in the cytoplasm *[1 mark]*. / A bacterial cell has a cell wall but a sperm cell only has a cell membrane *[1 mark]*.
[Maximum 2 marks available]

3.2 The flagellum requires ATP to move, which is generated by mitochondria *[1 mark]*.

3.3 E.g. a transmission/scanning electron microscope *[1 mark]* because these have a higher resolution than light microscopes, which would be needed to study the internal detail of mitochondria *[1 mark]*.

3.4 As the function of sperm is to deliver the genetic material to the egg, it isn't necessary for it to make lots of proteins for cell growth and repair / having lots of organelles may reduce its motility *[1 mark]*. A mitotic body cell is undergoing mitosis/division *[1 mark]*, so it requires ribosomes for cell growth prior to division *[1 mark]*.

Pages 19-21: Cell Structure and Division — 2

1.1 A cell that carries out a particular function *[1 mark]*.

1.2 E.g. each cell would only contain one nucleus. / Each nucleus would contain the same amount of genetic material. *[1 mark]*

1.3 The role of cell type A is to ingest invading pathogens because a greater percentage of the cell contains lysosomes than cell type B *[1 mark]*. Lysosomes are necessary to digest pathogens once they have been ingested by the cell *[1 mark]*. The role of cell type B is to secrete enzymes because a greater percentage of the cell contains rough endoplasmic reticulum than cell type A *[1 mark]*. This organelle is covered with ribosomes which synthesise proteins, such as enzymes / is responsible for folding and processing proteins, such as enzymes *[1 mark]*.

1.4 E.g. chloroplasts contain thylakoid membranes/grana, whereas mitochondria contain a folded membrane that form structures called cristae *[1 mark]* / Chloroplasts are the site of photosynthesis, whereas mitochondria are the site of aerobic respiration *[1 mark]*.

2.1 Any five from: clip the slide onto the stage *[1 mark]*. Select the lowest-powered objective lens *[1 mark]*. Use the coarse adjustment knob to bring the stage up to just below the objective lens *[1 mark]*. Look down the eyepiece and use the coarse adjustment knob to move the stage down until the image is roughly in focus *[1 mark]*. Adjust the focus with the fine adjustment knob until you get a clear image of what's on the slide *[1 mark]*. If a greater magnification is required, refocus using a higher-powered objective lens *[1 mark]*. *[Maximum of 5 marks available]*

2.2 One division of the stage micrometer is the same as four eyepiece divisions.
0.1 mm ÷ 4 = 0.025 mm
0.025 mm × 1000 = **25 μm**
[2 marks for the correct answer, otherwise 1 mark for the correct working]

2.3 The stage micrometer will appear larger, so each eyepiece division will be a smaller measurement *[1 mark]*.

2.4 E.g. length of cell = 36 mm
36 mm × 1000 = 36 000 μm
object size = image size ÷ magnification
= 36 000 μm ÷ 100
= **360 μm**
[accept values between 350 μm and 370 μm, 2 marks for the correct answer, otherwise 1 mark for the correct working]

3.1 The production of ATP *[1 mark]*.

3.2 Abnormal mitochondria might not produce as much ATP as normal mitochondria *[1 mark]*. This means the heart tissue may not have sufficient energy to work properly/for muscle contraction *[1 mark]*.

3.3 inner membrane *[1 mark]*

3.4 E.g. abnormal mice have smaller mitochondria/fewer cristae *[1 mark]*. This will reduce the surface area of the mitochondria and reduces ATP production *[1 mark]*. Abnormal mice have mitochondria with a less dense matrix *[1 mark]*. The matrix contains the enzymes needed for aerobic respiration, so this will also impair ATP production *[1 mark]*.

3.5 Object size = 1.5 μm ÷ 1000
= 0.0015 mm
magnification = image size ÷ object size
= 29 mm ÷ 0.0015 mm
= **× 19 333**
[accept values between × 18 667 and × 20 000, 2 marks for the correct answer, otherwise 1 mark for using the correct rearrangement of the magnification formula]

Pages 22-25: Cell Structure and Division — 3

1.1 E.g. they could add a buffer solution to the sample *[1 mark]* and grind the cells in a blender *[1 mark]*. They could then filter the solution to remove the cell and tissue debris *[1 mark]*.

1.2 At lower temperatures the activity of enzymes that break down organelles is reduced *[1 mark]*.

1.3

Contents of pellet	Sequence of Separation
Mitochondria and chloroplasts	2
Nuclei	1
Ribosomes	4
Endoplasmic reticulum	3

[1 mark]

1.4 It contains chloroplasts, which are responsible for photosynthesis, so would not be needed by root cells *[1 mark]*.

1.5 Ribosomes are made in the nucleolus *[1 mark]*. The nucleolus is found within the nucleus *[1 mark]*. If there was reduced function of the nuclear pore complexes, then fewer ribosomes could pass through the nuclear pore into the cytoplasm *[1 mark]*.

2.1 Both replicate inside a host cell *[1 mark]*. Both can cause a cell to burst (lysis) and release infective bodies *[1 mark]*. Viruses replicate by injecting their DNA or RNA into a host cell, whereas bacteria, such as *C. trachomatis*, replicate by binary fission/cell division *[1 mark]*.

2.2 E.g. the inhibition of ribosomes by azithromycin means that bacteria can't synthesise proteins *[1 mark]*. Protein synthesis is needed for mitosis/cell division, so the drug prevents bacteria multiplying *[1 mark]*.

2.3 Viruses don't have ribosomes *[1 mark]*.

2.4 During replication, plasmids can be replicated many times and can be shared unequally between the daughter cells *[1 mark]*. This means that the daughter cells can have a different number of plasmids, and therefore relative DNA content, to the parent cell and to each other *[1 mark]*.

3.1 Metaphase *[1 mark]*. The chromosomes are lined up along the middle of the cell *[1 mark]*.

3.2 A peak in the concentration of cyclin E occurs when the mass of DNA starts to increase *[1 mark]*. This suggests that cyclin E may trigger DNA replication in the cell / entry into the S stage of interphase *[1 mark]*. The peak in the concentration of cyclin B is followed by a decrease/halving in the mass of DNA *[1 mark]*. This suggests that cyclin B may trigger the cell to enter the mitosis stage *[1 mark]*.

4.1 DNA synthesis is needed to double the genetic content of the cell before it divides *[1 mark]*.

4.2 Because chemotherapy aims to reduce/control the rate of cell division in dividing cells *[1 mark]* and other non-cancerous body cells don't divide as often as hair follicle cells *[1 mark]*.

4.3 mitotic index = $\dfrac{\text{number of cells dividing}}{\text{total number of cells observed}}$

number of cells dividing = 0.9×200

                         = **180 cells**

[2 marks for the correct answer, otherwise 1 mark for using the correct formula]

4.4 The chromosomes would not line up in the middle of the cell and attach to the spindle fibres *[1 mark]*. This could mean that there isn't separation of the sister chromatids, and could result in there being an incorrect amount of genetic material in each daughter cell/mitosis would not progress to anaphase *[1 mark]*. This disruption of the cell cycle would kill the cancerous cells *[1 mark]*.

Pages 26-28: Cell Membranes — 1

1.1 Proteins are scattered amongst the phospholipids, like tiles in a mosaic *[1 mark]*. The phospholipids are constantly moving, so the structure is fluid *[1 mark]*.

1.2 The cholesterol molecules would restrict the movement of the phospholipids *[1 mark]*, making the structure less fluid and more rigid *[1 mark]*.

1.3 E.g. the cell-surface membranes are likely to have a high proportion of carrier or channel proteins *[1 mark]* in order to carry nutrients via facilitated diffusion or active transport *[1 mark]*. The cell-surface membrane is likely to have a large surface area/microvilli *[1 mark]* to maximise the rate of absorption of nutrients *[1 mark]*.

1.4 E.g. a large number of carrier or channel proteins *[1 mark]* in order to allow cations to cross the cell membrane quickly *[1 mark]*.

2.1 B *[1 mark]*

2.2 Phospholipids have a hydrophobic tail and a hydrophilic head *[1 mark]*. The hydrophilic heads are attracted to the water molecules in the cytoplasm or cell surroundings *[1 mark]*, and the hydrophobic tails are repelled from them, so a bilayer is formed *[1 mark]*.

2.3 The water will move from the exterior to the interior of the cell *[1 mark]* because the water potential of the exterior is higher/less negative than the water potential of the interior *[1 mark]*.

3 Any five from: e.g. sodium ions are actively transported out of the ileum epithelial cells into the blood *[1 mark]* by the sodium-potassium pump *[1 mark]*. This creates a concentration gradient of sodium ions between the lumen of the ileum and the interior of the epithelial cells *[1 mark]*. Sodium ions diffuse down this concentration gradient into the epithelial cells *[1 mark]* via sodium-glucose co-transporter proteins *[1 mark]*. The co-transporter proteins transport glucose into the cells along with the sodium ions *[1 mark]*.

4.1 To make sure any betalains/pigments released by the cutting of the beetroot were washed away *[1 mark]*.

4.2 Colorimetry analysis of distilled water *[1 mark]*.

4.3 Any four from: e.g. increasing the temperature from 20 °C to 40 °C increases the fluidity of the phospholipids in the beetroot cell membranes *[1 mark]*. At temperatures above 40 °C, the membrane starts to break down / proteins in the membrane start to denature *[1 mark]*. The membrane surrounding the vacuole therefore becomes more permeable with increasing temperature *[1 mark]*, meaning that betalains/pigments leak out into the distilled water *[1 mark]*. The more pigments released, the higher the absorbance reading *[1 mark]*.

4.4 Cell membranes contain channel proteins and carrier proteins *[1 mark]*. Proteins are denatured by extremes of pH / extremes of pH interfere with the bonding in proteins, causing them to change shape *[1 mark]*. If the proteins are not able to function and control what goes in or out of the cell, membrane permeability will increase *[1 mark]*.

Pages 29-30: Cell Membranes — 2

1.1

Concentration of sucrose solution to be made up / mol dm^{-3}	Volume of 1 mol dm^{-3} sucrose solution used / cm^3	Volume of water used / cm^3	Final volume of solution to be made up / cm^3
1	20	0	20
0.75	15	**5**	20
0.5	**10**	**10**	20
0.25	**5**	**15**	20
0	**0**	**20**	20

[2 marks for four rows correct, otherwise 1 mark for three rows correct]

1.2 Any two from: e.g. the temperature the potato samples were incubated at / the length of time the potato samples were incubated for / the volume of sucrose solution used / the variety of potato used / the age of potato used. *[2 marks]*

1.3 The line of best fit crosses the x-axis of Figure 1 halfway between 0.25 and 0.50, so the sucrose concentration of potato cells = approximately 0.375 mol dm^{-3}.
A 0.3 mol dm^{-3} sucrose solution has a water potential of −850 kPa. A 0.4 mol dm^{-3} sucrose solution has a water potential of −1130 kPa.
So a 0.375 mol dm^{-3} sucrose solution has a water potential of approximately:
$(-1130) - (-850) = 280 \times 0.75 = 210$
$-850 - 210 = \textbf{−1060 kPa}$

[2 marks for an answer > −850 and < −1130 kPa, otherwise 1 mark for estimating the sucrose concentration of the potato cells to be between 0.3 and 0.4 mol dm^{-3}]

1.4 The sweet potato tissue is likely to have a lower water potential than that of the white potato *[1 mark]* because it is likely to have a higher sucrose concentration *[1 mark]*.

The extra sucrose (with some other sugars too) is what makes the sweet potato sweet.

2.1 ATP is made inside the cell, rather than outside it, so the ATP binding site has to face inwards *[1 mark]*.

2.2 To catalyse the hydrolysis of ATP (into ADP and P_i) *[1 mark]* in order to release energy for the active transport of the calcium ions *[1 mark]*.

2.3 Ca^{2+} ions carry a charge, making them water soluble/ hydrophilic *[1 mark]*. This makes it difficult for them to travel directly through the hydrophobic centre of the phospholipid bilayer *[1 mark]*.

Pages 31-34: Cells and the Immune System — 1

1.1 A protein that binds to a specific antigen *[1 mark]*.

1.2 B-cells/B-lymphocytes / plasma cells *[1 mark]*

1.3 It has four variable regions, which form the antigen-binding sites *[1 mark]*. The tertiary structure of the variable regions varies between antibodies *[1 mark]*, giving the binding sites of each antibody a specific shape that is complementary to a specific antigen *[1 mark]*.

1.4 E.g. it allows the antibody to bind to more antigens at once *[1 mark]*, so there is a greater chance of agglutination occurring / more pathogens can be phagocytosed at once *[1 mark]*.

1.5 $2000 \times 60 \times 60 = 7200000$ *[1 mark]*
$= 7.2 \times 10^6$ *[1 mark]*

There are 60 seconds in a minute and 60 minutes in an hour. So, to work out how many molecules could be produced in an hour, multiply the number that can be produced in one second by 60, and then by 60 again.

2.1 Any two from: e.g. their age. / Their ethnicity. / Their sex. / If they are generally healthy/have a disease. / If they are currently taking any medication. / If they have previously been infected with the virus. *[2 marks]*

2.2 $\text{percentage change} = \dfrac{\text{final value} - \text{original value}}{\text{original value}} \times 100$

$((90 - 10) \div 10) \times 100 = \textbf{800\%}$ *[1 mark]*

2.3 It means that there is a greater than 5% probability that the results are due to chance *[1 mark]*, so there is no significant difference between the means *[1 mark]*.

2.4 The children who aren't vaccinated can be protected through herd immunity *[1 mark]*. If enough people are immune to a pathogen, it won't be able to spread easily through a population (even if not everyone is immune/has been vaccinated) *[1 mark]*.

2.5 Antigen variability means that a pathogen's antigens can change *[1 mark]*. If antigens change, memory cells produced as a result of a vaccine won't recognise them *[1 mark]*. Therefore, there won't be a fast secondary response to the pathogen / the person won't be immune to the pathogen *[1 mark]*.

3.1 E.g.

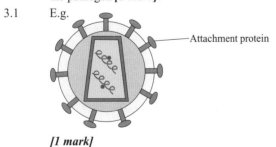

[1 mark]

3.2 The attachment proteins on the virus have a specific tertiary structure *[1 mark]* which allows them to bind to the complementary CD4 cell-surface receptor *[1 mark]*, but not any other receptors/membrane proteins *[1 mark]*.

3.3 The HTLV-I genetic material is RNA *[1 mark]*. Once inside the cell, reverse transcriptase is used to make a complementary DNA copy of the viral RNA *[1 mark]*. From this, double-stranded DNA is made and inserted into the T-cell DNA *[1 mark]*. The T-cell enzymes are then used to make HTLV-I proteins from the viral DNA, including Tax *[1 mark]*.

4.1 ELISA/enzyme-linked immunosorbent assay *[1 mark]*

4.2 Only antibodies that are complementary to the *Leishmania* antigen can bind to it *[1 mark]*.

4.3 To remove any unbound antibodies *[1 mark]* so that they don't affect the result / cause a false positive result *[1 mark]*.

4.4 The enzyme catalyses the reaction of solution X/its substrate, causing a colour change that indicates a positive result *[1 mark]*.

4.5 E.g. individuals may see colour change differently. / Colour change may be hard to detect by eye. *[1 mark]*

4.6 E.g. colorimetry *[1 mark]*

Pages 35-38: Cells and the Immune System — 2

1.1

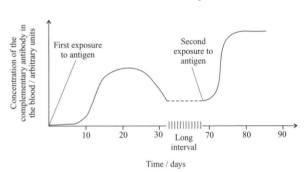

[1 mark]

A second exposure to the same antigen will always produce a quicker response, with a greater concentration of complementary antibodies.

1.2 E.g. the antibody concentration remains low for several days after exposure to the antigen because there aren't many B-cells that can produce the complementary antibody *[1 mark]*. Antibody concentration increases as activated B-cells divide to produce plasma cells, which start to rapidly produce lots of antibodies *[1 mark]*. Antibody concentration reaches a gradual peak and then falls as plasma cells die off *[1 mark]*. It doesn't fall back to pre-exposure levels because memory cells remain in the body *[1 mark]*.

2.1 E.g. so that the woman produces antibodies against the bacteria, which would be transferred to her baby (via the placenta) before it is born *[1 mark]*.

2.2 Any five from: e.g. the vaccine contains GBS antigens *[1 mark]*. Antigen-presenting cells present these antigens to helper T-cells *[1 mark]*. When the antigens bind to receptors on helper T-cell membranes, the helper T-cells are activated *[1 mark]*. The helper T-cells then activate B-cells *[1 mark]*, which divide to produce plasma cells that secrete antibodies against GBS *[1 mark]*. The activated T-cells and B-cells both produce memory cells *[1 mark]*. Memory cells remain in the body for a long time and result in a faster response to GBS antigens if they appear in the body again *[1 mark]*. *[Maximum of 5 marks available]*

2.3 Any two from: e.g. the immunity the baby receives from its mother is immediate, whereas immunity from a vaccine takes time to develop. / A vaccine involves exposing the baby to an antigen, whereas breastfeeding provides immunity without needing to expose the baby to an antigen. / The baby does not produce memory cells as a result of breastfeeding, but memory cells are produced as a result of a vaccine. / The immunity the baby gets from breastfeeding only lasts for a short time, whereas the immunity from a vaccine lasts much longer. *[2 marks]*

2.4 Viruses do not have cell walls *[1 mark]*.

3.1 E.g. the monoclonal antibodies bind to the (beta-amyloid) proteins in the plaque and form antigen-antibody complexes *[1 mark]*. This labels the proteins for destruction by phagocytosis, which breaks down the plaque *[1 mark]*.

3.2 The vehicle acted as a control *[1 mark]* so that the scientists could ensure that the drug caused the observed effect on plaque number and not the vehicle itself *[1 mark]*.

3.3 Any one from: e.g. gantenerumab cleared plaques that were less than 300 μm^2 in size. / Compared to the vehicle/control, gantenerumab reduced the number of plaques formed that were less than 600 μm^2 in size. / Gantenerumab had no effect on plaques that were greater than 600 μm^2 in size. *[1 mark]*

If the number of plaques in treated mice was less than the baseline, then you can conclude that the drug prevented plaque formation and removed some plaques. If it was less than the control but not the baseline, then the drug reduced the number of new plaques formed but didn't remove any.

3.4 Any four from: e.g. because the study was carried out in mice, not humans, so you don't know how effective the drug would be in humans *[1 mark]*. The data shows how the drug affected the number of beta-amyloid plaques, not how it affected the symptoms of Alzheimer's *[1 mark]*. Scientists don't know for certain that amyloid plaques cause Alzheimer's *[1 mark]*. The gantenerumab did not remove all the plaques in the mice's brains *[1 mark]*. The data does not record any side effects experienced by the mice, which might make the drug a less effective medical treatment *[1 mark]*. *[Maximum of 4 marks available]*

4.1 Different blood types have red blood cells with different antigens *[1 mark]*. The immune system of someone receiving the wrong blood type would not recognise the antigens on the donated red blood cells / would view the antigens on the donated red blood cells as foreign *[1 mark]*. This would stimulate an immune response, destroying the blood cells *[1 mark]*.

4.2 Any six from: e.g. phagocytes recognise foreign antigens on type B red blood cells and engulf them *[1 mark]*. They present the antigens on their surface *[1 mark]*. Receptors on helper T-cells bind to these antigens *[1 mark]*. This stimulates the helper T-cells to activate more phagocytes/cytotoxic T-cells to kill the type B red blood cells *[1 mark]*. The helper T-cells also activate B-cells *[1 mark]* which divide to produce plasma cells that secrete antibodies against the type B antigens *[1 mark]*. The antibodies bind to the type B antigens causing the type B blood cells to clump together/agglutinate *[1 mark]*, labelling them for destruction by phagocytosis *[1 mark]*. *[Maximum of 6 marks available.]*

4.3 Blood type O has no antigens, so no immune response will be triggered *[1 mark]*.

4.4 E.g. monoclonal antibodies specific to the antigen(s) of one blood type could be added to a sample of the person's blood *[1 mark]*. If agglutination is observed, then it can be concluded that the person has that blood type *[1 mark]*.

Topic Three — Exchange and Transport

Pages 39-42: Exchange and Transport Systems — 1

1.1 lamella *[1 mark]*

1.2 An arrow drawn across structure A in the opposite direction to the arrow showing water flow across the gill filament, e.g.

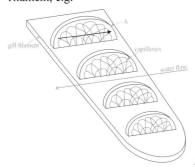

[1 mark]

Fish gills have a <u>counter</u>-current system, meaning the blood flows in the <u>opposite</u> direction to the water.

1.3 E.g.

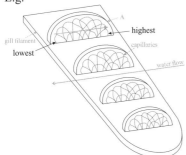

[1 mark]

1.4 E.g. the many lamellae give the gill a large surface area *[1 mark]*, increasing the rate of diffusion of gases *[1 mark]*.

2.1 E.g. dissecting scissors *[1 mark]*

2.2 A: spiracle *[1 mark]*
B: tracheae *[1 mark]*

2.3 E.g. pipette a drop of water onto a slide *[1 mark]*. Use tweezers to place a section of structures B/the tracheae onto the drop of water *[1 mark]*. Stand a cover slip upright on the slide, next to the water drop, then carefully tilt and lower it so it covers the specimen *[1 mark]*.

2.4 Any two from: e.g. it is able to close its spiracles when it is losing too much water *[1 mark]*. / It has a waterproof, waxy cuticle all over its body *[1 mark]*. / It has tiny hairs around the spiracles *[1 mark]*.

3.1 Mean number of stomata per 0.025 mm² =
$(5 + 6 + 7 + 4 + 3 + 8 + 5 + 5 + 3 + 4) ÷ 10 =$
$50 ÷ 10 = 5$
$150 \text{ mm}^2 ÷ 0.025 \text{ mm}^2 = 6000$
Number of stomata you'd expect to find in 150 mm² =
$5 × 6000 = $ **30 000 stomata**
[2 marks for correct answer, otherwise 1 mark for mean per 0.025 mm² = 5, or 1 mark for multiplying mean by 6000]

3.2 E.g. it is based on data from the lower epidermis only and stomata might not be evenly distributed across a leaf *[1 mark]*. It is based on a small sample size *[1 mark]*.

3.3 Mesophyll *[1 mark]*

3.4 The stoma is sunken in a pit *[1 mark]*, which traps moist air, reducing the concentration gradient of water between the leaf and the air *[1 mark]*. This reduces the diffusion and evaporation of water from the leaf *[1 mark]*.

4.1 *Lepus othus.* Having shorter ears gives the hare a smaller surface area to volume ratio *[1 mark]*, which means it loses heat less easily *[1 mark]*. This makes the hare better adapted to surviving at low temperatures *[1 mark]*.

4.2 Alaskan hares are likely to have a higher metabolic rate than polar bears because hares are smaller *[1 mark]*, so they have a higher surface area compared to their volume *[1 mark]*. This means they lose heat more easily, so need a high metabolic rate in order to generate enough heat to stay warm *[1 mark]*.

5.1

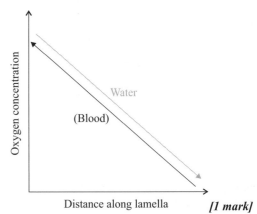

[1 mark]

5.2 In the parallel flow system, the oxygen concentration gradient between the water and the blood decreases with distance along the lamella *[1 mark]*, which will mean that the rate of oxygen diffusion will also decrease with distance along the lamella *[1 mark]*. This means that less oxygen diffuses into the blood than with a counter-current system, where the concentration gradient (and therefore rate of diffusion) is maintained *[1 mark]*.

Pages 43-45: Exchange and Transport Systems — 2

1 Bacterium B: $84 ÷ 22 = 3.8181...$, so $84 : 22 = 3.81 : 1$
Bacterium C: $15.75 ÷ 3.5 = 4.5$, so $15.75 : 3.5 = 4.5 : 1$
Bacterium with fastest gas exchange: Bacterium **A**
[1 mark for bacterium A, 1 mark for correct conversion of ratios]

Converting all the ratios into the form n : 1 makes it easier to see that Bacterium A has a bigger surface area compared to its volume, which means there is a larger surface for gases to diffuse across. This means the rate of gas exchange can be faster.

2.1 diaphragm *[1 mark]*, external intercostal muscles *[1 mark]*

You must specify the <u>external</u> intercostal muscles to get the mark here. The internal intercostal muscles only contract during forced expiration.

2.2 0-2 seconds *[1 mark]* because this is when the pressure inside the lungs/the intrapulmonary pressure is negative *[1 mark]*. Air travels down a pressure gradient, so air must be being taken into the lungs at this point *[1 mark]*.

2.3 3 seconds *[1 mark]*

Lung volume will be smallest when the pressure is highest (and the person is expiring).

3.1 Any two from: e.g. the alveolar epithelium is only one cell thick *[1 mark]*. / Alveolar epithelial cells are flat *[1 mark]*. / Alveoli have a large surface area for gas exchange to take place over *[1 mark]*.

3.2 Air flow into the emphysema patient's lungs is not restricted, so the inspiration line is relatively normal *[1 mark]*. The alveoli of the person with emphysema cannot recoil to expel air as well as those of the healthy person however, because of the loss of elastin in the alveoli walls *[1 mark]*. This limits/slows the flow of air out of the lungs, so the expiration line is lower and more concave *[1 mark]*.

3.3 1 dm³ = 1000 cm³
So 7.60 dm³ = 7.60 × 1000 = 7600 cm³
Volume of air in each breath = PVR ÷ breaths per minute
= 7600 ÷ 16
= **475 cm³**
[2 marks for the correct answer, otherwise 1 mark for 4.75 dm³ or for a correct conversion from dm³ to cm³.]

4.1 E.g. the scar tissue means that the lungs are less able to expand, so they can't hold as much air *[1 mark]*. To take in enough oxygen, the person has to breathe more quickly *[1 mark]*.

4.2 Any four from: e.g. the number of annual deaths from asbestosis increased after the ban in 1999, suggesting that the ban was not very effective *[1 mark]*. (However) it cannot be concluded that the ban was unsuccessful *[1 mark]*. We don't know whether the increase in deaths would have been greater without the ban *[1 mark]*. Asbestosis might not develop until many years after exposure / people might have asbestosis for a long time without dying *[1 mark]*. (Therefore) the annual death rate from asbestosis might be rising while the people who had already been exposed to asbestos before the ban die *[1 mark]*. Another explanation for the increase could be that doctors are getting better at diagnosing asbestosis or identifying it as a cause of death *[1 mark]*.
[Maximum of 4 marks available]

Pages 46-49: More Exchange and Transport Systems — 1

1.1 Any of the peptide bonds that are not at the end of the protein, e.g.

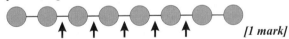
[1 mark]

1.2 Name: exopeptidases *[1 mark]*
Function: they hydrolyse peptide bonds at the ends of proteins *[1 mark]*.
Name: dipeptidases *[1 mark]*
Function: they hydrolyse peptide bonds in dipeptides *[1 mark]*.

1.3 E.g. amino acids are absorbed into the ileum epithelial cells by co-transport *[1 mark]*. This involves sodium ions being actively transported from the ileum epithelial cells into the bloodstream *[1 mark]*. This builds up a concentration gradient of sodium ions, with a higher concentration of sodium ions in the lumen of the ileum than in the ileum epithelial cells *[1 mark]*. Sodium ions then diffuse into the ileum epithelial cells through sodium-dependent transporter proteins *[1 mark]* carrying amino acids with them *[1 mark]*.

1.4 Without enteropeptidase, trypsin is not produced *[1 mark]*, which means that proteins cannot be fully digested *[1 mark]*. This may mean that not enough amino acids can be absorbed into the blood and used by body cells to keep the person healthy *[1 mark]*.

2.1 Lipase A is an enzyme with an active site that has a specific shape *[1 mark]* that is more complementary to the shape of Type B oil molecules than Type A or Type C oil molecules *[1 mark]*.

2.2 17.3 (Type B) ÷ 7.4 (Type C) = 2.3378...
2.3 : 1 *[1 mark]*

When a calculation gives you a number with a lot of decimal places, give your answer to the lowest number of significant figures that was used in the measurements for the calculation.

2.3 bile salts *[1 mark]*

2.4 monoglycerides *[1 mark]*
fatty acids *[1 mark]*

2.5 Micelles move the monoglycerides and fatty acids/products of lipid digestion towards the epithelial lining of the small intestine *[1 mark]*. As micelles break up, they release the monoglycerides and fatty acids/products of lipid digestion *[1 mark]*. Both monoglycerides and fatty acids/the products of lipid digestion are then able to freely diffuse across the epithelial cell membrane *[1 mark]*.

3.1 E.g. by setting up the equipment in the same way, but using the same volume of distilled water in the Visking tubing instead of amylase *[1 mark]*.

3.2 Any two from: e.g. In a real gut there are transporters/protein channels for active transport of food molecules across the gut wall *[1 mark]*. / Visking tubing doesn't have as large a surface area as the real gut *[1 mark]*. / The real gut is surrounded by blood that maintains a concentration gradient *[1 mark]*.

3.3 At the start of the experiment, the iodine test was positive for the Visking tubing contents, showing starch was present *[1 mark]* because it hadn't been digested by amylase yet *[1 mark]*. The iodine test was negative for the beaker contents because the starch molecules were too big to fit through the Visking tubing membrane and move into the beaker *[1 mark]*. At the end of the experiment, the iodine test was negative for the Visking tubing and the beaker contents because all the starch had been digested *[1 mark]*.

3.4 At the start of the experiment, the Benedict's test was negative for both the Visking tubing and beaker contents showing there was no sugar present *[1 mark]* because the starch hadn't been digested into maltose yet *[1 mark]*. At the end of the experiment, the Benedict's test was positive for the Visking tubing contents because the starch had been broken down into maltose *[1 mark]*. The Benedict's test was also positive for the beaker contents because the maltose molecules were small enough to move through the Visking tubing membrane and into the beaker *[1 mark]*.

Pages 50-52: More Exchange and Transport Systems — 2

1.1 Any five from: at low partial pressures of oxygen, the percentage saturation of haemoglobin with oxygen is low *[1 mark]* because the four polypeptide chains that make up haemoglobin are tightly bound, making it difficult for oxygen to bind *[1 mark]*. The curve rises steeply at medium partial pressures, as more haemoglobin is carrying oxygen *[1 mark]*. This is because once the first oxygen has bound, haemoglobin changes shape, making it easier for additional oxygen molecules to bind *[1 mark]*. At high partial pressures, the curve levels off/plateaus because more haemoglobin is saturated with oxygen *[1 mark]*, so it gets harder for oxygen molecules to bind *[1 mark]*. *[Maximum of 5 marks available]*

1.2 Llamas live at high altitudes where there is less oxygen *[1 mark]*, which means their haemoglobin has to have a higher affinity for oxygen than humans *[1 mark]*. This puts the llama oxygen dissociation curve to the left of the human curve, because their haemoglobin loads more oxygen at lower partial pressures *[1 mark]*.

1.3 The respiration rate increases during exercise, which increases the partial pressure of carbon dioxide in the blood *[1 mark]*. Higher concentrations of carbon dioxide increase the rate of oxygen unloading and the saturation of blood with oxygen is lower for a given pO_2 *[1 mark]*. This is called the Bohr effect *[1 mark]*.

2.1 Name of X = aorta *[1 mark]*
Name of Y = pulmonary vein *[1 mark]*

2.2 Any three from: e.g. wear gloves *[1 mark]* / wear a lab coat *[1 mark]* / disinfect the area and equipment afterwards *[1 mark]* / take care with the use of sharp equipment *[1 mark]*.

2.3 Any one from: e.g. use clear, continuous lines/no overlaps in lines *[1 mark]* / no shading *[1 mark]* / draw different components in proportion *[1 mark]* / include a scale *[1 mark]* / include relevant labels *[1 mark]*.

3.1 Inflammation and thrombosis in small and medium arteries would lead to reduced blood flow to the fingers and toes *[1 mark]*. Without an adequate supply of oxygen/glucose/nutrients etc., the tissue in the fingers and toes may die *[1 mark]*.

3.2 At the start of a capillary bed, the hydrostatic pressure inside the capillaries is higher than outside *[1 mark]*, so fluid is forced out of the capillaries, forming tissue fluid *[1 mark]*. At the venule end of the capillary bed, the loss of fluid means the water potential inside the capillaries is lower than in the tissue fluid *[1 mark]*, so some of the water in the tissue fluid re-enters the capillaries *[1 mark]* by osmosis *[1 mark]*.

3.3 E.g. capillaries have walls that are only one cell thick, which shortens the diffusion pathway *[1 mark]*.

Pages 53-55: More Exchange and Transport Systems — 3

1.1 They prevent the backflow of blood *[1 mark]* into the atria when the ventricles contract *[1 mark]*.

1.2 They open when pressure is greater below the valve / in the ventricle than in the artery *[1 mark]*.

1.3

	Standing up	Lying down
Mean heart rate / bpm	74	57
Mean cardiac output / cm³ min⁻¹	4700	4700
Mean stroke volume / cm³	63.5 (3 s.f.)	82.5 (3 s.f.)

[1 mark]

Stroke volume = cardiac output ÷ heart rate, so when standing up it's 4700 ÷ 74 = 63.5, and when lying down it's 4700 ÷ 57 = 82.5.

1.4 It gives the heart rate time to stabilise, as the act of changing position could cause it to increase *[1 mark]*.

1.5 Heart rate is lower when lying down as blood does not have to be pumped above the level of the heart / against gravity *[1 mark]*.

The heart has to work harder when a person is standing up, because blood has to flow against gravity. When you're lying down, the force of gravity is evenly distributed across the body.

1.6 Taking multiple measurements and calculating the mean reduces the effect of random error, so makes the results more precise *[1 mark]*.

2.1 60 ÷ 0.55 = 109.0909...
109 beats per minute *[1 mark]*

2.2 0.13 seconds or 0.68 seconds *[1 mark]*

The left atrium contracts before the left ventricle in the cardiac cycle, so you need to find a point on the graph where the pressure of the atrium increases before the pressure of the ventricle increases.

2.3 Any six from: at point A, pressure in the left ventricle exceeds pressure in the left atrium *[1 mark]*, because the left ventricle is contracting and the left atrium is relaxing *[1 mark]*. This causes the atrioventricular valve/the valve between the left atrium and left ventricle to close, preventing the backflow of blood into the left atrium *[1 mark]*.
At point B, pressure increases in the left ventricle to above that of the aorta *[1 mark]*, which forces the semi-lunar valve/the valve between the left ventricle and aorta open *[1 mark]*.
At point C, the left ventricular pressure falls below that of the aorta *[1 mark]*, because blood has moved into the aorta from the ventricle and the left ventricle is relaxing *[1 mark]*. As a result, the semi-lunar valve/the valve between the left ventricle and the aorta closes *[1 mark]*. Finally, at point D, pressure has been increasing in the left atrium as blood has been returning to the atrium from the body *[1 mark]*. As the atrial pressure exceeds ventricular pressure *[1 mark]*, the atrioventricular valve/valve between the left atrium and left ventricle opens, allowing blood to flow into the left ventricle *[1 mark]*.
[Maximum of 6 marks available]

2.4 The left ventricle has a higher maximum pressure than the left atrium because it has a thicker muscle wall and so is able to generate more force when it contracts *[1 mark]*.

2.5 The wall of the aorta is thick and muscular / the wall of the aorta contains elastic tissue to stretch and recoil / the inner lining of the aorta is folded so it can stretch *[1 mark]*, which helps to maintain the high pressure of the blood coming out of the left ventricle *[1 mark]*.

Pages 56-58: More Exchange and Transport Systems — 4

1.1 Water on the leaves would reduce the water potential gradient between inside the leaf and outside *[1 mark]*, reducing water loss/transpiration *[1 mark]*.

1.2 The higher the temperature, the faster the rate of transpiration *[1 mark]*. At higher temperatures, water molecules have more kinetic energy so they evaporate more quickly from the cells inside the leaf *[1 mark]*. This increases the water potential/concentration gradient between the inside and outside of the leaf, so water diffuses out of the leaf faster *[1 mark]*.

2.1 Light intensity is higher at 12:00, so more stomata are open *[1 mark]*, which increases the transpiration rate *[1 mark]*. This draws water molecules up the xylem at a quicker rate, due to cohesion and tension *[1 mark]*.

At 00:00, it would be dark, whereas there is sunlight at 12:00.

2.2 To prevent the plant tissue from drying out *[1 mark]*.

2.3 Dyeing the tissue with a stain/named stain *[1 mark]*.

3.1 Translocation requires energy/ATP *[1 mark]*. If metabolism stops, respiration cannot occur so ATP is not produced / energy is not released *[1 mark]*.

3.2 The level of pressure at point A is higher than that at point B *[1 mark]*. This is because, at point A, the water potential is being lowered by the solutes entering from the companion cell, causing water to enter from the xylem and companion cell *[1 mark]*, and raising the pressure *[1 mark]*.

3.3 The concentration of solutes at point A would increase because the solutes are still being loaded from the companion cell and can't flow down the phloem *[1 mark]*, as phloem is removed when a ring of bark is taken *[1 mark]*.

3.4 E.g. in a tracer experiment, a leaf could be supplied with radioactively labelled CO_2 *[1 mark]*, which would then be incorporated into the organic substances produced by the leaf *[1 mark]*. The movement of these substances around the plant could then be tracked by detecting the radioactively labelled carbon *[1 mark]*.

Topic Four — Genetic Information and Variation

Pages 59-62: DNA, RNA and Protein Synthesis

1.1 The DNA is wound around histone proteins *[1 mark]* and then tightly coiled into compact chromosomes *[1 mark]*.

1.2 Any one from: e.g. prokaryotic DNA is not associated with proteins *[1 mark]*. / Prokaryotic DNA is condensed by supercoiling *[1 mark]*.

1.3 The total length of DNA is 2 m.
1.5% of the DNA encodes proteins.
Therefore, $(1.5 \div 100) \times 2 = 0.03$ m of DNA corresponds to protein-encoding genes.
There are 20 000 protein-encoding genes.
Therefore, the average length of a gene is:
$0.03 \div 20\,000 = \textbf{0.0000015 m}$ or $\mathbf{1.5 \times 10^{-6}}$ m
[2 marks for the correct answer, 1 mark for 0.03 m]

1.4 genome *[1 mark]*

1.5 proteome *[1 mark]*

1.6 E.g. prokaryotes don't have introns/non-coding sequences within genes *[1 mark]*. Prokaryotes have shorter/fewer multiple repeat sequences between genes *[1 mark]*.

1.7 E.g. genes encoding ribosomal RNA *[1 mark]*. Genes encoding tRNAs *[1 mark]*.

2.1 Any two from: e.g. mitochondrial DNA is shorter while the DNA in the nucleus is longer *[1 mark]*. / Mitochondrial DNA is circular while the DNA in the nucleus is linear *[1 mark]*. / Mitochondrial DNA is not associated with proteins, while DNA in the nucleus is associated with proteins/histones *[1 mark]*.

2.2 D *[1 mark]*

2.3 E.g. valine is coded for by four DNA codons *[1 mark]*.

'Degenerate' means that multiple DNA codons can code for one amino acid, so any evidence that shows this from the table could gain a mark.

2.4 The mRNA codon GAC will become GCC / an A at mRNA codon position 156 will be swapped for a C *[1 mark]*.

2.5 An arginine amino acid will be produced at position 156 instead of a leucine *[1 mark]*.

2.6 It could change the shape of the enzyme *[1 mark]* so that the substrate is no longer able to fit into its active site *[1 mark]*, preventing the enzyme from being able to catalyse the reaction *[1 mark]*.

2.7 Any five from: e.g. the mRNA attaches to a ribosome *[1 mark]*. tRNA molecules carry amino acids to the ribosome *[1 mark]*. The tRNAs attach to the mRNA via complementary/specific base pairing *[1 mark]*. The amino acids on adjacent tRNAs join together with peptide bonds *[1 mark]*. ATP provides the energy for peptide bond formation *[1 mark]*. The ribosome moves along the mRNA and the amino acid chain is extended *[1 mark]*. The process continues until a stop signal on the mRNA is reached *[1 mark]*. *[Maximum of 5 marks available]*

3.1 Any four from: e.g. after the DNA has been unwound *[1 mark]*, RNA polymerase lines up free RNA nucleotides along the template strand *[1 mark]* according to the rules of complementary base pairing *[1 mark]*. RNA polymerase then joins the RNA nucleotides together as it moves along the DNA template strand *[1 mark]*. Once RNA polymerase reaches a stop signal, it detaches and the mRNA is released *[1 mark]*. *[Maximum of 4 marks available]*

3.2 The original DNA contains introns, while the cDNA does not / the cDNA only contains exons *[1 mark]*. This is because the cDNA is made from mRNA, which has been spliced / had the introns removed *[1 mark]*.

3.3 The levels of mRNAs 2 and 3 were only slightly affected by the drug *[1 mark]*. If RNA polymerase was inhibited, the levels of all of the mRNAs would have decreased by a large amount *[1 mark]*.

3.4 Only the level of mRNA 1 has been significantly reduced *[1 mark]*. This indicates that mRNA 1 contains the particular sequence destroyed by the drug *[1 mark]*.

Pages 63-65: Diversity, Classification and Variation — 1

1.1 A species is a group of similar organisms able to reproduce to give fertile offspring *[1 mark]*.

1.2 four *[1 mark]*

The genera shown on the phylogenetic tree are Panthera, Meles, Lutra and Canis. You know that these are the genera because the binomial name for a species is made up of two parts, e.g. Panthera leo, and the first part is always the genus.

1.3 *Canis aureus* and *Canis lupus* because they both belong to the same genus *[1 mark]*.

1.4 Family *[1 mark]*

2.1 Both types of selection increase the likelihood of organisms with the beneficial traits surviving *[1 mark]*. However, the selection acting on population A increases the chances of organisms with an extreme phenotype surviving *[1 mark]*, whereas the selection acting on population B increases the chance of organisms with an average trait surviving *[1 mark]*.

2.2 Population A, because this is showing directional selection / selection for an extreme phenotype *[1 mark]*. Taller plants are likely to be selected for in dense forest because these could more easily gain access to sunlight *[1 mark]*.

2.3 E.g. the environmental conditions in the grassland and the forest are different. / In an open field, being too tall would be a disadvantage due to the risk of damage by wind. *[1 mark]*

2.4 E.g. if a female lays too many eggs then she may be unable to care for them all *[1 mark]*. If she doesn't lay enough eggs then there is a chance that no chicks would survive to adulthood *[1 mark]*. So, an intermediate number of eggs is selected for, and variation in the clutch size decreases over time *[1 mark]*.

Figure 3 shows that clutch size is undergoing stabilising selection — the mean stays roughly the same, but variation (shown by the error bars) is decreasing.

3.1 Proteins consists of amino acids which are encoded by DNA base sequences *[1 mark]*. The more similar the proteins are, the more similar the DNA is between two species *[1 mark]*, and so the more closely related they are *[1 mark]*.

3.2 Species A is the least closely related to humans, as it has the greatest number of differences in amino acid sequence from the human protein *[1 mark]*. Species C is the most closely related to humans as it's amino acid sequence has the fewest differences *[1 mark]*.

3.3 E.g. both species have seven differences in their amino acid sequence from the human protein, but they could be unique differences / at different points in the sequence, so you can't tell how closely related they are to each other *[1 mark]*.

Pages 66-69: Diversity, Classification and Variation — 2

1.1

Species	Number of individual plants counted in different quadrats					Mean number counted
Rapeseed	24	46	32	28	32	**32.4**
Common sunflower	1	0	2	1	1	**1**
Common poppy	8	12	6	10	8	**8.8**
Creeping thistle	13	14	7	15	13	**12.4**

[1 mark]

1.2
$$N = 32.4 + 1 + 8.8 + 12.4$$
$$= 54.6$$
$$d = \frac{54.6(54.6 - 1)}{32.4(32.4 - 1) + 1(1 - 1) + 8.8(8.8 - 1) + 12.4(12.4 - 1)}$$
$$= \frac{2926.6}{1227.4}$$
$$d = \textbf{2.38} \text{ (to 3 s.f.)}$$

[2 marks for the correct answer, otherwise 1 mark for N(N − 1) = 2926.6 or Σn(n − 1) = 1227.4. Allow full marks if incorrect answers to 1.1 used correctly.]

1.3 The scientists could have used a t-test *[1 mark]* as this would have allowed them to compare two mean values *[1 mark]*.

1.4 E.g. animal grazing prevents some plants from growing, reducing plant biodiversity *[1 mark]*. This would mean there are fewer habitats and food resources to support other organisms, further reducing biodiversity *[1 mark]*.

2.1 Because an index of diversity takes into account both the number of species and the number of individuals *[1 mark]*, which means that it takes into account species that are only present in small numbers, which species richness does not *[1 mark]*.

2.2 Any three from: e.g. there were fewer ladybird species on the conventional farm than on the organic farm. / The standard deviation bars do not overlap, so the difference was significant/the standard deviation bars are short, showing that the data is precise. / However, there is no indication of how many samples were taken, so the data may not be representative of all organic/conventional farms. / There may be factors other than the way in which the fields were farmed, which influenced the number of ladybird species present. / The scientists' conclusion is correct for this data, but further investigation is needed to ensure that these results are valid *[1 mark for each correct answer]*.

2.3 E.g. the scientists could have taken random samples, to prevent sampling bias *[1 mark]*. / They could have had a large sample size, to reduce the risk of results being due to chance *[1 mark]*.

3.1 To sterilise it *[1 mark]* and prevent contamination of the investigation which could affect the results *[1 mark]*.

3.2 Any five from: e.g. disinfect work surfaces/wash hands to prevent contamination of cultures *[1 mark]*. Work near a Bunsen burner flame *[1 mark]*. Flame the neck of the glass bottle of bacterial culture just before use *[1 mark]*. Use a sterile pipette to transfer the bacteria from the broth to the agar plate *[1 mark]*. Spread the bacteria over the plate using a sterile plastic spreader *[1 mark]*. Soak a paper disc in each type of hand sanitiser and use sterile forceps to place each disc on the plate *[1 mark]*. Lightly tape a lid onto the plate *[1 mark]*. Invert and incubate at 25 °C for 48 hours *[1 mark]*. *[Maximum of 5 marks available]*

3.3 To act as a control *[1 mark]* and ensure that it was only the antibacterial hand sanitiser that was preventing growth, and not the paper disc itself *[1 mark]*.

3.4

Disc	Area of Inhibition Zone / mm²
B	**346** (to 3 s.f.)
C	**908** (to 3 s.f.)
D	**227** (to 3 s.f.)

[1 mark]

4.1 The crossing over of homologous chromosomes in meiosis I *[1 mark]* leads to the four daughter cells containing different combinations of alleles *[1 mark]*. Independent segregation in meiosis I *[1 mark]* leads to the daughter cells containing any combination of maternal and paternal chromosomes *[1 mark]*.

4.2 $n = 23$ in humans
$2^{23} = $ **8 388 608** *[1 mark]*

4.3 Non-disjunction *[1 mark]* means that chromosome 13 *[1 mark]* fails to separate properly during meiosis, leaving one daughter cell/gamete with an extra copy of chromosome 13 and another with no copies *[1 mark]*. If a gamete with an extra copy of chromosome 13 is fertilised, the resulting zygote will have three copies, leading to Patau syndrome *[1 mark]*.

Pages 70-72: Diversity, Classification and Variation — 3

1.1 For species A, B, D and E, there is a less than 5% probability that the results are due to chance *[1 mark]*. For species C, there is a greater than 5% probability that the results are due to chance *[1 mark]*.

1.2 Any two from: e.g. the time of year the traps were set. / The length of time the traps were left for. / The depth at which the traps were set. / The type of traps used. / The age/size of the fish caught. / The health of the fish caught. *[2 marks — 1 mark for each correct answer]*

1.3 E.g. the scientists could have compared the DNA/mRNA base sequence of the same gene in different individual fish *[1 mark]*. This would have allowed them to estimate the number of different alleles the population has for that particular gene, giving them an indication of genetic diversity *[1 mark]*.

1.4 E.g. it allows natural selection to take place. / It allows the population to adapt to environmental changes. *[1 mark]*

2.1 E.g. from 0 to approximately 15 µg cm⁻³, the number of strain B bacteria decreases more rapidly with increasing ampicillin concentration than the number of strain A bacteria *[1 mark]*. Above an ampicillin concentration of approximately 15 µg cm⁻³, the number of strain A bacteria remains fairly constant at about 1000 cells, but the number of strain B continues to decrease. *[1 mark]*

2.2 E.g. ionising radiation is a mutagenic agent / increases the chance of mutations arising *[1 mark]*. A mutation may have caused the active site of the strain A transpeptidase to change shape *[1 mark]*, so that ampicillin could no longer bind to and inhibit the enzyme *[1 mark]*. So strain A bacteria with the mutation were more likely to survive and reproduce in increasing ampicillin concentrations than strain B bacteria *[1 mark]*.

3.1 Courtship behaviours are species-specific *[1 mark]*. They allow organisms to recognise members of their own species *[1 mark]*, to ensure that mating leads to the production of fertile offspring *[1 mark]*.

3.2 As a result of mutation, some males had an allele/alleles for larger horn size *[1 mark]*. These males would have had a greater chance of defeating their rivals during fights over females *[1 mark]*, so they would have been more likely to reproduce and pass on their beneficial alleles to the next generation *[1 mark]*. After many generations, the frequency of the allele/alleles for large horn size would have increased in the population of male wild bighorn sheep *[1 mark]*.

3.3 Stabilising selection *[1 mark]*. The hunting exerts a selection pressure against large horns *[1 mark]* but there is still selection pressure against small horns, due to males fighting for mates *[1 mark]*.

3.4 E.g. the wild sheep have a greater genetic diversity than the agricultural sheep *[1 mark]*. This means that the wild population can more easily withstand environmental changes / a new disease arriving *[1 mark]*.

Pages 73-74: Diversity, Classification and Variation — 4

1.1 E.g. if three consecutive bases were deleted/a base triplet was deleted, the amino acid they/it coded for would be lost *[1 mark]*.

1.2 A change in the amino acid sequence could affect the tertiary structure of the CFTR protein *[1 mark]*. This could impair the function of the protein, and affect the transport of chloride ions across cell membranes in the lungs *[1 mark]*. This could affect the water potential of the cells in the lungs, leading to increased water absorption *[1 mark]*.

1.3 E.g. the effect of the mutations on the amino acid sequence of the CFTR protein and its tertiary structure is relatively minor *[1 mark]* and therefore the function of the CFTR protein is less impaired *[1 mark]*.

2.1 $0.7 \times 0.5 \times 0.4 \times 0.6 = \textbf{0.084}$ *[1 mark]*

2.2 To prevent members of different species from mating *[1 mark]*, as only females of the correct species will respond to a particular birdsong *[1 mark]*.

2.3 Both the populations have a similar pattern of courtship behaviour / the same courtship behaviours in roughly the same sequence *[1 mark]*, which suggests that they are closely related *[1 mark]*. However, there are key differences in their behaviour, e.g. preening females is an important step for the first population, but doesn't directly lead to mating in the second population / bobbing the head can lead to mating in the second population but not in the first *[1 mark]*. These differences suggest that the two are separate species / may be becoming two separate species *[1 mark]*.

2.4 It may mean that only a limited number of males get to mate and pass on their alleles *[1 mark]*, so the number of alleles in the gene pool decreases *[1 mark]*.

Topic Five — Energy Transfers

Pages 75-78: Photosynthesis and Respiration — 1

1.1 Chlorophyll a absorbs most light at 410-425 nm and 675 nm *[1 mark]*. There is no/very little absorption between 450-600 nm *[1 mark]*. / Chlorophyll a absorbs violet/blue light and orange/red light *[1 mark]*. There is no/very little absorption of green/yellow light *[1 mark]*.

1.2 Light energy is absorbed by chlorophyll in the thylakoid membranes *[1 mark]*. The light energy excites the electrons in the chlorophyll, leading to their release / the chlorophyll is photoionised *[1 mark]*.

1.3 Carbon dioxide concentration / temperature *[1 mark]*.

2.1 E.g. rate of uptake of carbon dioxide *[1 mark]*.

2.2 By controlling all the variables, so only the effect of light intensity on the rate of photosynthesis was being tested *[1 mark]*.

2.3 Any four from: e.g. at both low and high CO_2 concentrations, the rate of O_2 release increases with decreasing distance from the lamp, up until 0.5 m *[1 mark]*, so light is the limiting factor up until 0.5 m *[1 mark]*. Then at 0.5 m for each CO_2 concentration the rate of O_2 release levels off *[1 mark]*, as CO_2 becomes the limiting factor *[1 mark]*. The values for high CO_2 concentration level off at a higher O_2 release rate as high CO_2 concentration becomes limiting less quickly *[1 mark]*. *[Maximum of 4 marks available]*

2.4 E.g. set up more than one beaker containing an aquatic plant at each CO_2 concentration and record a mean *[1 mark]*.

2.5 Plot distance on the *x*-axis and the rate that O_2 is released on the *y*-axis *[1 mark]*. Plot data as a line graph *[1 mark]*, because the data is continuous *[1 mark]*.

2.6 light intensity = $1 / d^2$
light intensity = $1 / 0.5^2 = \textbf{4}$ arbitrary units *[1 mark]*

In the table, from 0.5 m to 0.25 m, the rate of O_2 release does not increase for the aquatic plant exposed to a low CO_2 concentration, so 0.5 m is the distance at which photosynthesis has become limited.

3.1 Any five from: e.g. the student should grind up several leaves in anhydrous sodium sulfate, and add a few drops of propanone *[1 mark]*. Next they should transfer the liquid into a test tube and add petroleum ether *[1 mark]*, then gently shake the tube until two layers form *[1 mark]*. Some of the liquid from the top layer should be transferred into a second test tube with some anhydrous sodium sulphate *[1 mark]*. The liquid from the second test tube should then be used to build up a single concentrated spot on the chromatography paper/ to form the point of origin, allowing the spot to dry between each application of the liquid *[1 mark]*. Once the spot has dried, the chromatography paper should be placed into a glass tube containing a small volume of a solvent/a mixture of propanone, cyclohexane and petroleum ether, so that it is below the point of origin *[1 mark]*. The student should then place a bung in the glass tube and allow time for the solvent to spread up the paper *[1 mark]*. When the solvent has almost reached the top of the chromatography paper, they should then remove the paper and mark the solvent front *[1 mark]*. They should repeat the experiment for each type of leaf *[1 mark]*. The results/chromatogram for each type of leaf should be compared to determine whether the two types of leaves contain similar pigments *[1 mark]*. *[Maximum of 5 marks available]*

3.2 E.g. wear gloves / wear goggles because many of the chemicals involved are toxic *[1 mark]*. Use a fume cupboard when using volatile chemicals like petroleum ether because the vapours are hazardous *[1 mark]*.

3.3 The mobile phase moves through/over the stationary phase *[1 mark]*. The pigments spend different amounts of time in the mobile phase and the stationary phase *[1 mark]*. The pigments that spend longer in the mobile phase travel faster/further, so different pigments are separated out *[1 mark]*.

3.4 They could demonstrate that their results are repeatable by repeating the experiment themselves and getting similar results *[1 mark]*. They could demonstrate that their results are reproducible by someone else repeating the experiment and getting similar results *[1 mark]*.

3.5 R_f value = distance travelled by spot ÷ distance travelled by solvent
R_f value = 9.3 cm ÷ 9.7 cm = 0.958... = 0.96
Pigment X = carotene *[1 mark]*
You can see from table 1 that the closest R_f value to 0.96 is 0.95, which is the R_f value for carotene, so pigment X is most likely carotene.

3.6 A different proportion of pigments allows the shade-tolerant leaves to absorb the wavelengths of light available to them, to maximise the rate of photosynthesis *[1 mark]*.

Pages 79-82: Photosynthesis and Respiration — 2

1.1 Any four from: e.g. the electrons from photoionisation pass down a chain of electron carriers in the thylakoid membrane *[1 mark]*, which results in the release of energy *[1 mark]*. Some of this energy is used to generate a proton gradient across the thylakoid membrane *[1 mark]*. Protons move down their concentration gradient into the stroma via ATP synthase, which releases energy allowing ADP and P_i to combine and form ATP *[1 mark]*. This is called the chemiosmotic theory *[1 mark]*. *[Maximum of 4 marks available]*.

1.2 If dehydrogenase activity is taking place, there will be an observable colour change from blue to colourless *[1 mark]*.

1.3 1. The midribs are tough and so difficult to blend *[1 mark]*.
2. To break open cells / release chloroplasts from cells *[1 mark]*.
3. To reduce enzyme activity / prevent damage to chloroplasts *[1 mark]*.

1.4 To show that any colour change is due to the presence of chloroplast extract / to act as a negative control *[1 mark]*.

1.5

Tube	Colour of solution at the beginning of the experiment	Colour of solution at the end of the experiment
1	blue	blue
2	blue	blue
3	blue	colourless

[2 marks for three correct answers, otherwise 1 mark for two correct answers]

1.6 E.g. the student could set up additional test tubes each exposed to different light intensities, by positioning the test tubes at different distances from a lamp *[1 mark]*. Then the student could use a colorimeter to detect the colour/absorbance of the solution at the end of the experiment *[1 mark]*, and could compare the results to determine how light intensity affects the rate of dehydrogenase activity *[1 mark]*.

2.1 The electrons will no longer travel along the electron transport chain, thus the fish would have a severe lack of ATP *[1 mark]*, which would mean that they are unable to carry out biological processes, e.g. muscle movement *[1 mark]*.

2.2 Pyruvate *[1 mark]*, as it is able to cross the mitochondrial membrane *[1 mark]*.

3.1 X = cytoplasm, Y = mitochondrial matrix *[1 mark]*

3.2 Glucose is phosphorylated using a phosphate from a molecule of ATP *[1 mark]*. This creates one molecule of glucose phosphate *[1 mark]* and one molecule of ADP *[1 mark]*.

3.3 Pyruvate is oxidised using one molecule of NAD *[1 mark]* and decarboxylated using one molecule of CO_2 *[1 mark]*. This creates one molecule of acetate *[1 mark]* and one molecule of reduced NAD *[1 mark]*. Acetate then combines with coenzyme A to produce acetyl CoA *[1 mark]*.

3.4 During anaerobic respiration pyruvate is converted into lactate *[1 mark]* using reduced NAD *[1 mark]*. This regenerates oxidised NAD *[1 mark]*, which can be used to oxidise substance B, triose phosphate, into pyruvate and therefore maintain glycolysis *[1 mark]*.

3.5 Excess water in the soil means that conditions for these cells become anaerobic due to a low oxygen concentration *[1 mark]*. As a result, oxygen is unable to combine with electrons from the electron transport chain, so respiration can't progress past glycolysis / to further aerobic stages that require oxygen, e.g. the link reaction *[1 mark]*.

3.6 Pyruvate is decarboxylated by losing/releasing one molecule of CO_2 *[1 mark]* to produce ethanal *[1 mark]*. Ethanal is reduced to ethanol *[1 mark]* using one molecule of reduced NAD *[1 mark]*.

4.1 NAD *[1 mark]*
FAD *[1 mark]*

4.2 She could have added methylene blue to glucose in the absence of yeast / in the presence of boiled/inactive/dead yeast *[1 mark]*. All other conditions would be kept the same *[1 mark]*.

4.3 E.g. temperature *[1 mark]* – used a water bath *[1 mark]*.
pH *[1 mark]* – added a buffer *[1 mark]*.

4.4 Shaking the tube would mix the solution with oxygen *[1 mark]*. This would oxidise methylene blue / methylene blue would give up its electrons *[1 mark]*.

4.5 Any four from: e.g. in oxidative phosphorylation, reduced coenzymes/NAD/FAD, from aerobic respiration are oxidised *[1 mark]*. The electrons released pass down the electron transport chain, releasing energy *[1 mark]*. This energy is used to pump protons from the mitochondrial matrix to the intermembrane space, forming a proton/electrochemical gradient *[1 mark]*. Protons then diffuse back into the mitochondrial matrix down their proton gradient through ATP synthase, resulting in the generation of ATP *[1 mark]*. This is called the chemiosmotic theory *[1 mark]*. At the end of the transport chain in the mitochondrial matrix, the protons, electrons and O_2 combine to form water *[1 mark]*. *[Maximum of 4 marks available]*

Pages 83-84: Photosynthesis and Respiration — 3

1.1   As more CO_2 is released by the respiring yeast, the pH of the solution may fall, which will affect the results *[1 mark]*. This decreases the validity of the experiment because not all of the variables have been controlled *[1 mark]*.

1.2   The curves plateau/level off *[1 mark]*. This is because glucose is used up / the yeast cells start to die due to toxic build up of ethanol *[1 mark]*.

1.3   E.g.

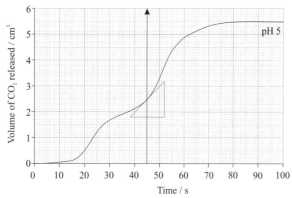

Rate at pH 5: $1.4 \div 14 = 0.10 \ cm^3 \ s^{-1}$
[1 mark — accept answers between 0.09 and 0.11 $cm^3 s^{-1}$]

1.4   Because the Krebs cycle only occurs in aerobic respiration *[1 mark]*. During this process, one molecule of CO_2 is lost when a six-carbon compound/citrate becomes a five-carbon compound *[1 mark]* and another is lost when the five-carbon compound becomes a four-carbon compound/oxaloacetate *[1 mark]*. For each molecule of glucose the Krebs cycle happens twice, therefore four more molecules of CO_2 are produced *[1 mark]*.

2.1   rubisco *[1 mark]*

2.2   RuBP allows the light-independent reaction to continue because CO_2 reacts with RuBP to form GP *[1 mark]*. Glucose is used as an energy source for respiration / used to make other important molecules, e.g. cellulose *[1 mark]*.

2.3   The amount of GP being made would decrease *[1 mark]*, as there is less CO_2 available for RuBP to combine with *[1 mark]*. The amount of RuBP would increase *[1 mark]*, because there is less CO_2 to combine with it *[1 mark]*.

2.4   At a lower light intensity the products of the light-dependent reaction/reduced NADP and ATP will be in short supply *[1 mark]*. So the amount of GP will rise *[1 mark]* and the level of RuBP will fall *[1 mark]*.

When working out the answers to questions on the light-independent reaction it's a good idea to sketch out the reaction (like below) to see exactly what will be affected when different factors are changed.

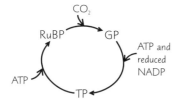

Pages 85-86: Energy Transfer and Nutrient Cycles — 1

1.1   To replace the nitrates and phosphates/mineral ions lost from the nutrient cycles when the crops are harvested *[1 mark]*.

1.2   Proteins/amino acids/nitrogen-containing compounds are broken down/converted into ammonia by saprobionts in the soil *[1 mark]*. Ammonia is converted to ammonium ions *[1 mark]*. Then nitrifying bacteria convert ammonium ions to nitrites *[1 mark]* and other nitrifying bacteria convert nitrites to nitrates, which growing plants can use as a source of nitrogen *[1 mark]*.

1.3   The hyphae of this fungus can increase the surface area of the plant's root system *[1 mark]*. This helps the plant to absorb more inorganic/mineral ions and water from the soil *[1 mark]*, which would improve plant growth and therefore increase crop yield *[1 mark]*.

1.4   Under anaerobic conditions, there is a greater number of denitrifying bacteria, which convert nitrates into nitrogen gas *[1 mark]*, so waterlogging would reduce the amount of nitrates in the soil *[1 mark]*. This reduces the amount of nitrates available to the plants for growth, so will reduce crop yield *[1 mark]*.

2.1   E.g. carbohydrates / amino acids *[1 mark]*

2.2   The chemical energy store in plant biomass after respiratory losses to the environment have been taken into account / that is available for plant growth and reproduction *[1 mark]*.

2.3 1.9×10^{10} kJ $\div$ 120 ha $= 1.58 \times 10^8$ kJ ha^{-1}
1.58×10^8 kJ ha$^{-1} \times 4 = 6.3 \times 10^8$ kJ ha^{-1} yr^{-1}
$NPP = GPP - R$
        $= 6.3 \times 10^8$ kJ ha^{-1} yr$^{-1} - 3.0 \times 10^8$ kJ ha^{-1} yr^{-1}
        $= \mathbf{3.3 \times 10^8}$ **kJ ha^{-1} yr^{-1}** (to 2 s.f.)
[2 marks for the correct answer, otherwise 1 mark for the correct working]

Here, you first need to get the gross primary productivity into the right units (kJ ha^{-1} yr^{-1}). Start by dividing the amount of energy produced by 120 to get per hectare, and then multiply by 4 to get per year (as the question states the energy produced was over 3 months).

2.4   E.g. dry one of the palm tree saplings in an oven set to a low temperature *[1 mark]*. Burn the dry sapling and use the heat energy given off to heat a known volume of water *[1 mark]*. Use the change in water temperature to calculate the chemical energy of the sapling *[1 mark]*.

2.5   E.g. weathering of rocks releases phosphorus/ phosphate ions into the soil, that plants can then absorb *[1 mark]*. Saprobionts in the soil can break down the organic compounds in animal waste products, releasing phosphorus/phosphate ions *[1 mark]*.

Pages 87-89: Energy Transfer and Nutrient Cycles — 2

1.1 $N = I - (F + R)$
        $7150 - (4361 + 2288) = 501$
        $(501 \div 7150) \times 100 = \textbf{7.0\%}$ (to 2 s.f.)
        [2 marks for the correct answer, otherwise 1 mark for the correct working]

Efficiency of energy transfer is the percentage of the net production from one trophic level that makes up the net production of the next trophic level. Here only 501 kJ of the 7150 kJ ingested from the plant material goes on to form the farm animal's net production.

1.2   E.g. the value of *R*/energy lost through respiration would be greater *[1 mark]* because the rate of respiration would have increased in order to maintain body temperature *[1 mark]*.

1.3   E.g. restricting movement of animals in the pens minimises their respiratory losses *[1 mark]* so net production increases *[1 mark]*.

1.4   The net production of these farm animals may be reduced due to the increased energy loss from activating the immune system against disease *[1 mark]*.

1.5   Any four from: e.g. eutrophication may have occurred, whereby the excreted waste from the farm animals entered the pond and the excess nitrogen and phosphate caused an algal bloom *[1 mark]*. The algae have blocked out the light, so plants under the surface have died as they couldn't photosynthesise (enough to meet their needs) *[1 mark]*. The number of bacteria then increased as they fed on the increased amount of dead plant matter *[1 mark]*. The increase in aerobic respiration by these decomposers reduced the oxygen concentration of the water *[1 mark]*. The fish then died because there wasn't enough dissolved oxygen in the water *[1 mark]*.
        [Maximum of 4 marks available]

2.1   As the mass of fertiliser increases, the yield of crop increases *[1 mark]*, until a peak in crop yield is reached at 160 kg ha^{-1}, after which the crop yield begins to decrease *[1 mark]*.

2.2 $7.3 - 4.5 = 2.8$
        $(2.8 \div 4.5) \times 100 = \textbf{62\%}$ (to 2 s.f.) *[1 mark]*

2.3   E.g. the water content of the harvested crop plants may vary, which would create variation in the mass, that is unrelated to the investigation *[1 mark]*.

2.4   E.g. test the fertiliser in different soils/different locations. / Test the fertiliser on different crop plants. / Test the fertiliser at different times of the year/seasons. *[1 mark]*

2.5   The water potential in the soil around the plant would be more negative/lower than in the plant *[1 mark]*. Water would move out of the plant, down this concentration gradient via osmosis, limiting growth of the plants/killing them *[1 mark]*.

2.6   Natural fertilisers are made of organic matter *[1 mark]*, which needs to be broken down by microorganisms in the soil before they can be absorbed by plants *[1 mark]*. This means the release of mineral ions is more controlled and they are less likely to be leached into ponds and rivers *[1 mark]*.

3.1   There may be parts of the organism that the secondary consumer cannot ingest, such as bones *[1 mark]*.

3.2   Energy transferred from producer to primary consumer 1
        $= (2.5 \times 10^4 \text{ kJ m}^{-2} \text{ yr}^{-1} \div 100) \times 2 = 500 \text{ kJ m}^{-2} \text{ yr}^{-1}$
        Energy transferred from crop plant to primary consumer 1
        $= 1305 \text{ kJ m}^{-2} \text{ yr}^{-1} - 500 \text{ kJ m}^{-2} \text{ yr}^{-1} = 805 \text{ kJ m}^{-2} \text{ yr}^{-1}$
        Energy transferred from crop plant to primary consumer 2
        $= (2.3 \times 10^4 \text{ kJ m}^{-2} \text{ yr}^{-1} \div 100) \times 6 = 1380 \text{ kJ m}^{-2} \text{ yr}^{-1}$
        Energy transferred from crop plant to humans =
        $(2.3 \times 10^4 \text{ kJ m}^{-2} \text{ yr}^{-1} \div 100) \times 0.5 = 115 \text{ kJ m}^{-2} \text{ yr}^{-1}$
        Energy available to humans if pests are eliminated =
        $805 \text{ kJ m}^{-2} \text{ yr}^{-1} + 1380 \text{ kJ m}^{-2} \text{ yr}^{-1} + 115 \text{ kJ m}^{-2} \text{ yr}^{-1} = \textbf{2300 kJ m}^{-2} \textbf{ yr}^{-1}$
        [2 marks for the correct answer, otherwise 1 mark for the correct working]

You know the net production of primary consumer 1 but this comes from the producer and the crop plant. As you know the efficiency of energy transfer from the producer to this consumer, you can calculate how much energy is transferred from just the crop plant to primary consumer 1 (this is the only energy that will become available to humans). Then just work out the energy transferred to the primary consumer 2 and to humans, and add them all together.

Topic Six — Organisms Respond

Pages 90-92: Stimuli and Responses — 1

1.1 It conducts the waves of electrical activity, after a short delay, from the SAN to the bundle of His *[1 mark]*.

1.2 The layer of collagen prevents the wave of electricity passing straight from the atria into the ventricles *[1 mark]*. This makes sure that the ventricles only respond to signals from the AVN, transferred via the bundle of His/Purkyne tissue *[1 mark]*.

2.1 E.g. the heart rate will increase *[1 mark]*. Binding of norardenaline at receptors on the sinoatrial node will increase the rate at which the sinoatrial node generates electrical impulses/action potentials / will cause the sinoatrial node to fire more frequently *[1 mark]*.

2.2 Pressure receptors/baroreceptors in the aorta/carotid arteries detect the high blood pressure *[1 mark]*. This information is relayed to the medulla oblongata/brain *[1 mark]*, which sends impulses along parasympathetic neurones to the sinoatrial node *[1 mark]*. This decreases the rate at which the sinoatrial node generates impulses and slows down heart rate, bringing blood pressure back to normal *[1 mark]*.

3.1 The lamellae will deform and press on the sensory nerve ending *[1 mark]*. This will cause the sensory neurone's cell membrane to stretch, opening the stretch-mediated sodium ion channels *[1 mark]*. The resulting influx of sodium/Na^+ ions will change the potential difference of the Pacinian corpuscle / produce a generator potential *[1 mark]*.

3.2 The generator potential established as a result of the change may not reach the threshold needed to trigger an action potential *[1 mark]*.

3.3 E.g. each type of receptor only responds to a specific stimulus *[1 mark]*, so different types of receptor are needed to detect the different types of mechanical stimuli *[1 mark]*.

4.1 Area A because it contains more rod cells than area B *[1 mark]*. Rod cells are more sensitive to light than cone cells *[1 mark]*. Therefore, there will be a greater number of action potentials initiated in dim light from area A than from area B *[1 mark]*.

4.2 Area B contains more cone cells than area A *[1 mark]* and cone cells give greater visual acuity than rod cells *[1 mark]*. This is because a single cone cell connects to a single sensory neurone, whereas three rod cells connect to a single sensory neurone *[1 mark]*. This means that cone cells allow a person to distinguish between two points that are close together, but rod cells don't *[1 mark]*.

4.3 E.g. red-sensitive/green-sensitive cone cells / cone cells with the optical pigments that detect red/green light *[1 mark]*.

Pages 93-95: Stimuli and Responses — 2

1.1 positive phototropism *[1 mark]*

1.2 The results suggest that indoleacetic acid/IAA is produced in the shoot tip *[1 mark]*, because seedling B didn't curve towards the light but seedling D did *[1 mark]*.

1.3 **A**: light did not reach the shoot tip since it was covered in tin foil, so light couldn't influence the distribution of indoleacetic acid/IAA and affect cell elongation *[1 mark]*. **B**: the shoot tip had been removed, so indoleacetic acid/IAA didn't diffuse down the shoot and affect cell elongation *[1 mark]*.

1.4 The light caused the indoleacetic acid/IAA to accumulate on the shaded side of the shoot in both seedlings *[1 mark]*.

2.1 Any two from: e.g. the temperature in each chamber. / The light intensity in each chamber. / The humidity in each chamber. / The species of mosquito used. / The time the mosquitoes were left for when released from the holding chamber. *[2 marks — 1 mark for each correct answer]*

2.2 The mosquitoes showed a tactic response *[1 mark]*, because it was a response to a directional stimulus / they moved towards a directional stimulus *[1 mark]*.

2.3 Organisms exhale carbon dioxide when they respire *[1 mark]*. This means that by being attracted to carbon dioxide, mosquitoes will be better able to locate respiring organisms *[1 mark]* which will improve their chances of finding a blood meal *[1 mark]*.

2.4 Chemical C, because far fewer mosquitoes entered the treatment chamber compared to the control chamber *[1 mark]*, suggesting that it had a repellent effect on many of the mosquitoes *[1 mark]*.

2.5 E.g. the chi-squared/χ^2 test *[1 mark]*, as this will allow the scientist to determine if there is a significant difference between the expected and observed results *[1 mark]*.

Pages 96-99: Nervous Coordination — 1

1.1 There are more positive ions outside the cell than inside the cell *[1 mark]*.

1.2 E.g. at rest, sodium-potassium pumps move sodium ions/Na^+ out of the neurone cell / across the cell membrane to side A *[1 mark]*. This means that there will be more sodium ions outside of the cell compared to inside the neurone cell, as is shown in Figure 1 *[1 mark]*.

1.3 When a neurone is at rest sodium ion channels are not open / the cell membrane is not permeable to sodium ions *[1 mark]*.

1.4 The potassium ions are moved into the cell by sodium-potassium pumps using active transport *[1 mark]*, so the concentration of potassium ions is higher inside the cell than outside the cell *[1 mark]*. This causes potassium ions to diffuse out of the cell, along a concentration gradient, through potassium ion channels in the cell membrane *[1 mark]*.

1.5 The sodium ion channels will mainly be found at the nodes of Ranvier *[1 mark]*. This is because the rest of the axon is covered with a myelin sheath which acts as an electrical insulator *[1 mark]*. As depolarisation only takes place at the nodes of Ranvier, this is where the sodium ion channels are most densely located *[1 mark]*.

2.1 The tibialis anterior muscle contracts and pulls the metatarsal bones upwards *[1 mark]*, while the calf muscle relaxes and allows the heel bone to move downwards *[1 mark]*.

2.2 Being incompressible means they can act as levers, which gives the muscles in the leg something to pull against *[1 mark]*.

2.3 Any five from: e.g. the erector spinae muscles are likely to contain a high proportion of slow-twitch fibres *[1 mark]*, as they will need to contract for long periods of time *[1 mark]*. The calf muscle is likely to contain a higher proportion of fast-twitch muscle fibres compared to the erector spinae muscles *[1 mark]*, as the calves are used for fast movement *[1 mark]*. The erector spinae muscles are likely to have a larger number of mitochondria *[1 mark]* and more blood vessels supplying them than the calf muscles *[1 mark]*. This is because slow-twitch muscle fibres are adapted to mainly use aerobic respiration, whereas fast-twitch muscle fibres are adapted to use anaerobic respiration *[1 mark]*. A high proportion of myoglobin in slow-twitch muscle fibres will mean that the erector spinae muscles may be more red than the calf muscle *[1 mark]* which contains a smaller proportion of slow-twitch muscle fibres *[1 mark]*. Erector spinae muscles may be able to work for a long time without getting tired, whereas calf muscles get tired quickly *[1 mark]*. This is because the calf muscles have a smaller proportion of slow-twitch muscle fibres compared to the erector spinae muscles *[1 mark]*. *[Maximum of 5 marks available]*

3.1

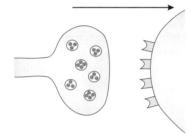

[1 mark for drawing an arrow pointing to the right]

3.2 The receptors for the neurotransmitter are only found on the postsynaptic membrane *[1 mark]*, so the neurotransmitter can only trigger an action potential at the postsynaptic membrane *[1 mark]*.

3.3 The action potential depolarises the sarcolemma *[1 mark]*, and this depolarisation spreads down the T-tubules to the sarcoplasmic reticulum *[1 mark]*. The depolarisation of the sarcoplasmic reticulum causes the release of calcium ions throughout the muscle fibre *[1 mark]*.

3.4 Calcium ions result in tropomyosin being pulled out of the actin-myosin binding site *[1 mark]*, which allows the attachment between myosin and actin to occur *[1 mark]*. Calcium ions activate ATP hydrolase *[1 mark]*, which hydrolyses/breaks down ATP to provide energy used in muscle contraction *[1 mark]*.

3.5 E.g. at neuromuscular junctions, curare would compete with acetylcholine for acetylcholine receptors on the postsynaptic membrane *[1 mark]*. At a high dose, curare would block all of the acetylcholine receptors and prevent acetylcholine binding *[1 mark]*. This means that acetylcholine released from the motor neurone wouldn't lead to the generation of a response in the muscle cell *[1 mark]*. So the presence of curare would inhibit muscle contraction / prevent muscle contraction being triggered *[1 mark]*.

You could have talked about the hyperpolarization of the postsynaptic membrane preventing the generation of an action potential instead. As curare is acting as an inhibitory neurotransmitter this is also a valid answer.

4.1 I-band *[1 mark]*

4.2 H-zone *[1 mark]*, because this part contains only myosin filaments and no actin filaments *[1 mark]*.

4.3 H-zone and I-band *[1 mark]*.

4.4 E.g. the myosin heads bind to the binding sites on the actin filaments, forming cross bridges *[1 mark]*. The myosin heads then bend and pull the actin filaments along the length of the myosin *[1 mark]*. The myosin heads detach from the actin filaments once they've moved *[1 mark]*. The heads reattach at binding sites further along the actin *[1 mark]*.
The cycle is repeated many times, moving the actin filaments along the myosin, and shortening the sarcomeres *[1 mark]*.

Pages 100-103: Nervous Coordination — 2

1.1 Saltatory conduction *[1 mark]*

1.2 E.g.

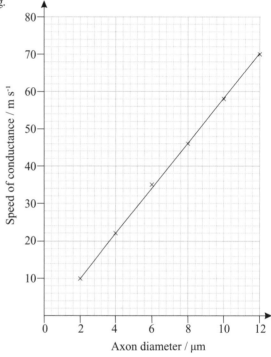

[2 marks — 1 mark for scatter graph with axon diameter on the x-axis (with correct units) and speed of conductance on the y-axis (with correct units), 1 mark for correct plotting of data points and correct line of best fit]

A line of best fit should pass through or near to as many data points as possible, ignoring any anomalous results.

1.3 40 m s⁻¹ *[1 mark for an answer between 38 and 42]*

1.4 As the diameter of the axon increases, the speed of conductance increases *[1 mark]*. This is because the larger the axon diameter, the lower the resistance to the flow of ions *[1 mark]*, and therefore the faster the wave of depolarisation travels along the neurone *[1 mark]*.

1.5 The speed of conductance would have been slower at each axon diameter, compared to the myelinated neurones *[1 mark]*.

1.6 E.g. temperature should have been kept constant *[1 mark]*. At different temperatures, ions diffuse at different speeds through the axon *[1 mark]*.

2.1 E.g. the refractory period acts as a time delay between action potentials *[1 mark]*. This means that action potentials don't overlap so the impulses are discrete *[1 mark]*, and that there is a limit to the frequency at which nerve impulses can be transmitted *[1 mark]*. The refractory period also means that action potentials are unidirectional/only travel in one direction *[1 mark]*.

2.2 E.g. this means that the neurone cell membrane is less permeable to potassium ions / fewer potassium ions can diffuse out of a neurone *[1 mark]*. So the potential difference across the cell membrane takes longer to change *[1 mark]* and therefore slows down the repolarisation stage of an action potential *[1 mark]*.

2.3 E.g. disopyramide can increase the duration of the action potentials, which may slow down the rate of heart muscle contractions, and therefore slow the beating of the heart/ heart rate *[1 mark]*.

3.1 Acetylcholine is an excitatory neurotransmitter, because when neurones A and B are stimulated together, an action potential is initiated in neurone D *[1 mark]*. GABA is an inhibitory neurotransmitter, because when neurone C is stimulated along with either neurone A or B, it prevents an action potential being initiated in neurone D *[1 mark]*.

3.2 When neurones A, B and C are stimulated, the spatial summation of neurones A and B is enough to counteract the inhibitory effect of neurone C *[1 mark]*. However, when only neurones A and C are stimulated, there is not enough excitation to overcome the inhibition and generate an action potential *[1 mark]*.

3.3 Metrifonate would prevent the breakdown of acetylcholine by inhibiting acetylcholinesterase/AChE *[1 mark]*. This would mean that acetylcholine would remain on the receptors on the postsynaptic membrane of neurone Y, so neurone Y would continue to be depolarised/generate an action potential *[1 mark]*.

4.1 Individual 3: $= ((96 - 81) \div 81) \times 100 = $ **18.5%** *[1 mark]*
Individual 4: $= ((85.8 - 69) \div 69) \times 100 = $ **24.3%** *[1 mark]*

The formula for calculating percentage difference is:
% difference = ((final value − original value) ÷ original value) × 100

4.2 Mean percentage increase $=$
$(22.7 + 7.9 + 18.5 + 24.3) \div 4 = $ **18.4%** *[1 mark for correct answer, and if incorrect answer(s) are carried forward from 4.1, give full marks for correct working]*

4.3 E.g. as creatine is part of phosphocreatine, creatine supplements might increase the amount of phosphocreatine available in the muscles *[1 mark]*. This could mean that the muscles will be able to generate more ATP in a given time, as phosphocreatine is broken down to make ATP *[1 mark]*. More ATP present could mean that there's more energy available for muscle contraction, which might improve a weightlifter's performance *[1 mark]*.

4.4 E.g. the weightlifters may have been tired already since they had lifted weights previously in the same day, which may have meant they were not fully recovered before the second lifting session and performed worse as a result. / The creatine may only be effective over a long period of time/when taken at particular times before or after exercising, therefore the investigation might not have assessed the impact of taking creatine effectively *[4 marks available — 1 mark for a reason and 1 mark for a supporting explanation]*.

There are other possible answers for this question. Award yourself marks for other reasonable reasons (and explanations) too.

Pages 104-107: Homeostasis — 1

1.1 To maintain a stable internal environment within restricted limits *[1 mark]*, so that enzymes can function normally / to prevent damage to enzymes *[1 mark]*.

1.2 When a physiological level deviates from its normal state, a mechanism returns the level back to within the normal range *[1 mark]*.

1.3 So that blood pH can be actively increased or decreased to return it to normal *[1 mark]*, giving greater control over changes in blood pH *[1 mark]*.

1.4 E.g. blood glucose concentration *[1 mark]*, blood water potential *[1 mark]*

1.5 A temperature above 40 °C may cause enzymes to be denatured *[1 mark]*. This changes the shape of the enzyme's active site so that it no longer works as a catalyst, and as such the metabolic reactions are less efficient *[1 mark]*.

1.6 Positive feedback *[1 mark]* because the body will no longer be cooled by sweating and so the body temperature will continue to rise *[1 mark]*.

2.1 Glucose is large / not lipid soluble, so it cannot cross the membrane *[1 mark]*.

2.2 Insulin binds to specific receptors on the liver and muscle cells/target cells *[1 mark]*. It increases the permeability of the muscle/liver/target cells to glucose (e.g. by increasing the number of channel proteins in the membrane) *[1 mark]*.

2.3 E.g. insulin activates enzymes responsible for the conversion of glucose to glycogen/glycogenesis *[1 mark]*.

2.4 Glucagon acts to increase the concentration of glucose circulating in the blood *[1 mark]*.

2.5 E.g. glucagon activates enzymes involved in the breakdown of glycogen into glucose/glycogenolysis *[1 mark]*. Glucagon activates enzymes involved in the production of glucose from glycerol and amino acids/ gluconeogenesis *[1 mark]*.

2.6 Any four from: e.g. glucagon binds to specific receptors on the surface membrane of target cells *[1 mark]*. This activates an enzyme called adenylate cyclase *[1 mark]*, which converts ATP into cAMP/cyclic AMP *[1 mark]*. cAMP/cyclic AMP then activates an enzyme called protein kinase A *[1 mark]*, which triggers a cascade of reactions that convert glycogen into glucose/ glycogenolysis / which triggers a cascade of reactions that convert glycerol and amino acids into glucose/ gluconeogenesis *[1 mark]*. *[Maximum of four marks available]*

2.7 E.g. adrenaline activates glycogenolysis/the breakdown of glycogen to glucose *[1 mark]*, which increases the amount of glucose available for muscle cells to respire *[1 mark]*.

3.1 $9.8 - 7.6 = 2.2$ mmol dm^{-3}
$(2.2 \div 9.8) \times 100 = $ **22.4%** (to 3 s.f.) *[1 mark]*

3.2 The high GI food with the supplement caused the blood glucose concentration to rise more slowly after the food was eaten *[1 mark]* and to reach a lower maximum value of 6.7 mmol dm^{-3} compared to the high GI food without the supplement *[1 mark]*.

3.3 Type II diabetes arises due to β cells not producing enough insulin / receptors not responding to the presence of insulin *[1 mark]*. This means that the blood glucose concentration gets too high *[1 mark]*, so the food supplement could be useful as it would help people with Type II diabetes manage their blood glucose concentration *[1 mark]*.

3.4 Any two from: losing weight (if necessary) / eating a healthy, balanced diet / taking regular exercise / taking glucose-lowering medication / using insulin injections *[2 marks]*.

4.1

Test tube	Final concentration of glucose / mM
1	4.0
2	2.0
3	1.0
4	0.5
5	0.25

[1 mark for four correct glucose concentrations]

4.2 Any four from: the student could carry out the Benedict's test on each known glucose solution *[1 mark]*. He could then use a colorimeter to measure the absorbance value of each glucose solution *[1 mark]*. The known values could then be used to plot a calibration curve *[1 mark]*. A Benedict's test could then be carried out on each urine sample and a colorimeter measurement taken *[1 mark]*. The absorbance value for each sample would then be read off the calibration curve to find the associated glucose concentration *[1 mark]*. *[Maximum of 4 marks available]*

4.3 E.g. 10 cm³/the same volume of distilled water *[1 mark]*.

4.4 To demonstrate that only the colour of the solution/the presence of glucose is affecting the readings *[1 mark]*.

4.5 E.g. not all glucose in the blood of people with diabetes is lost in urine / some glucose in the blood of people with diabetes is reabsorbed by the kidneys *[1 mark]*, so it wouldn't be a very accurate method *[1 mark]*.

Pages 108-111: Homeostasis — 2

1.1 E.g. the epithelium of the wall of the proximal convoluted tubule/PCT has lots of microvilli *[1 mark]*. This provides a large surface area for reabsorption of useful materials from the glomerular filtrate back into the capillaries *[1 mark]*.

1.2 Glucose is filtered out of the capillaries at point A/in the glomerulus, so the concentration of glucose in the filtrate will be high *[1 mark]*. At point D/the distal convoluted tubule/DCT, the concentration of glucose in the filtrate will be much lower, as most of the glucose will have been selectively reabsorbed at the proximal convoluted tubule/PCT/point B *[1 mark]*.

1.3 loop of Henle *[1 mark]*

1.4 Any four from: the structure at point C/loop of Henle maintains a sodium ion gradient, so that water can be reabsorbed *[1 mark]*. The structure at point C/loop of Henle is made up of a descending limb which is permeable to water, and an ascending limb which is impermeable to water *[1 mark]*. Near the top of the ascending limb, sodium ions are pumped out into the medulla by active transport *[1 mark]*, and near the bottom of the ascending limb, sodium ions diffuse out into the medulla *[1 mark]*. This lowers the water potential of the medulla, and so water moves from the descending limb into the medulla by osmosis *[1 mark]*. The water in the medulla can then be reabsorbed into the blood by the capillary network *[1 mark]*. *[Maximum of 4 marks available]*

1.5 Frogs and toads tend to live in aquatic environments, so do not need to conserve water *[1 mark]*.

1.6 Desert animals may have long loops of Henle *[1 mark]*, to conserve more water to survive in their dry environment *[1 mark]*.

2.1 Any four from: the process of ultrafiltration occurs *[1 mark]* when blood passes through the afferent arterioles under high pressure due to the smaller diameter of the efferent arteriole *[1 mark]*. This forces liquid and small molecules out of the blood and into the Bowman's capsule *[1 mark]*, through the capillary wall, the basement membrane and an epithelial layer *[1 mark]*. Larger molecules (e.g. protein and blood cells)cannot pass through so they remain in the blood *[1 mark]*. *[Maximum of 4 marks available]*

2.2 Any two from: e.g. amino acids / fatty acids / ions / glycerol / glucose / water / hormones / vitamins *[2 marks]*.

2.3 Blood volume = 70 cm³ × 65 kg = 4550 cm³
Glomerular filtration rate per day = 110 cm³ min⁻¹ × 60 × 24 = 158 400 cm³ day⁻¹.
Blood filtration = 158 400 cm³ ÷ 4550 cm³ = **34.8 times**
[2 marks for the correct answer, otherwise 1 mark for correct working]

2.4 Most of the water from the glomerular filtrate is reabsorbed into the blood *[1 mark]* by the distal convoluted tubule and collecting ducts *[1 mark]*.

2.5 E.g. the glomerulus becomes damaged due to high blood pressure *[1 mark]*, which means that some large molecules such as proteins are also filtered out of the capillaries into the glomerular filtrate, so end up in the urine *[1 mark]*.

2.6 The concentration of blood glucose is higher than normal in people with diabetes, so the kidneys are unable to reabsorb all of the glucose from the filtrate *[1 mark]*. This means that some glucose remains in the latter part of the nephron, which lowers the water potential of the filtrate *[1 mark]*. This causes less water to be reabsorbed from the nephron into the blood via osmosis, so more water passes out of the body in urine *[1 mark]*.

3.1 osmoregulation *[1 mark]*

3.2 When the level of ADH is decreased, the distal convoluted tubule/DCT and collecting ducts become less permeable *[1 mark]*, so less water is reabsorbed into the blood by osmosis *[1 mark]*. This results in a large amount of dilute urine being produced, so more water is lost from the body *[1 mark]*.

3.3 Water moves out of osmoreceptors in the hypothalamus by osmosis *[1 mark]*, causing their volume to decrease *[1 mark]*. This sends a signal to other cells in the hypothalamus, which sends a signal to the posterior pituitary gland to release more ADH *[1 mark]*.

3.4 When the level of ADH is increased, the distal convoluted tubule/DCT and collecting ducts become more permeable *[1 mark]*, so more water is reabsorbed into the blood by osmosis *[1 mark]*. This increases the volume of the blood and so reduces the concentration of sodium in the blood *[1 mark]*.

If you add water to a salt solution, the solution becomes less concentrated and more dilute.

4.1 To ensure that the blood glucose concentration was not affected by any food consumed *[1 mark]*.

4.2 People with Type I diabetes have a much higher blood glucose concentration than those without diabetes *[1 mark]*. This is because their β cells/islets of Langerhans in the pancreas produce no/little insulin *[1 mark]*, so they can't regulate their blood glucose concentration *[1 mark]*.

4.3 Student's t-test *[1 mark]*, because the mean values of two groups are being compared *[1 mark]*.

4.4 There is a significant difference between the blood glucose concentrations of patients with Type I diabetes and those without diabetes *[1 mark]*, and there is a less than 5% probability that the results are due to chance *[1 mark]*.

4.5 If the glucose concentration is too high, the water potential of the blood is reduced and water molecules diffuse out of cells by osmosis *[1 mark]*. This can cause the cells to shrivel up and die *[1 mark]*. If blood glucose concentration is too low, cells are unable to carry out normal activities as there isn't enough glucose for respiration to provide energy *[1 mark]*.

Topic Seven — Genetics, Populations, Evolution and Ecosystems

Pages 112-115: Genetics — 1

1.1 The son with DMD must have inherited the DMD-causing allele from his mother, but Figure 1 shows she does not have the disease *[1 mark]*. If a person carries an allele that is not expressed in their phenotype, it must be recessive *[1 mark]*.
Boys have one X chromosome, which they always inherit from their mother — so the son with DMD must have inherited the DMD-causing allele from his mother.

1.2 Mother: $X^M X^m$
Father: $X^M Y$
[1 mark for both correct answers.]

1.3 50% / 0.5 / 1 in 2 *[1 mark]*
There's a 50:50 chance of the daughter inheriting either of her mother's X chromosomes, and so a 50:50 chance of her inheriting the DMD allele.

1.4 25% / 0.25 / 1 in 4 *[1 mark]*
If you struggled with this question, you could have sketched a quick genetic diagram to work out the answer, e.g.

	X^M	Y
X^M	$X^M X^M$ Unaffected	$X^M Y$ Unaffected
X^m	$X^M X^m$ Unaffected	$X^m Y$ Has DMD

1.5 The unaffected son cannot be a carrier of the DMD allele because males only have one copy of the X chromosome, so the unaffected son's copy must carry a normal allele for the dystrophin gene *[1 mark]*. The son with DMD must have a copy of the allele that causes DMD *[1 mark]*. As the genotypes of both sons are known, genetic testing would give no new information *[1 mark]*.

1.6 3:1 *[1 mark]*

1.7 The chi-squared test *[1 mark]*

2.1 Because both alleles are expressed in the phenotype, so the insects appear both red and purple *[1 mark]*. Neither allele is recessive / dominant over the other *[1 mark]*.

2.2 A homozygous genotype is one where the organism has two copies of the same allele, e.g. $P^R P^R$ / $P^P P^P$ / $P^y P^y$ *[1 mark]*. A heterozygous genotype is one where the organism has two different alleles for the same gene, e.g. $P^R P^y$ / $P^P P^y$ / $P^P P^R$ *[1 mark]*.

2.3 E.g.

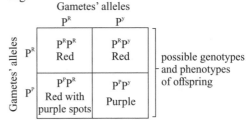

Gametes' alleles

	P^R	P^y
P^R	$P^R P^R$ Red	$P^R P^y$ Red
P^P	$P^P P^R$ Red with purple spots	$P^P P^y$ Purple

possible genotypes and phenotypes of offspring

Expected phenotypic ratio: **2:1:1 (red : red with purple spots : purple)**
[3 marks — 1 mark for the correct gametes, 1 mark for the correct genotypes of offspring, plus 1 mark for the correct phenotypic ratio]

2.4 $88 \div 4 = 22$
        $22 \times 2 = \mathbf{44}$
[1 mark — allow mark if incorrect ratio from 2.3 used correctly here.]

Divide the total number of offspring by the ratio total (2 + 1 + 1 = 4). Then multiply this number by the expected number of offspring with a red cuticle (2).

2.5   There is no significant difference between the observed results and the expected results *[1 mark]*.

2.6   The null hypothesis cannot be rejected because the chi-squared value is lower than the critical value *[1 mark]*.

2.7   There is a greater than 5% probability that the difference between the observed and expected results is due to chance *[1 mark]*.

3.1   coloured full and colourless shrunken *[1 mark]*

3.2   E.g. there are more coloured full and colourless shrunken offspring than expected *[1 mark]*. This suggests that the heterozygous parent plant produced mostly CS and cs gametes *[1 mark]*. For the alleles to be inherited together like this, the colour and shape genes must be autosomally linked / on the same chromosome/autosome *[1 mark]*.

Pages 116-118: Genetics — 2

1.1   E.g.

Gametes' alleles

	G	g	
G	Gg grey	gg non-grey	possible genotypes and phenotypes of offspring
g	Gg grey	gg non-grey	

(Gametes' alleles — left axis labels: g, g)

Expected phenotypic ratio: **1:1 (grey : non-grey)**
[3 marks — 1 mark for the correct gametes, 1 mark for the correct genotypes of offspring, plus 1 mark for the correct phenotypic ratio]

1.2   Epistasis *[1 mark]*.

1.3

Genotype	Pigment produced
EeWw	none
Eeww	black
eeww	red

[1 mark for three correct phenotypes]

1.4   E.g. parental genotypes: WwEe × wwee
So the genotypes of the offspring and pigments produced are:

	WE	wE	We	we
we	WwEe (white/ none)	wwEe (black)	Wwee (white/ none)	wwee (red)

Probability of offspring producing black pigment:
¼ / 25% / 0.25
[3 marks — 1 mark for the correct parental genotypes/ correct gametes, 1 mark for the correct genotypes of the offspring, and 1 mark for the correct probability.]

1.5   It means that the genes are (autosomally) linked *[1 mark]*. This means that their alleles are more likely to be inherited together by the offspring *[1 mark]*, which will alter the phenotypic ratio in the offspring *[1 mark]*.

2.1   The genotype is the genetic constitution of an organism and the phenotype is the expression of the genetic constitution, and its interaction with the environment *[1 mark]*.

2.2   RM and rm *[1 mark]*

2.3   All offspring will have multiple red flowers per stem *[1 mark]*.

All of the offspring would have the genotype RrMm.

2.4

	Multiple red flowers	Single red flower	Multiple yellow flowers	Single yellow flower
Expected number of offspring	9	3	3	1

[1 mark]

2.5   7.82 *[1 mark]*

Degrees of freedom = number of classes (in this case phenotypes) − 1. There are 4 phenotypes, so this test has 3 degrees of freedom.

2.6   Yes there is a significant difference, because the chi-squared value is larger than the critical value *[1 mark — allow mark for incorrect answer to 2.5 used correctly here]*.

2.7   Any two from: e.g. the genes could exhibit autosomal linkage *[1 mark]*, making some certain combinations of alleles in the gametes more likely than others *[1 mark]*. / The genes could exhibit epistasis *[1 mark]*, resulting in some genotypes being hidden/overrepresented in the phenotypic ratio *[1 mark]*. / The genes could be sex-linked *[1 mark]*, resulting in the phenotype being more likely in males than females or vice versa *[1 mark]*.

Pages 119-122: Populations and Evolution

1.1   E.g. the Hardy-Weinberg principle assumes that immigration/emigration isn't happening, but the flow of genes suggests that it is *[1 mark]*.

1.2   E.g. mutation / meiosis / the random fertilisation of gametes during sexual reproduction *[1 mark]*.

1.3   Because the two populations are geographically isolated, alleles are not passed between them *[1 mark]*. Due to different selection pressures/genetic drift, the allele frequencies will change independently in each population *[1 mark]*. This could increase the differences/variation between the gene pools of the two populations *[1 mark]*, eventually leading to reproductive isolation *[1 mark]*.

1.4   The flow of genes may reduce/stop *[1 mark]* because members of population two are no longer able to attract members of population one *[1 mark]* and the two populations stop interbreeding *[1 mark]*.

2.1

Latitude / ° N	Allele frequency 'W'	Allele frequency 'w'
64	0.62	**0.38**
66	**0.67**	0.33
68	**0.83**	0.17
70	0.92	0.08

[1 mark]

The allele frequencies should add up to 1.0 here.

2.2   E.g. $p^2 + 2pq + q^2 = 1$
Here, $p = 0.92$ and $q = 0.08$.
Frequency of white fur phenotype = $p^2 + 2pq$ = $(0.92^2) + (2 \times 0.92 \times 0.08) = $ **0.99** (to 2 s.f.) *[2 marks for the correct answer, otherwise 1 mark for recognising that the frequency of the white fur phenotype = $p^2 + 2pq$]*

The question tells you that the 'W' allele is dominant, so to work out the frequency of the white fur phenotype you need to calculate the frequency of the heterozygous individuals (2pq) as well as the frequency of the homozygous dominant individuals (p^2).

2.3   E.g. the snowy weather acts as a selection pressure on the rodents *[1 mark]*. The 'W' allele results in the white fur phenotype, which will provide camouflage in snow *[1 mark]*. Rodents with the white fur phenotype at higher latitudes are more likely to survive and pass on their alleles (including the 'W' allele) than rodents with the brown fur phenotype *[1 mark]*. After many generations, the frequency of the 'W' allele will have increased in the populations at higher latitudes *[1 mark]*.

2.4   The allele frequencies do not add up to 1, suggesting that there are more than two alleles for fur colour in this population *[1 mark]*.

3.1 $p^2 + 2pq + q^2 = 1$
$p + q = 1$
Here, q^2 = the yellow phenotype frequency = 0.25,
so $q = \sqrt{0.25}$
$p = 1 - q = 1 - \sqrt{0.25}$
The frequency of the heterozygous genotype = $2pq$
$= 2 \times (1 - \sqrt{0.25}) \times (\sqrt{0.25}) = $ **0.5**
[3 marks for the correct answer, otherwise 1 mark for $q^2 = 0.25$ and 1 mark for recognising that the frequency of the heterozygous genotype = $2pq$]

Because the yellow phenotype can only arise when the individual contains two copies of the recessive allele, the frequency of the homozygous recessive phenotype (yellow) is equal to the frequency of the homozygous recessive genotype (q^2), which is why you can use '$q^2 = 0.25$' in this equation.

3.2   The phenotype frequencies seem to be changing randomly *[1 mark]*, but if selection was acting on the trait then there would be a trend/direction to the change *[1 mark]*. This is because one phenotype would increase an individual's chance of survival, so it would become more common *[1 mark]*.

3.3   E.g. because of genetic drift *[1 mark]*.

3.4   The two groups aren't living in the same area and so don't have the potential to interbreed *[1 mark]*.

4.1   E.g. disruptive selection would have resulted in a selective advantage for those individuals in the ancestral population with either large wide beaks or long narrow beaks / beaks that were better adapted for feeding on either larger seeds or nectar *[1 mark]*. Individuals with the alleles for these beaks would have been more likely to survive and pass on their alleles to the next generation than individuals with medium-sized beaks *[1 mark]*. Over time, two separate breeding populations would have developed *[1 mark]*. Eventually, changes in allele frequency between the two populations would have led to them becoming reproductively isolated *[1 mark]*.

4.2   During the drought, the individuals of the species with very large beaks (adapted for consuming the largest, toughest seeds) would have been unable to find as much food *[1 mark]*. Individuals with slightly smaller beaks would have been able to feed on different/smaller food sources that those with larger beaks couldn't *[1 mark]*. Because those individuals with the largest beaks were less likely to survive than those with smaller beaks, the average beak size fell the following year *[1 mark]*.

4.3   E.g. because a population of Galapagos finches is likely to be smaller than a population of finches on the mainland *[1 mark]*.

Pages 123-125: Populations in Ecosystems — 1

1.1   Sandwort and sea couch *[1 mark]*.

1.2   Their organic material is decomposed after they die, forming a basic soil *[1 mark]*. They make the abiotic conditions less hostile, so new organisms can survive there *[1 mark]*.

1.3   Any one from: e.g. woodland is the most complex community that the ecosystem can support *[1 mark]*. / Woodland is the steady state reached when the ecosystem has passed through all stages of succession *[1 mark]*.

1.4   Any four from: e.g. marram grass would only have been able to survive after a thin layer of soil was created by plants such as sandwort and sand couch *[1 mark]*. Marram grass may have adaptations that make it particularly suited to growing at the third stage, e.g. being able to survive without much shelter *[1 mark]*. Once the marram grass had stabilised the sand dunes, a larger number of plants were able to survive there *[1 mark]*. More plants colonising the area created more interspecific competition *[1 mark]*. As the abiotic and biotic conditions changed, the marram grass was no longer the best adapted plant species, and was out-competed by the shrubs *[1 mark]*. *[Maximum 4 marks available]*

2.1   A community is made up of the populations of different species in an area *[1 mark]*, whereas an ecosystem is made up of a community and the abiotic components of the area *[1 mark]*.

2.2   Any one from: e.g. temperature / soil type / soil pH / availability of space *[1 mark]*.

2.3   E.g. the quadrats could have been placed (at regular intervals) along a belt transect *[1 mark]*.

2.4   The student could plot a scatter graph *[1 mark]* because he is seeing whether there is a correlation between two discrete variables (ground vegetation cover and light intensity) *[1 mark]*.

2.5   E.g. if the measurements were not taken simultaneously, they will not account for the fact that light levels will vary depending on the time of day/the weather *[1 mark]*.

3.1 rate = change in y / change in x
Number of bacteria at 5 hours = 10^3
Number of bacteria at 12 hours = $10^{7.8}$
$(10^{7.8} - 10^3) \div 7 = 9013533.492...$
= **9 013 533 cells hour^{-1}**
[2 marks for correct answer, otherwise 1 mark for $(10^{7.8} - 10^3) \div 7]$

3.2 E.g. abiotic factors, such as availability of nutrients *[1 mark]*, and intraspecific competition *[1 mark]* have caused the flask of broth to reach its carrying capacity *[1 mark]*.

Pages 126-129: Populations in Ecosystems — 2

1.1 Sustainability means meeting the needs of people today without reducing the ability of people in the future to meet their own needs *[1 mark]*.

1.2 The grazing animals will feed on plants, including young shrubs and trees, preventing the larger plants from growing *[1 mark]*. This interrupts succession *[1 mark]*, preventing the fens from developing into carr woodland / maintaining the fens ecosystem *[1 mark]*.

1.3 E.g. mowing / cutting *[1 mark]*

1.4 E.g. there may be a conflict between the need to conserve the habitat for the species that live there, and the need to allow tourists to visit and generate income for the area *[1 mark]*.

2.1 Total population size = (number caught in 1st sample × number caught in 2nd sample) ÷ number marked in 2nd sample = $(24 \times 23) \div 7 = 78.857... = $ **79**
[2 marks for correct answer, otherwise 1 mark for evidence of correct formula]

When a question is about whole objects, you should round to the nearest whole number — in this example, there wouldn't be 0.857 of a sand martin.

2.2 To give the ringed sand martins time to mix back in with the rest of the population *[1 mark]*.

2.3 The population size is more likely to change during a period of several months, due to births / deaths / migration in and out of the nature reserve *[1 mark]*.

3.1 Their spiny fur protects them against predators *[1 mark]*.

3.2 As the population size increased, there were fewer resources (e.g. food, water, space) available per individual, so intraspecific competition increased *[1 mark]*. Eventually, the amount of resources became limiting and the population declined *[1 mark]*. When the population size was low, there was less intraspecific competition for resources. This meant more of the golden spiny mice could survive and reproduce, causing the population to grow again *[1 mark]*.

3.3 65 (accept between 60 and 70) *[1 mark]*

The population size is fluctuating around the carrying capacity. When it's below the carrying capacity, it's able to increase, and when it gets too far above the carrying capacity, it decreases.

3.4 E.g. if the temperature becomes higher or lower than the optimum external temperature of golden spiny mice, then they would have to use more energy to maintain the right internal temperature *[1 mark]*. This would mean the mice have less energy available for growth and reproduction, so their population size would fall *[1 mark]*.

3.5 The two species occupy a similar niche in the ecosystem *[1 mark]*, because they live in similar habitats and have similar diets *[1 mark]*. Therefore, they are avoiding interspecific competition by being active at different times *[1 mark]*.

3.6 Capture a sample of mice, e.g. using pitfall traps, and count them *[1 mark]*. Mark the mice in a way that doesn't affect their chances of survival *[1 mark]*. Release them, and wait a week *[1 mark]*. Take a second sample from the same area, counting the number that are marked, and use these figures to calculate an estimate of the total population size *[1 mark]*.

4 Any five from:
Evidence that the project was successful:
E.g. the population sizes of Marsh Fritillaries on Dartmoor and High Brown Fritillaries on Exmoor increased overall between 2005 and 2016 *[1 mark]*. After 2008, the population of Marsh Fritillaries on Dartmoor was larger than the national population *[1 mark]*. The Marsh Fritillary population on Dartmoor was bigger at the end of the project than at the beginning, despite the national population being smaller than it was at the beginning *[1 mark]*. From 2013, the population size of High Brown Fritillaries on Exmoor was higher than the national average *[1 mark]*. There was a large increase in the High Brown Fritillary population on Exmoor from 2010 to 2014 *[1 mark]*.
Evidence that the project was not successful:
E.g. the High Brown Fritillary became more common in the UK as a whole from 2012, so the increases seen on the moors may not have been because of the conservation project *[1 mark]*. The population of the High Brown Fritillary on Dartmoor was smaller at the end of the project, whereas the national population had grown *[1 mark]*. *[Maximum 5 marks available]*

Topic Eight — Gene Expression

Pages 130-132: Mutations and Gene Expression — 1

1.1 E.g. it could increase the rate at which the gene is transcribed *[1 mark]*. This would mean that more lactase mRNA gets produced, so more lactase will be made, compared to a wild-type adult without the lactase persistence mutation *[1 mark]*.

1.2 Because substitution mutations only change one base triplet *[1 mark]* and due to the degenerate nature of the genetic code, many amino acids are coded for by more than one base triplet *[1 mark]*.

1.3 total number of patients = 11 + 196 = 207
percentage lactose intolerant = (11 ÷ 207) × 100
= **5.3%** (to 2 s.f.) *[1 mark]*

1.4 E.g. there may have been other factors that prevented the person's blood sugar level from rising *[1 mark]*.

2.1 E.g. to slow down cell division / cause apoptosis *[1 mark]*.

2.2 E.g. a mutation in the lung cell DNA could prevent the PTEN protein from functioning / could stop the PTEN protein being produced *[1 mark]*. As a result, the PTEN protein would no longer be able to regulate the cell cycle *[1 mark]*, and the cells in the lung could start dividing uncontrollably *[1 mark]*. This would lead to the development of a tumour *[1 mark]*.

2.3 E.g. increased methylation of the *PTEN* gene *[1 mark]* would prevent the *PTEN* gene from being transcribed, so the regulatory protein it produces would not be made *[1 mark]*.

2.4 E.g. cigarette smoke contains mutagenic agents *[1 mark]* which increase the rate of mutation in DNA *[1 mark]*. Therefore, regularly smoking cigarettes increases the chances of acquiring a mutation that could lead to cancer *[1 mark]*.

2.5 Because malignant tumours can invade surrounding tissues and spread to other parts of the body *[1 mark]* but benign tumours cannot *[1 mark]*.

3.1 Gamma radiation is a mutagenic agent *[1 mark]*, so it will increase the rate at which random mutations are introduced into the crop's DNA *[1 mark]*.

3.2 Any two from: e.g. most mutations will not occur in/affect a gene that improves crop yield *[1 mark]*. / Mutations in a gene that improves crop yield may not lead to a change in the amino acid sequence it codes for, so protein function will not be altered *[1 mark]*. / Changes in the amino acid sequence of a protein affecting crop yield may have no effect/a negative effect, so crop yield will not be affected/ will be negatively affected *[1 mark]*.

3.3 The first mutation is an inversion, from the sequence TTA to ATT *[1 mark]*. The second mutation is the addition of a guanine base/G *[1 mark]*.

3.4 Unlike the first mutation, the second mutation causes a change in the number of bases *[1 mark]*, leading to a frameshift *[1 mark]*. This means that all of the codons downstream of the mutation will be changed, which may cause significant changes to the amino acid sequence of the protein *[1 mark]*.

3.5 The mutation could cause a change in the amino acid sequence of the enzyme, which could lead to a change in the enzyme's tertiary structure *[1 mark]*. This might improve the function of the enzyme / improve the enzyme's ability to bind to its substrate, and so increase the rate of photosynthesis *[1 mark]*.

Pages 133-135: Mutations and Gene Expression — 2

1.1 E.g. oestrogen can stimulate breast cells to divide *[1 mark]*. Increased cell division would increase the chance of cancer-causing mutations occurring / increased cell division of cancerous cells would help tumours to grow rapidly *[1 mark]*. / Oestrogen may be able to introduce mutations directly into the DNA of breast cells *[1 mark]*. Mutations in tumour suppressor genes/proto-oncogenes could lead to the development of cancer in breast tissue *[1 mark]*. *[Maximum 2 marks available]*

1.2 E.g. patients may be able to be treated with drugs that specifically target oestrogen/the oestrogen receptor *[1 mark]*.

1.3 Identical twins are genetically identical *[1 mark]*, so any differences between them must be caused by environmental factors *[1 mark]*.

1.4 E.g. the mean difference in the age of onset was lower for identical twins than non-identical twins, whether the identical twins were raised apart or together *[1 mark]*. This suggests genetic factors influence the age of onset of menstruation *[1 mark]*. However, the mean difference in age of onset was lower for twins who were raised together than twins who were raised apart, whether they were identical or not *[1 mark]*. This suggests environmental factors also have an influence *[1 mark]*.

If the results were only due to genetic factors then you would expect there to be no difference between identical twins who were raised together and those who were raised apart (because identical twins are genetically identical). As there is a difference, the results must have been influenced by environmental factors too.

2.1 Proto-oncogenes are genes that promote cell division *[1 mark]*. In the development of cancer, proto-oncogenes mutate to become oncogenes *[1 mark]*. In doing so, they become over-active, causing cells to divide uncontrollably, resulting in a tumour *[1 mark]*.

2.2 Transcription factors like MYC are produced in the cytoplasm and move into the nucleus *[1 mark]*. Once in the nucleus, they bind to DNA *[1 mark]*, at a specific site near to their target genes *[1 mark]*. Once bound to DNA, they increase the expression of their target genes by increasing the rate of transcription *[1 mark]*.

2.3 E.g. the drug might change the shape of MYC so that it was no longer complementary to its target DNA sequence *[1 mark]*. This would prevent MYC from binding to DNA and activating the transcription of genes that promote cell division *[1 mark]*. This could slow down/prevent tumour growth *[1 mark]*.

2.4 E.g. the drug would also likely inhibit the activity of *MYC* in normal/non-cancerous cells *[1 mark]*.

2.5 Cancers can be caused by a wide variety of different mutations *[1 mark]*. This drug would only be effective in cancers that are caused by a mutated *MYC* gene / overexpression of the *MYC* gene *[1 mark]*.

3.1 Mutation is a change to the DNA base sequence *[1 mark]*, whereas methylation is the addition of methyl groups to the DNA *[1 mark]*.

3.2 Increased methylation may alter the structure of the promoter region *[1 mark]* so that RNA polymerase is unable to bind *[1 mark]*. This will mean that *BRCA1* is not transcribed and the BRCA1 tumour suppressor protein is not produced *[1 mark]*. This will allow breast cells to divide uncontrollably *[1 mark]*.

3.3 DNA methylation has an important role in regulating gene expression in normal cells *[1 mark]*. Therefore, drugs that affect DNA methylation have to be specifically targeted to tumour cells to avoid damaging normal cells *[1 mark]*.

3.4 E.g. decreased acetylation of the histones associated with a tumour suppressor gene *[1 mark]* would prevent the gene from being transcribed and its protein produced, allowing cells to divide uncontrollably *[1 mark]*.

Pages 136-138: Mutations and Gene Expression — 3

1.1 The signalling molecules caused transcription factors to move from the cytoplasm to the nucleus *[1 mark]*. These transcription factors activated the expression of genes required for the formation of a specific cell type and inhibited the expression of genes required for the formation of other cell types *[1 mark]*. As a result, in each type of cell, only proteins required for the formation of the specific cell type were produced *[1 mark]*. These proteins modified the structure and function of the cell so that it became the specific cell type *[1 mark]*.

1.2 Totipotent cells are only found during the first few embryonic divisions and can mature into any type of body cell, including those that make up the placenta *[1 mark]*. After the first few divisions, embryonic cells lose their ability to form placental cells and become pluripotent *[1 mark]*.

1.3 Adult body cells *[1 mark]* are made to express transcription factors associated with pluripotent stem cells *[1 mark]*.

1.4 Advantage: e.g. the creation of induced pluripotent stem cells does not involve the destruction of an embryo, which is necessary to obtain embryonic stem cells *[1 mark]*, so there are fewer ethical issues surrounding the use of induced pluripotent stem cells *[1 mark]*.
Disadvantage: e.g. induced pluripotent stem cells may not behave in exactly the same way as embryonic stem cells *[1 mark]*, which could affect the accuracy of the results *[1 mark]*.

1.5 Unipotent stem cells can only differentiate into one type of cell *[1 mark]*. Therefore, changing the signalling molecules that the cells were exposed to would not cause them to differentiate into different types of cell *[1 mark]*.

2.1 It prevents the target mRNA/gene from being translated into a protein *[1 mark]*.

2.2 The mutation in the base sequence of the gene could alter the base sequence of the transcribed mRNA *[1 mark]* so that it is no longer complementary to the siRNA *[1 mark]*. The siRNA would longer be able to bind to the mRNA and cut it into fragments *[1 mark]*.

2.3 It is being used as a negative control *[1 mark]* to determine whether any effects seen are due to the specific sequence of the siRNA targeting gene *X* or due to the presence of siRNA in general *[1 mark]*.

2.4 After approximately five days, the percentage of target mRNA remaining in the cells began to rise *[1 mark]*. This may be because the siRNA molecules began to be degraded, preventing them from cutting up the mRNA *[1 mark]*.

2.5 E.g. she could repeat her experiment using test siRNA and scramble siRNA concentrations between 5 and 50 nM *[1 mark for any sensible range of concentrations]*. The concentration of both the test siRNA and scramble siRNA should be the same each time *[1 mark]*. To make the experiment valid, she should control variables such as the volume of siRNA used/the temperature the reaction is carried out at/the type of cell used/the culture the cells come from *[1 mark]*.

Pages 139-142: Genome Projects and Gene Technologies — 1

1.1 Any five from: the DNA sample is mixed with free nucleotides, primers and DNA polymerase *[1 mark]*. The DNA sample is then heated to 95 °C to break the hydrogen bonds between the DNA strands and separate them *[1 mark]*. The mixture is then cooled to 50–65 °C so that the primers can bind to the separated strands *[1 mark]*. The mixture is then heated to 72 °C, which is the temperature at which the DNA polymerase enzyme can work effectively *[1 mark]*. DNA polymerase then catalyses the formation of complementary DNA strands, thus replicating the DNA molecule *[1 mark]*. Many cycles of this process are repeated to produce many copies of the original DNA molecule *[1 mark]*. *[Maximum 5 marks available]*

1.2 The blood sample will only contain very small amounts of DNA *[1 mark]*, so amplification is needed to provide enough DNA for the bands produced by genetic fingerprinting to be visible *[1 mark]*.

1.3 The genome contains areas of variable number tandem repeats/VNTRs *[1 mark]*. Different individuals have different numbers of repeats at different loci *[1 mark]*. In genetic fingerprinting, DNA fragments corresponding to different numbers of repeats are separated according to size *[1 mark]*. The pattern of bands produced corresponds to the number of repeats an individual has at each locus *[1 mark]*.

1.4 The blood from the crime scene is a mixture of the victim's and suspect C's *[1 mark]*.

1.5 Compare genetic fingerprints from the child and the possible fathers *[1 mark]*. As the child will have inherited around half of its variable number tandem repeats/ VNTRs from its father *[1 mark]*, the candidate with the most bands matching the child's is the most likely father *[1 mark]*.

2.1 Genetic testing involves a labelled DNA probe with a complementary sequence to the target allele *[1 mark]*. If the allele is present, then the DNA probe hybridises with it, allowing the allele to be identified *[1 mark]*.

2.2 E.g. genetic testing could indicate which drugs would be most effective in treating his condition *[1 mark]*.

2.3 E.g. if the result shows that she has not inherited the mutation, she can be reassured that she does not have a higher than normal risk of developing colon cancer *[1 mark]*. If the result shows that she has inherited the mutation, she can take necessary precautions (e.g. regular screening) to reduce her risk of dying from colon cancer *[1 mark]*.

186

2.4 Any one from: e.g. it could lead to discrimination by insurance companies/employers *[1 mark]*. / It may cause her undue stress if she never goes on to develop colon cancer *[1 mark]*.

3.1 E.g. the fragments were transferred from the electrophoresis gel to a nylon membrane *[1 mark]*. The membrane was incubated with a fluorescently labelled DNA probe that was complementary to the mutated allele *[1 mark]*. The membrane was then viewed under UV light *[1 mark]*.

3.2 The positive control is carried out to show what a positive result looks like *[1 mark]*. The negative control is used to check that the DNA probe is only detecting/binding to the DNA samples *[1 mark]*.

3.3 Any one from: e.g. it could indicate which drugs are likely to be effective in treating the condition *[1 mark]*. / It could indicate how likely the individual is to pass the condition on to his or her children *[1 mark]*. / It could help predict the severity of the condition *[1 mark]*. / It could help to predict the patient's prognosis *[1 mark]*.

3.4 E.g. a DNA fragment containing the functional IL2RG gene could be isolated from a healthy cell using restriction enzymes/endonucleases *[1 mark]*. The virus DNA is then cut open using the same restriction enzyme/ endonuclease *[1 mark]*, so that it has sticky ends that are complementary to the sticky ends of the DNA fragment *[1 mark]*. A DNA ligase enzyme is then used to join the gene fragment and viral DNA together, so that the virus has recombinant DNA *[1 mark]*.

3.5 The virus infects the white blood cells and inserts its DNA into their DNA *[1 mark]*. This provides the white blood cells with a functional copy of the IL2RG gene *[1 mark]*.

3.6 Any two from: e.g. the virus vector may make the person ill *[1 mark]*. / The gene may be overexpressed with adverse consequences *[1 mark]*. / The treatment would not affect the germ line so the patient's children could still inherit the disease *[1 mark]*.

Pages 143-146: Genome Projects and Gene Technologies — 2

1.1 The genetic code and mechanisms of transcription and translation are universal / the same in all species *[1 mark]*.

1.2 E.g. because all the *E. coli* cells produce the enzyme, whereas only some of the plant cells produce the enzyme. / Because the *E. coli* produce the enzyme all the time, whereas the plant cells only produce the enzyme at certain times *[1 mark]*.

1.3 Restriction enzymes/endonucleases recognise specific DNA sequences either side of the gene of interest *[1 mark]*. They then catalyse a hydrolysis reaction that breaks the DNA at these sequences (cutting the gene of interest out of the plant DNA) *[1 mark]*.

1.4 The ampicillin gene serves as a marker gene for cells that have successfully taken up the plasmid *[1 mark]*. Only *E. coli* that have successfully taken up the plasmid and possess the ampicillin resistance gene will be able to grow on the growth medium *[1 mark]*.

1.5 The promoter region tells the RNA polymerase where to start producing mRNA *[1 mark]*. This allows the gene of interest to be transcribed by the *E. coli* so that the enzyme it codes for can be produced *[1 mark]*.

2.1 4 *[1 mark]*

2.2 Digested DNA was loaded onto a gel and an electrical current was passed through the gel *[1 mark]*. DNA fragments are negatively charged, so they moved towards the positive electrode *[1 mark]*. Different sized fragments move at different speeds, so the fragments separated out, producing a banding pattern when the DNA was made visible *[1 mark]*.

2.3 Male A and Female A are both carriers of the recessive IGS allele *[1 mark]*, so any puppies produced from this pairing will be at risk of developing IGS *[1 mark]*.

2.4 Male B and Female B *[1 mark]*. They are the only pair that aren't both carriers of any of the same conditions, so there is no risk of their offspring inheriting two alleles for the same condition *[1 mark]*.

2.5 It shows how closely related two individuals are *[1 mark]*, so that inbreeding can be avoided *[1 mark]*.

2.6 Compare:
Any two from: e.g. both use gel electrophoresis to separate DNA fragments *[1 mark]*. / Both require PCR to amplify the DNA sample *[1 mark]*. / Both use labelled DNA/require a method to visualise the DNA *[1 mark]*.
Contrast:
E.g. genetic fingerprinting analyses variable number tandem repeats/VNTRs in the genome, whereas genetic testing using DNA probes looks for specific alleles in the genome *[1 mark]*. *[Maximum 3 marks available]*

3.1 More complex organisms like fish have more non-coding DNA and regulatory genes in their genomes than bacteria *[1 mark]*, which means that knowledge of the genome cannot be translated into knowledge of the proteome as easily *[1 mark]*.

3.2 E.g. $240\,000 \times 6 = 1\,440\,000$ base pairs to be read in total $1\,440\,000 \div 12\,000 = 120$ minutes = **2 hours** *[1 mark]*

3.3 E.g. they are now automated *[1 mark]*.

3.4 The mRNA sample could be mixed with free DNA nucleotides and reverse transcriptase *[1 mark]*. The reverse transcriptase will use the mRNA as a template to synthesise a complementary DNA strand using the free DNA nucleotides *[1 mark]*.

3.5 Copies of the DNA fragment are made inside a living organism *[1 mark]*.

3.6 Advantages: any two from: e.g. the new crop could help increase global food production/reduce the risk of famine *[1 mark]*. / The new crop could allow maize to be grown on land that is currently unusable because it is too cold *[1 mark]*. / The new crop could allow maize to be produced locally in cold areas, reducing the need for transport of the crop and the associated energy cost/ pollution *[1 mark]*. *[Maximum 2 marks available]*
Disadvantages: any two from: e.g. there is a risk of the gene being transferred to other plants, potentially creating 'superweeds' *[1 mark]*. / Farmers may begin to practice monoculture with the new crop, making crops more susceptible to disease/reducing biodiversity *[1 mark]*. / The genetically modified crops could contaminate nearby organic crops, making them unsaleable *[1 mark]*. / If a large corporation owns the patent to the technology, it may be very expensive for farmers *[1 mark]*. / Contamination of non-GM crops with the GM crop may lead to disputes regarding ownership and patent laws *[1 mark]*. / There are ethical issues associated with the use of GM crops/some people may not want to eat the GM crop *[1 mark]*. *[Maximum 2 marks available]*

Mixed Questions

Pages 147-150: Mixed Questions — 1

1.1 D *[1 mark]*

1.2 E.g. the reaction/breakdown of lactose is a hydrolysis reaction *[1 mark]*, which requires the addition of a water molecule *[1 mark]*.

1.3 E.g. that lactase is only active below pH 8 / lactase is inactive at pH 8 or above *[1 mark]*. Lactase breaks lactose down into glucose and galactose *[1 mark]*. Therefore, if glucose is present/the strip is green, it indicates lactase is active / if glucose is absent/the strip is yellow, it indicates that lactase is inactive *[1 mark]*.

1.4 Above and below its optimum pH, every enzyme is affected by the H^+ and OH^- ions found in acids and alkalis *[1 mark]*. These ions interfere with the ionic and hydrogen bonds that hold the enzyme's tertiary structure together *[1 mark]*. This changes the shape of the enzyme's active site *[1 mark]*.

1.5 Any two from: e.g. the temperature of the solutions. / The concentration of the lactose and lactase solutions. / The type of glucose test strip used. / The person observing the colour change of each glucose test strip. *[2 marks available — 1 mark for each reasonable suggestion]*

For this question there are other correct answers that aren't listed here. For an answer to be valid, the variable needs to have an impact on the results, and be something that's possible to control in an experiment.

1.6 E.g. increase the number of reactions carried out between pH 7 and 8 *[1 mark]* because it is between these pH values that lactase activity stops *[1 mark]*.

Accurate results need to be close to the true answer, so increasing the number of reactions carried out between pH 7 and 8 would let the student narrow down where lactase activity stops. E.g. the investigation could show that the activity stops between pH 7.2 and 7.3 rather than between pH 7 and 8.

1.7 E.g. it allows the breakdown products of lactose to be immediately absorbed from the ileum into bloodstream *[1 mark]*.

1.8 E.g. the mutation produced an allele which increased people's chance of survival in Europe *[1 mark]*. This meant individuals with the mutation were more likely to survive, reproduce and pass on the beneficial allele to the next generation *[1 mark]*. The frequency of this allele increased from generation to generation in the European population *[1 mark]*.

2.1 spindle fibre *[1 mark]*

2.2 Cell B because the diagram shows the homologous pairs being separated, not the sister chromatids *[1 mark]*.

2.3 20 *[1 mark]*

2.4 Meiosis because the chromosome number changes from diploid/2n in the sporophyte to haploid/n in the spores *[1 mark]*.

2.5 When a sperm fertilises an egg, a diploid/2n fertilised gametophyte is formed *[1 mark]*. This must mean that both the egg and sperm are haploid/n *[1 mark]*. The spores are also haploid/n and to maintain a haploid number of chromosomes between the spores and gametophytes, stages 1 and 2 must represent mitosis *[1 mark]*.

3.1 Cl^- ions move from the epithelial cells lining the ileum, through the open Cl^- channel proteins and into the ileum lumen *[1 mark]*. The build up of Cl^- ions lowers the water potential of the lumen *[1 mark]*. This causes water to move by osmosis out of the epithelial cells into the lumen *[1 mark]*. This lowers the water potential of the epithelial cells, causing water to move out of the blood into the cells *[1 mark]*.

3.2 E.g. *V. cholerae* will have a cell wall, the ileum epithelial cell will not *[1 mark]*. / *V. cholerae* will not have a nucleus/membrane-bound organelles, the ileum epithelial cell will *[1 mark]*. / *V. cholerae* will have smaller ribosomes than the ileum epithelial cell *[1 mark]*.

You're being asked to compare the structure of a prokaryotic cell (V. cholerae) to that of a eukaryotic animal cell (the ileum epithelial cell) here.

3.3 E.g. an attachment protein on HIV attaching to a receptor protein on a helper T-cell. *[1 mark]*

Pages 151-153: Mixed Questions — 2

1.1 A: glycerate 3-phosphate/GP *[1 mark]*
B: NADP *[1 mark]*
C: ribulose bisphosphate/RuBP *[1 mark]*

1.2 E.g. a low temperature would reduce the activity of the enzyme rubisco, which would reduce the rate of the first reaction / the reaction of CO_2 with ribulose bisphosphate/RuBP *[1 mark]*.

1.3 E.g. the rate at which glucose is produced as a result of the light-independent reaction would be reduced *[1 mark]*. This would mean that there is less glucose available for respiration, and so less energy available for plant growth *[1 mark]*. / The rate at which amino acids are produced as a result of the light-independent reaction would be reduced *[1 mark]*. This would mean that there are less amino acids available for making proteins, and so less proteins available for plant growth *[1 mark]*.

1.4 GPP/gross primary production is the total amount of chemical energy converted from light energy by plants, in a given area *[1 mark]*. NPP/net primary production is GPP/gross primary production, minus the energy lost to the environment through respiration *[1 mark]*.

2.1 Any two from: e.g. it takes time for the depolarisation caused by the action potential to spread from the sarcolemma of the muscle fibre to the sarcoplasmic reticulum. / It takes time for the sarcoplasmic reticulum to release its stored calcium/Ca^{2+} ions into the sarcoplasm. / It takes time for calcium/ Ca^{2+} ions to bind to the protein that moves tropomyosin out of the way. / It takes time for the actin-myosin cross bridges to form. *[2 marks — 1 mark for each correct answer]*

2.2 Calcium/Ca^{2+} ions leave their binding sites and are transported back into the sarcoplasmic reticulum *[1 mark]*. This causes the tropomyosin molecules to move back so that they block the actin-myosin binding sites again *[1 mark]*. This allows the muscles to relax because no myosin heads are attached to the actin filaments/there are no actin-myosin cross bridges and the actin filaments slide back to their relaxed position *[1 mark]*.

2.3 E.g. the cycle would be shorter / the peak would be narrower / the contraction and relaxation would happen faster *[1 mark]*.

2.4 E.g. because slow twitch muscle fibres release energy through oxidative phosphorylation *[1 mark]*, whereas fast twitch muscle fibres mainly release energy through glycolysis *[1 mark]*. This produces much less ATP than oxidative phosphorylation, so less energy can be released *[1 mark]*.

3.1 Glycogenolysis *[1 mark]*, which is the process of breaking down glycogen into glucose *[1 mark]*.
Gluconeogenesis *[1 mark]*, which is the process of forming glucose from non-carbohydrate sources *[1 mark]*.

3.2 The mRNA molecules are isolated from the pancreatic cells *[1 mark]*. Then the mRNA is mixed with free DNA nucleotides and reverse transcriptase *[1 mark]*. The reverse transcriptase uses the mRNA as a template to synthesise a new strand of complementary DNA/cDNA *[1 mark]*.

3.3 The fragment of DNA containing the insulin gene would be treated with a restriction endonuclease so that it has sticky ends *[1 mark]*. The vector DNA would be cut open using the same restriction endonuclease, to create sticky ends that are complementary to those on the DNA fragment *[1 mark]*.
The vector DNA and the insulin DNA fragment would then be mixed together with ligase, to join the sticky ends together *[1 mark]*.

3.4 The T7 RNA polymerase will only be transcribed in the presence of IPTG *[1 mark]* and so the human insulin gene will only be transcribed in the presence of IPTG *[1 mark]*. This means the expression of the human insulin gene, and so the production of insulin, can be controlled *[1 mark]*.

Pages 154-156: Mixed Questions — 3

1.1 tactic response/taxis *[1 mark]*

1.2 E.g. the scientists could have used the polymerase chain reaction/PCR *[1 mark]*.

1.3 A fluorescent tag would have been added to the DNA fragments *[1 mark]*. The DNA fragments would have been separated by gel electrophoresis *[1 mark]*. The two genetic fingerprints would have been compared under UV light to see the differences in the banding patterns *[1 mark]*.

1.4 The genetic fingerprints would have similar banding patterns because the number of VNTRs wouldn't vary as much at each locus *[1 mark]*.

1.5 The genetic variation between the two deer populations may increase *[1 mark]*. This is because the geographical isolation of the two species means they may experience slightly different environmental conditions and so different selection pressures *[1 mark]*. This may cause different changes in the allele frequencies of the populations *[1 mark]*.

2.1 E.g. the mutation occurs in the gene for a protein that is essential for mitochondria to function *[1 mark]*. The mutation causes a change in the amino acid sequence of the protein *[1 mark]*. This results in a change in the 3D/tertiary structure of the protein, which means that the protein can no longer function *[1 mark]*.

2.2 Petite mutants are able to grow on a substrate containing glucose because they can still generate energy from glucose via glycolysis *[1 mark]*, which occurs in the cytoplasm and does not require the mitochondria *[1 mark]*. However, they form smaller colonies than normal cells because glycolysis alone produces much less ATP from each molecule of glucose than the full respiratory chain *[1 mark]*, so the cells will not be able to release as much energy for growth as normal cells *[1 mark]*.

2.3 As petite mutants have inactive mitochondria/can only form small colonies, they are less fit than non-mutant cells and are therefore less likely to survive and reproduce *[1 mark]*. As a result, a lower proportion of the next generation will inherit the petite mutation, and the petite mutants will largely be eliminated from the population by natural selection *[1 mark]*.

2.4 Ethidium bromide acts as a mutagenic agent *[1 mark]*. By disrupting DNA replication it causes mutations to be introduced into the cells' DNA, which can lead to the production of petite mutants *[1 mark]*.

2.5 The NRF-1 transcription factor binds to specific DNA sequences near the start of its target genes *[1 mark]*. It then increases the rate of transcription of these genes *[1 mark]*.

2.6 Because the genome of a complex organism, like a human, contains large sections of non-coding DNA and regulatory genes *[1 mark]*. These make it more difficult to translate the genome into the proteome *[1 mark]*.

Pages 157-158: Mixed Questions — 4

1   *21-25 marks:*
The answer includes material from a variety of different topic areas and clearly shows its link to the question title. No irrelevant material is included. The answer includes a range of detailed and accurate biological facts that are all of A-level standard. No incorrect material is included. Appropriate scientific terminology is used. Explanations are clear and the overall essay is very well written.
(To get top marks, evidence of wider reading beyond the specification must be shown.)
16-20 marks:
The answer includes material from several relevant topic areas and links these to the question title. An irrelevant topic may be included. The answer includes a range of biological facts that are accurate and of A-level standard but may sometimes be lacking in detail. There may be one significant error in the scientific content. Appropriate scientific terminology is used. Explanations are clear.
11-15 marks:
The answer includes material from several relevant topic areas but doesn't link them to the question title. More than one irrelevant topic may be included. The biological facts included in the answer are mostly correct and of A-level standard but material is lacking in detail. There may be a few significant errors in the scientific content. Appropriate scientific terminology is usually used. Explanations are usually clear.

6-10 marks:

The answer includes material from one or two relevant topic areas but doesn't link them to the question title. Several irrelevant topic areas may be included. Some A-level content may be included but it will be lacking in detail and may contain several significant scientific errors. There may be limited use of scientific terminology. Explanations lack clarity.

1-5 marks:

The answer includes material that is only vaguely linked to the question title. Material is presented as a series of facts. Most of the material is irrelevant. The content is below A-level standard and contains a large number of scientific errors. Scientific terminology is not used or is below A-level standard. Explanations are poor or absent.

0 marks:

Nothing relevant is included in the answer or nothing has been written.

Here are some topic areas you might write about:

- the importance of ATP hydrolysis in releasing energy for energy-requiring reactions in cells and in releasing inorganic phosphate for the phosphorylation of other compounds;

- the importance of ATP in providing energy for the movement of molecules across cell membranes by active transport (allowing, e.g. translocation in plants/the establishment of a resting potential in animal neurones);

- the importance of ATP in providing energy for the bond between an amino acid and tRNA molecule to form in protein synthesis;

- the importance of ATP in providing energy for the light-independent reaction of photosynthesis, leading to the formation organic substances such as glucose;

- the importance of ATP in the reactions of glycolysis in aerobic and anaerobic respiration;

- the importance of ATP in muscle contraction.

This is not a full list of all the topic areas you could write about — it's just to give you an idea. Remember, you should aim to write about at least five of these topic areas. Whatever topic areas you include, you must relate them to the essay title — so in this case, don't just write about ATP, make it really clear how ATP is important to living organisms.

Acknowledgements

Graph on page 37 reprinted from Journal of Alzheimer's Disease, 28, Bohrmann et al, Gantenerumab: A Novel Human Anti-Aβ Antibody Demonstrates Sustained Cerebral Amyloid-β Binding and Elicits Cell-Mediated Removal of Human Amyloid-β, pages 49–69, copyright 2012, with permission from IOS Press.

Graph on page 45 contains public sector information published by the Health and Safety Executive and licensed under the Open Government Licence.

Table on page 100 based on data from Conduction Velocity and Diameter of Nerve Fibers, J. B. Hursh, Vol. 127, Issue 1, July 1939, pages 131-139.

Maize graph on page 115 based on the data from "The linkage of certain aleurone and endosperm factors in maize, and their relation to other linkage groups" by C.B. Hutchison, published in Ithaca, N.Y. : Cornell University, 1922.

Graphs on page 129 based on the data from the Butterfly Conservation.

Bar chart on page 133 based on the data from "Resemblance for Age at Menarche in Female Twins Reared Apart and Together" by Nancy L. Segal and Joanne Hoven Stohs. © 2007 Wayne State University Press.

Every effort has been made to locate copyright holders and obtain permission to reproduce sources. For those sources where it has been difficult to trace the originator of the work, we would be grateful for information. If any copyright holder would like us to make an amendment to the acknowledgements, please notify us and we will gladly update the book at the next reprint. Thank you.